Sir Philip Sidney

A STUDY OF HIS LIFE AND WORKS

TO
THE MASTER AND FELLOWS OF
ST JOHN'S COLLEGE, CAMBRIDGE
FOR THE PLEASURE OF
THEIR COMPANY
1974–5

Sir Philip Sidney

A STUDY OF HIS LIFE AND WORKS
by
A. C. HAMILTON
Professor of English, Queen's University
Kingston, Ontario

CAMBRIDGE UNIVERSITY PRESS

CAMBRIDGE

LONDON · NEW YORK · MELBOURNE

Published by the Syndics of the Cambridge University Press
The Pitt Building, Trumpington Street, Cambridge CB2 1RP
Bentley House, 200 Euston Road, London NW1 2DB
32 East 57th Street, New York, NY 10022, USA
296 Beaconsfield Parade, Middle Park, Melbourne 3206, Australia

First published 1977

Printed in Great Britain by
Western Printing Services Ltd, Bristol

Library of Congress cataloguing in publication data
Hamilton, A. C.
Sir Philip Sidney: a study of his life and works.
Bibliography: p.
Includes index.
1. Sidney, Philip, Sir, 1554–1586. 2. Authors,
English–Early modern, 1500–1700–Biography.
PR2343.H3   821'.3 [B]   76–47410
ISBN 0 521 21423 8

35, 225

Contents

Preface

The following pages attempt a general survey of Sidney as a writer. From an awareness of his life in the context of his age, and his works in their literary traditions, I seek to relate the life to the works. I admit that I wish to proselytize: I greatly admire Sidney as a writer, and in showing why, I hope to persuade others to appreciate him. Since his works are seminal in English literature, they may provide the reader with an imaginative centre for all his literary experience. For this reason I have enjoyed lecturing on Sidney, and I record with gratitude the opportunities to do so: at my own University, at the University of Cambridge in 1967 in a joint seminar with Professor Harry Levin, at the Johns Hopkins University in 1972 on the occasion of the annual Tudor and Stuart lecture, at Carleton University in 1973 in a lecture series on 'The writer and society in Renaissance England', at York University, Canada, in the same year, at the University of Missouri in 1974 at the conference of the Renaissance Society of America, and finally at Cambridge once again in 1975 when Dr Helen Cooper kindly included me in her 'lecture-circus'. I am grateful to the editors of the following journals for permission to include, in much revised form, material previously published by them: *Comparative Literature*, *ELH*, *English Literary Renaissance*, and *Review of English Studies*. Also I am grateful to the Canada Council for a summer grant and a leave fellowship, and to St John's College, Cambridge for a visiting overseas fellowship, which gave me the opportunity to write under ideal conditions.

With all students of Sidney, I am indebted to his editors, especially William A. Ringler, jr, Jean Robertson, Katherine Duncan-Jones, Jan van Dorsten, C. S. Levy, the late James M. Osborn, and Geoffrey Shepherd. I am especially indebted to Jean Robertson for her valuable comments on the final draft of the manuscript. I wish to thank my wife for reading the manuscript in its various versions: except for her skilled editorial labour, the pages would be blotted with many more infelicities. Also I must thank her for her constant encouragement: although she never read the *Arcadia*, she promised to do so many times. Finally, I thank the typist, Mrs Ann Waites of Swavesey, England.

Spelling has been modernized throughout in order to agree with the Oxford editions of the *Old Arcadia* and Sidney's *Miscellaneous Prose*.

Queen's University   A. C. HAMILTON

Sidney in life, legend, and in his works

'Some are born great, some achieve greatness, and some have greatness thrust upon them': the aphorisms are used by Maria, in *Twelfth Night*, to gull Malvolio. To the Renaissance mind, an aspiration to greatness is overweening in a pompous major-domo. He is mocked by greatness when his actions prove him to be only a great fool. Yet the aspiration itself, the intense desire for worldly honour and fame, 'that last infirmity of noble mind', marks most men of the time. In particular, it marks Sir Philip Sidney. Because he was born great, great expectations were held for him throughout his life; after his death, his reputation for personal greatness helped to establish the legend that he was the ideal Renaissance gentleman. Like Malvolio, however, he has been mocked by greatness: the legend thrust upon him has prevented any understanding of the life he actually lived by placing a barrier between his life and works, and between both and the modern reader.

Sidney was born great. He was the eldest son of a family distinguished on his father's side for several generations by personal service to English kings. This lineage was acknowledged by the French king when he elevated him to a Gentleman Ordinary, 'considerans combien est grande la maison de Sydenay en Angleterre'.[1] He was even more distinguished on his mother's side. His father told him to remember 'the noble blood you are descended of by your mother's side; and think that only by virtuous life and good action you may be an ornament to that illustrious family'.[2] Later Sidney boasted that 'though in all truth I may justly affirm that I am by my father's side of ancient and always well esteemed and well matched gentry, yet I do acknowledge, I say, that my chiefest honour is to be a Dudley'.[3] Such great birth, particularly as he was for much of his life the prospective heir of his rich – and childless – uncles, the earls of Leicester and Warwick, gave great hope for advancement, as Hubert Languet, his chief mentor and tutor, indicated to the ambassador of Poland during Sidney's tour of Europe:

His father is the Viceroy of Ireland, with whom, I am told, scarcely anyone among the nobility of England can compare in *virtus* and military experience.

His mother is a sister of the Earl of Warwick and of Robert the Earl of Leicester, the most favoured at Court: since neither has children, this gentleman [i.e. Sidney] will probably be their heir.

His father's sister is married to the Earl of Sussex. . . .His mother's sister is the wife of the Earl of Huntingdon, who is related to the Royal family.

Neither nobleman has any sons: so that on this one person they have placed their hopes, and him they have decided to advance to honour after his return.[4]

Sidney's own recognition of his position is suggested by his emblem, '*Spero*'.[5] For few in that age were prospects through high birth more dazzling.

Yet Sidney was not born great enough. His mother's family was tainted by treason. His great-grandfather was executed by Henry VIII for extortion; the year before he was born, his grandfather, John Dudley, Duke of Northumberland, was executed for treason; and in the year that he was born, his uncle, Guilford, was also executed for treason. Although Sidney boasted 'I am a Dudley in blood', he did so in the course of defending his uncle, the Earl of Leicester, against the anonymous libel that 'from his ancestors, this Lord receiveth neither honour nor honesty, but only succession of treason and infamy'.[6] He could excuse the fall of his family only on grounds that it was high enough to fall:

Our house received such an overthrow, and [as?] hath none else in England done; so I will not seek to wash away that dishonour with other honourable tears. I would this island were not so full of such examples; and I think, indeed, this writer, if he were known, might in conscience clear his ancestors of any such disgraces. They were too low in the mud to be so thunder-stricken.[7]

Sidney's mixed pride in his ancestors, and his recognition that he must act himself, is nicely registered in the motto which he wore under his arms: *Vix ea nostra voco* (I hardly dare call our ancestors' deeds our own).[8]

But worse than this, his father's family was blighted by poverty. The Sidney family was, as he admits, 'so youngly a fortuned family':[9] it was, in fact, impoverished, and became increasingly so. The family place at Penshurst was granted to his grandfather only two years before Sidney was born, and his father always lacked the means to maintain his state. Sir Henry's lengthy service to the Queen – he was thrice Lord Deputy Governor of Ireland besides being Lord President of the Marches of Wales – was rewarded only by new service which left him deeper in debt. He was forced to refuse a barony because he could not afford to maintain the rank. As a result, Sidney more than most experienced the special crisis of the Elizabethan aristocracy: being forced to attend court, courtiers so neglected their own affairs that they became increasingly dependent on the Queen for their support.[10] Fulke Greville records how for him – and it would be the same for Sidney – the Queen's actions 'fell heavy in crossing a young man's ends', and how she 'made me live in her court a spectacle of disfavour, too long as I conceived'.[11] For reasons of her own, she withheld her favours from the Sidney family, forcing them to beg, usually in vain, for the means to live. As a consequence, Sidney was in debt all his life; and not only did he die bankrupt, but left such debt that his father-in-law, in discharging it, became bankrupt.

The promise of Sidney's birth proved to be only disappointing. If Leicester had married the Queen, if Warwick had left him his wealth, if the Queen had favoured him: but none of these things happened. Leicester married instead the widow of the Earl of Essex, and their son, born in 1581, became heir to the family fortunes. At the next tilt-day, according to Camden, Sidney wore the impresa 'SPERAVI, thus dashed through, to show his hope therein was dashed'.[12] Although Leicester's son died three years later, Sidney's two rich uncles outlived him. The Queen never favoured him, and knighted him only because the Prince of Orange, who was to receive the Order of the Garter, named him his proxy, an office that protocol required should bear a title. Two minor events reveal his position at court. When the Queen granted him stipends from lands confiscated from Roman Catholics, he protested: 'I think my fortune very hard that my reward must be built upon other men's punishments';[13] then he accepted the gift. When the Earl of Oxford called him a 'puppy' during a quarrel on a tennis court, Sidney challenged him to a duel, but the Queen forced him to withdraw, laying before him 'the difference in degree between Earls and Gentlemen; the respect inferiors ought [owed] to their superiors'.[14] All his life Sidney lived only on the fringe of the establishment and under the shadow of greatness.

Sidney was expected to achieve greatness through public service, as his father recognized when he advised his sons 'that if they meant to live in order, they should ever behold whose sons, and seldom think whose nephews, they were'.[15] Sir Henry spent his life in public service, fulfilling what Malcolm Wallace describes as his 'engrossing conviction that only in disinterested service for prince and country could a man find a worthy end toward the achieving of which he could bend the whole of his energies'.[16] Sidney was expected to follow his father's example. He was groomed for public service first by his education at Shrewsbury School and Christ Church, Oxford, and then by an extended continental tour from 1572–5. By the end of that tour, he was poised to play a major role in England's affairs. In 1576, the dying Essex said of him: 'he is so wise, so virtuous and godly; and if he go on in the course he hath begun, he will be as famous and worthy a gentleman as ever England bred'.[17] His youth – he was only 22 – was bright with promise. Yet all his effort to achieve greatness came to little: apart from one embassy in 1577, he was not employed by the Queen in any important office until the year of his death. His life had a promising beginning and an heroic end, but no middle in public service. A recent biographer, Roger Howell, quite rightly concludes that the central event of Sidney's career was his death.[18] The explanation of his failure – if any is needed for a man who died in his thirty-first year – is simply that 'his short life and private fortune were. . .no proper stages to act any greatness of good or evil upon'.[19]

Sidney had greatness thrust upon him by his death. The circumstances which led to his death, the death itself, and the national orgy of grief on the occasion of his extravagant funeral in London four months later, promoted the legend that he embodied all the values cherished by the age: the ideal man, the perfect knight and pattern of the courtier, the mirror of princes and 'the world's delight'.[20]

In the previous year, by forcing the Queen's hand, Sidney initiated the sequence of events which led to his death. Frustrated at his failure to be appointed to the English expeditionary force to Holland, he was determined to accompany Drake to Virginia. Before he could sail, the Queen forbade him to leave, and promised to appoint him Governor of Flushing and General of the Horse. His appointment was confirmed on 9 November 1585, and he arrived in the Netherlands later that month. For the next nine months he was engaged in preparing the defences for the coming war against Spain. After waiting almost a decade to serve his country, at last he was given his great opportunity. As governor of Flushing, he could embody Sir Thomas Elyot's governor, that ideal of civic humanism expressed in Erasmus's claim that 'there is no better way to gain the favor of God, than by showing yourself a beneficial prince for your people'.[21] In leading a successful assault against the city of Axel, he was able to display himself as the ideal captain. As Stow records, Sidney addressed his men before the assault with an oration that 'did so link the minds of the people, that they desired rather to die in that service, than to live in the contrary'.[22] In the assault, not one English soldier was lost while all the defenders were massacred. George Whetstone, who may have served under Sidney, records that 'he always was a special favourer of soldiers'.[23] Then on 22 September in a minor skirmish at Zutphen against some Spanish forces, he was mortally wounded because he had discarded his leg-armour when he saw a fellow-knight not wearing his. Fulke Greville's account of what followed is too well known to be omitted:

The horse he rode upon. . .forced him to foresake the field, but not his back, as the noblest and fittest bier to carry a martial commander to his grave. In which sad progress, passing along by the rest of the army. . .and being thirsty with excess of bleeding, he called for drink, which was presently brought him; but as he was putting the bottle to his mouth, he saw a poor soldier carried along, who had eaten his last at the same feast, ghastly casting up his eyes at the bottle. Which Sir Philip perceiving, took it from his head, before he drank, and delivered it to the poor man, with these words, 'Thy necessity is yet greater than mine'. And when he had pledged this poor soldier, he was presently carried to Arnheim.[24]

Sidney's failure to wear leg-armour displays the conspicuous bravery, or bravado, of the Renaissance courtier. That act is closely related to his act of offering water to the soldier. A gesture which is flamboyant in not caring for himself has its counterpart in caring for another. Both acts are private, yet become fully public in that they display ideals of personal and social behaviour.

The twenty-five days between being wounded at Zutphen and dying of gangrene poisoning at Arnheim allowed Sidney to act out his death in a fitting manner. While his preparations for death enact the ritual of holy dying expected of any Christian, some details are personal. He asked that a song which he entitled 'La cuisse rompue' (The Broken Thigh) be set to music and played to him; but he also asked that his *Arcadia* be burned, for 'he then discovered, not only the imperfection, but vanity of these shadows'.[25] He repented what his closest friend, Fulke Greville, terms obliquely 'the secret sins of his own heart', which an attending chaplain, George Gifford, spells out as the final vanity which Sidney feared would prevent his salvation: 'a vanity wherein I had taken delight, whereof I had not rid myself. It was my Lady Rich. But I rid myself of it, and presently my joy and comfort returned.'[26] Greville records also that Sidney asked 'the opinion of the ancient heathen touching the immortality of the soul; first, to see what true knowledge she retains of her own essence, out of the light of herself; then to parallel with it the most pregnant authorities of the Old, and New Testament, as supernatural revelations, sealed up from our flesh, for the divine light of faith to reveal, and work by'.[27] Orthodoxy allowed that knowledge of the soul's immortality was attainable by natural reason, and the concern to fuse reason and revelation is characteristic of most men of the age; but what seems deeply personal is Sidney's concern, surprising at this late hour, with what reason alone may reveal and how it may lead to faith. Interest in what reason may discover of Christian truth had led to his translating De Mornay's *De la verité de la religion Chrestienne*;[28] and interest in reason working apart from faith may have encouraged him to use the classical Arcadia as the setting for his prose fiction: his characters debate moral virtue, and even answer atheism, without the support of revelation. His concern with man as a rational being shows why his writings remain profoundly secular despite his strongly religious nature.

The basis of the Sidney legend was laid during his life by the great expectations held out for him: for example, in Essex's dying prophecy cited above, that he 'will be as famous and worthy a gentleman as ever England bred', and in his father's eloquent judgment, which seems sincere, when he advised his son Robert to 'imitate his [Sidney's] virtues, exercises, studies, and actions; he is a rare ornament of this age, the very formular that all well-disposed young gentlemen of our court do form also their manners and life by. In truth, I speak it without flattery of him, or of myself, he hath the most rare virtues that ever I found in any man.'[29] While Sidney aroused some envy, praise of him by his contemporaries was almost uniformly extravagant, even by Renaissance standards. Later, when the Elizabethan age was idealized, as it was by Daniel, for example, Sidney became its exemplar.[30] It is surprising to learn that the legend continued in later centuries. In *Adonais*, Shelley writes: 'Sidney, as he fought / And as he fell and as he lived and loved / Sublimely mild, a Spirit without spot'.[31] The legend survives even today, for example, in Yeats's poem, 'In memory of Major Robert Gregory'. Sidney's best biographer, Malcolm Wallace, tries his best to be impartial by listing his faults:

He was foolishly extravagant in the spending of money, and was sometimes forced to seek to improve his financial position by means which were at least not dignified. He was somewhat arrogant and hot-headed. He was inclined to be egotistical. . . .To us there appears something strangely simple in Sidney's attitude toward most of life's problems. It is scarcely possible that he had been seriously touched by the philosophic and scientific stirrings of his time. His religious beliefs were as simple as those of a little child. None of the daring speculations of Bruno or the scepticism of the intellectuals of his day finds utterance in his writings. His only religious doubts had to do with his failure to be obedient to the God who was his heavenly Father. His political creed could hardly have been more simple. The enemies of England and of Protestantism were his enemies.

Yet he allows that 'no one can have familiarized himself with the details of Sidney's life without realizing what a large measure of truth there is in the popular conception of his character'.[32]

The legend may strike us simply as a legend, one that may be challenged by Sidney's own argument in the *Defence* for placing the poet's image of an ideal man above the work of Nature: 'Nature never set forth. . .so excellent a man every way.' One may wonder if there is any conflict between the life and the legend. Katherine Duncan-Jones refers to the gap 'which is often to be found between the magnificence of his personality and reputation, and the prosaic or even sordid facts of his life'.[33] Yet nothing that we know reveals any clash in Sidney himself between 'reality' and the ideal: there is no man apart from the legend, no face under the mask. From the beginning he seems to have lived a fully public life, which he sought to shape into an ideal of virtue expressed in public service. From all that we know, he dedicated his life to fulfil what was expected of him by his family and friends. As a result, his life satisfies Milton's dictum that the poet 'ought himself to be a true poem, that is, a composition, and pattern of the best and honourablest things, not presuming to sing high praises of heroic men, or famous cities unless he have in himself the experience and the practice of all that which is praise-worthy'.[34] If there is no man *behind* the legend, there is a man *in* it – one who tried to live as he ought, and succeeded.

The problem about the legend is not only that it overwhelms Sidney's life as known from his biography, but also that it all but ignores his life as a writer. Outside his circle of close friends, few of his contemporaries knew enough to praise him as a poet. One is Scipio Gentili:

Others admire in you, Philip Sidney, the splendour of your birth – your genius in your childhood, capable of all philosophy – your honourable embassy undertaken in your youth, and...the exhibition of your personal valour and prowess in the public spectacles and equestrian exercises, in your manhood: let others admire all these qualities. I not only admire, but I love and venerate you, because you regard poetry so much as to excel in it.[35]

No contemporary, except Greville, seems to have suspected that Sidney would achieve greatness through his literary works. Since his works were not published during his lifetime, except by the circulation of manuscripts among close friends, he remained largely unknown as a writer.

More letters to Sidney, and by him – 165 and 117 respectively, by Osborn's count – survive than for any other writer of his age; yet none reveals any plans for writing or comments even indirectly upon what he had written. For the poetry there is only one reference in a letter to a friend urging him to sing his songs; for the prose fiction, the promise in a letter to his brother to send him his 'toyful book' and the reported death-bed wish to have the *Arcadia* burned. As a consequence, none of his works may be dated with certainty, and even their titles are confused.[36] Only when it is known that he was not busy at court may one infer that he was free to write. He seems to have lived two separate lives: a known life as a Renaissance courtier seeking political office, and a private life as a poet. Accordingly, the standard biography by Malcolm William Wallace treats Sidney's writings separately, and so does the most recent biography by Roger Howell. James M. Osborn's extended study of *Young Philip Sidney 1572–1577* provides only one fact directly relevant to Sidney as a writer, a passing reference to his songs.

That the legend and known facts of Sidney's life all but ignore him as a writer is astonishing when one considers what he achieved in his writings simply in terms of comprehensiveness and orginality, and the commitment which that achievement demanded of him.

When Sidney began writing in the late 1570s or early 1580s, the English literary scene was barren. As he notes in the *Defence of poetry*, apart from a few works of worth such as Surrey's lyrics and Spenser's *Shepherd's Calendar*, a wasteland stretched back to Chaucer. Of Chaucer he wonders 'whether to marvel more, either that he in that misty time could see so clearly, or that we in this clear age go so stumblingly after him'. One may infer what he intended to do about this lamentable state from what he did, that is, by his literary criticism, writings, and influence, create a Renaissance of English literature. He was seen as the leader of such a Renaissance by Daniel in an address to Sidney's sister in 1594:

> Now when so many pens (like spears) are charg'd,
> To chase away this tyrant of the north;
> Gross Barbarism, whose power grown far enlarg'd
> Was lately by thy valiant brother's worth
> First found, encountered, and provoked forth:
> Whose onset made the rest audacious,
> Whereby they likewise have so well discharg'd,
> Upon that hideous beast encroaching thus.

When *Astrophel and Stella* appeared in 1591, Nashe heralded it as a work which ushers in the golden age: '*Tempus adest plausus; aurea pompa venit*: so ends the scene of idiots, and enter Astrophel in pomp', and Thomas Newman, who published the first edition, called it a work 'wherein the excellence of sweet poesy is concluded'.[37] Ringler concludes that 'no previous English poet, from Old English to Tudor times, even approached Sidney in the variety and complexity of metrical forms that he used'.[38] Henry Olney, the first editor of the *Defence of poetry*, refers to 'excellent poesy, so created by this *Apology*'.[39] Finally, the *Arcadia* is the first work of original prose fiction in our language, the first prose work of European stature in English, and one in which, as Virginia Woolf saw, 'as in some luminous globe, all the seeds of English fiction lie latent'.[40] Through these three works Sidney became the seminal writer of the Elizabethan age: *Astrophel and Stella* initiated the Petrarchan sonnet cycle in English as a literary form, the *Defence* provided the critical basis for Elizabethan literature, and the *Arcadia* promoted first a school of Arcadian fiction and later, through Richardson's *Pamela*, the English novel. At a time when the English literary scene was barren, and it was necessary to demonstrate that the English language was, as he claimed in the *Defence*, 'indeed capable of any excellent exercising of it', Sidney appeared as the one right man at the right time. Through his critical insight and literary craftsmanship, he pointed to what should be done and showed how it could be done.

To achieve such originality in poetry, literary criticism, and prose fiction, Sidney read widely and thoroughly in earlier literature. As sources of his poetry, Ringler cites Ovid, Virgil, Horace, Petrarch, Sannazaro, Montemayor and his continuators, and Tottel's *Songs and Sonnets*.[41] As sources of the *Defence*, Shepherd cites Scaliger, Elyot, Agrippa, Landino, Horace, Plato, and Aristotle, and adds Sidney's wider reading in humanist writing: 'he read in Petrarch, Boccaccio, Tasso, Mantuan, Pontanus, Sannazaro, Erasmus, More, Ascham, Ramus, Bembo, Patrizi, Bodin, Buchanan, Ronsard, du Bartas. He knew the old Roman poets, historians, moralists, and dramatists well. Certain books and authors were particularly congenial to him: Plutarch notably, and the Bible; also Xenophon, Virgil, and Seneca.'[42] While the sources of the *Arcadia* are few – chiefly Sannazaro, Montemayor, *Amadis of Gaul*, and Heliodorus – they reveal that Sidney drew comprehensively upon what earlier literature could provide as models in the classical, medieval, and modern periods. Further, he thoroughly assimilated his reading so that each of his writings is a well-wrought artifact, uniquely his own, and characterized by an original argument and careful, deliberate structure. Even in size these works are considerable, particularly *Astrophel and Stella* with its 108 sonnets and 11 songs, and the *Arcadia* with its 180,000 words in its first version (later expanded to more than 230,000 words) interlaced with over 70 poems either set within the prose or organized into the eclogues that conclude the separate books. Yet the biography of Sidney provides almost no record of this labour.

One might conclude that Sidney's works are unrelated to his life and to the age in which he lived. Ringler notes that his poetry 'is remarkable for what he did not write about':

He was a courtier, but except for some passages in *The Lady of May* he never wrote in praise of the Queen. He was sincerely religious, but he never wrote a poem of personal devotion. He placed a high value upon friendship, but except for his 'Two Pastorals' and a single mention of Languet he never wrote a commendatory or memorial poem for a real person. The major interest of his life was politics, but only once did he deal with problems of government, and then under the veil of a beast fable. Except for *Astrophil and Stella* his verse was neither official nor personal and dealt almost entirely with imagined situations.[43]

One may add that he chose to write a defence of poetry, which he himself refers to as 'this ink-wasting toy of mine', while his friends wrote political and religious tracts in defence of liberty and the Protestant faith, and that the setting of his *Arcadia*, which he refers to as 'a trifle, and that triflingly handled', is classical Greece rather than one which could have easy allegorical reference to contemporary England. According to Coleridge's distinction, Sidney would seem to be the kind of impersonal poet, like Shakespeare, who leaves no trace of himself in his works, and not the personal poet, like Milton, who may be found in every line that he writes.

Yet Sidney's presence dominates all his works. In the *Old Arcadia*, he inserts himself into the story as the character Philisides; and as narrator everywhere controls and directs the reader's response. *Astrophel and Stella* centres upon Astrophel, whom no reader may fail to associate with Sidney. The argument of the *Defence* is persuasive chiefly because of Sidney's persuasive voice. The ideals treated in the *New Arcadia* are Sidney's as well as those of his class and age. While his writings are never personal in the sense of treating the stuff of biography – courtly gossip, quarrels, rumours of appointments, or whatever is simply personal – they are always centrally concerned with the business of a man (and that man is Sidney) living at a certain moment and place in human history. Equally his writings are never impersonal in the sense of treating man or mankind: they are dominated by the presence of an individual man responding to the immediate pressures of his life and times.

I see a close and significant relationship between Sidney and his writings, and between both and his age. That relationship is not direct: the writings do not reveal his actual life – whatever that may have been like; instead, his life provides the setting, occasion, or point of departure for what he writes. While the personal is included in all that he writes, it is transcended. He was not a Romantic poet for whom poetry could record the spontaneous overflow of emotions. He is never personal, as Spenser is, and could never begin a poem, as Spenser does, with the line, 'Lo I the man, whose Muse whilom did mask' – not even with Virgil's authority. On the other hand, in reading Sidney one never reaches the point as one soon does with Spenser, where the writer's life and times become irrelevant. If one could strip the mask from Sidney's *persona*, most likely one would uncover another mask, and another under that. The reason, I suspect, is that from his birth he began to live the legend confirmed by his death; and, to adapt Keats's phrase, his works are comments on it. By his own nature, as well as by nurture, education, and the urging of his friends, he shaped his life into an image of virtue. Or to adapt his own words in the *Defence,* his essential life is not recorded in what is, but rather in 'what may be and should be'. He lived on the level of art; or, as he might say, he lived by rules of decorum which required him to fulfil the promise of his birth and place in society.

As a result of the kind of life that he lived, his life and works are closely related to his age. In retrospect, it seems inevitable that of all those who attended Elizabeth's court, he should be singled out as the ideal Renaissance gentleman, the one alone who may be awarded the praise given the young Hamlet: 'the courtier's, soldier's, scholar's, eye, tongue, sword; / Th' expectancy and rose of the fair state, / The glass of fashion and the mould of form, / Th' observ'd of all observers'. As with his life, his works have become the norm by which we may understand the nature of the English literary Renaissance. Accordingly, Richard B.

Young interprets Sidney as the English Petrarch; C. S. Lewis sees the *Arcadia* as a kind of touchstone or work of distillation that 'gathers up what a whole generation wanted to say'; and Shepherd notes of the *Defence* that Sidney's 'articulations are moments of European self-consciousness'.[44] One reason why his life is so closely related to his age is that his mind was receptive to ideas, comprehensive in scope, and constantly eclectic and assimilative. By virtue of his birth, position, promise of political power, and apparently great personal charm, he was sought out by the chief men of his day: there was no movement in politics, philosophy, or religion to which he was not exposed. One may say of all his writings what Shepherd says of the *Defence*, that the more it is studied, 'the more astonishing appears Sidney's sensitivity to contemporary intellectual development, in the arts, in religion, in politics, and in science'.[45] The movements in current thought to which he was exposed did not lead him to endorse any personal or independent position, in part because he sought instead a synthesis in which opposing points of view were balanced; in part because he had a unifying, rather than a unified, sensibility; and in chief part because of an introspective nature which separated him from the world even while he was deeply engaged in it. Greville, who knew him best, understood this Christian position of being in the world yet not of it:

...When Sir Philip found this, and many other of his large and sincere resolutions imprisoned within the plights of their fortunes, that mixed good and evil together unequally; and withal discerned how the idle-censuring faction at home had won ground of the active adventurers abroad; then did this double depression both of things and men lift up his active spirit into an universal prospect of time, states, and things: and in them made him consider what possibility there was for him, that had no delight to rest idle at home, of repropounding some other foreign enterprise, probable and fit to invite that excellent Princess's mind and moderate government to take hold of. The placing of his thoughts upon which high pinnacle laid the present map of the Christian world underneath him.[46]

One consequence was that while Sidney led a fully public life, one in which he always played a role on the public stage, and his writings respond fully to the pressures of his time, his life and writings are not submerged by the age. Both remain highly individual. In Geoffrey Whitney's *A choice of emblems* (1586), the emblem addressed to Sidney is entirely fitting: it shows a plumed horseman on a prancing war-horse, with the motto: *non locus virum, sed vir locum ornat.* Another consequence is that Sidney gained the perspective of the poet, of one not being subject to nature but 'having all. . .under the authority of his pen'.[47] While the world 'mixed good and evil together unequally', he was free to assume the poet's task of separating them, what Jonson aptly describes as the 'proper embattling' of the virtues and vices.[48]

In later chapters I shall argue my claim that Sidney's life is closely related to his works, and both to the age, but I may illustrate it briefly here by tracing his use of a common motif: life as a prison which tests man's worth. The motif is based on the religious view that the soul is imprisoned by the body, as in the Psalmist's cry, 'Bring my soul out of prison.' For Sidney, that view would be confirmed on the secular level by his own confined life, largely spent waiting impatiently, and finally in despair, for some public appointment. The image of man's body or mind confined in a dungeon is found throughout his poetry, as in Pyrocles's lament in the *Old Arcadia*:

> . . .the stormy rage of passions dark
> (Of passions dark, made dark by beauty's light)
> With rebel force hath closed in dungeon dark
> My mind ere now led forth by reason's light. (179–80)

The testing of man's worth by imprisonment provides the climax to that work: when Pyrocles and Musidorus are imprisoned and then sentenced to death, they fully reveal their virtue.[49] So, too, at the end of *Astrophel and Stella*: even when his life as the lover of the star is reduced to a 'dungeon dark', he rejoices in his love, and thereby proves himself to be one 'loving in truth'. At the climax to the *New Arcadia*, the two princesses, Philoclea and Pamela, manifest their virtue when they are imprisoned in Amphialus's castle. Behind all these works is the view, implicit in Sidney's poetic theory, that man's virtue is tested by the confines of life, and the faith that virtue makes man free.

'Our erected wit maketh us know what perfection is, and yet our infected will keepeth us from reaching unto it': this observation in the *Defence*[50] may serve as an epigraph to Sidney's life and works. Central to his thought is an awareness of the gulf between man's life as it is and as it should be. In his poetry and prose he shows how reality falls short of the ideal, and in the

Defence he justifies the work of the poet on the grounds that it may best move the reader's 'infected will' to embrace the perfection which he knows by his 'erected wit'. His phrases, 'erected wit' and 'infected will' suggest generally the central secular and religious movements of the age, which H. J. C. Grierson identifies as its cross-currents, and specifically the two traditional views of man's nature, the one optimistic as it affirms man's perfectibility and the other pessimistic as it affirms his corruption.[51] The former is associated with the neo-Platonists, such as Pico della Mirandola whose *Oration on Human Dignity* allows man freedom so to fashion himself that he may become at one with Godhead itself. This view of human nature tends to ignore original sin, manifest in the 'infected will', and allows man to depend in some measure upon himself, upon good works apart from grace. The latter is associated with the Calvinists who stress man's radical imperfection in his fallen state: since man is deprived of his original perfection and depraved through sin, his will is so infected that he must depend entirely upon God's grace.

As a humanist, Sidney acknowledges man's 'erected wit': he believes with Erasmus that man may be shaped through education – *homines non nascuntur, sed finguntur*. As a Protestant, he notes man's 'infected will': the doctrine of the Fall provides the basis of his religious beliefs. His careful balancing of the two phrases reveals him to be a Christian humanist who believes that man is radically imperfect, but stresses the possibility of his regeneration. Douglas Bush's comment on the confidence in the goodness and greatness of man among the chief writers of the Renaissance applies, above all, to Sidney: 'that confidence was one element in Christian humanism, but it was kept in check by a religious sense of man's littleness and sinful frailty. . . . With a simultaneous double vision they see man as both a god and a beast. That double vision is, to be sure, the mark of the greatest writers of all ages, especially the ancients; but the Christian religion intensified the paradox by exalting man's sense of his divinity and deepening his sense of bestiality.'[52] In this double view of man, the secular and religious need not conflict: the end of learning is not to rival God but, in Milton's words, 'to repair the ruins of our first parents'.[53] Sidney would agree with Milton's complaint in *Tetrachordon* that 'nothing nowadays is more degenerately forgotten than the true dignity of man, almost in every respect'.[54] Yet his full awareness of man's 'true dignity' is based upon his full acceptance of the doctrine of man's 'infected will'. While he was receptive to the most radical intellectual currents of his time, he 'made the religion he professed the firm basis of his life'.[55] As a result, his writings reveal the central conflicts in his age between the Renaissance and the Reformation. Since they treat man's life comprehensively in relation both to his own nature and to his society, Sidney deserves his legend as the representative Elizabethan – representative, that is, of the age at its best.

Sidney and the pastoral:
The Lady of May and the *Old Arcadia*

Sidney's life was too brief, varied, and forced, to fall into distinct periods. His works were written in too short a space of time to show any dramatic development or change as a writer.[1] Further, we know little about when they were written, and in what order. However, this much seems clear: up to 1575 he was being groomed for some high political office; from 1575 to 1577 he hoped that the Queen would employ him; from 1577 to 1579 he began to despair that she would ever do so; and 1580 marks his turning towards a life as a poet while waiting for a public appointment. His masque, *The Lady of May,* belongs to the first stage of his career as a courtier–poet; and the pastoral romance, the *Old Arcadia,* and the *Certain sonnets* belong to the next stage as a poet writing privately, apart from the court even while he belongs to it. From 1580 until the final year of his life, the pattern is more definite: his essential life took place in his writings, however outwardly busy he may have been in affairs at court. Within the period 1580 to 1582 he wrote his major poem *Astrophel and Stella* and his *Defence of poetry.* As a manifesto, the *Defence* declares his emergence as a public poet, a role which he fulfils by revising and recasting the *Old Arcadia* into the work known as the *New Arcadia.* The years from 1582 to 1584 seem largely to have been taken up with that work; and the two final years of his life seem to have been totally dedicated to serving his country.

In the *Old Arcadia* Sidney describes his life until 1575 through his namesake, the character Philisides, a melancholy knight disguised as a shepherd.[2] He relates that he was born in Samothea (the legendary name for England in its golden age[3]), of a family neither so great that he was envied nor so base that he was subject to contempt, and 'brought up from my cradle age with such care as parents are wont to bestow upon their children whom they mean to make the maintainers of their name'. His parents gave

him a religious education, 'that kind that teacheth what in truth
and not in opinion is to be embraced, and what to be eschewed',
and also 'the natural knowledge of things so far as the narrow
sight of man hath pierced into it'. To this exercise of the mind
was added physical exercise and, later, travel to 'ripen my judgement':

> Then being home returned, and thought of good hope (for the world
> rarely bestows a better title upon youth), I continued to use the benefits
> of a quiet mind; in truth (I call him to witness that knoweth hearts) even
> in the secret of my soul bent to honesty – thus far you see, as no pompous
> spectacle, so an untroubled tenor of a well guided life.

The phrase, 'thought of good hope', describes exactly Sidney's
state in 1575: his family and friends expected a brilliant future
for him.[4] Whatever his personal ambition – and at times, one suspects, for lack of it – he was driven by the expectations of others.
Typical is Languet's response when he feared that Sidney would
be led into danger by his desire to gain knowledge by travel: 'To
offend *me* is of little consequence, but reflect how grievously you
would be sinning against your excellent father, who has placed
all his hopes in you, and who being now in the flower of life, expects to see the full harvest of all those virtues, which your character promises so largely to produce.'[5] As noted earlier, such expectations of greatness haunted Sidney throughout his life. In the *Old
Arcadia*, Evarchus characterizes 'overshooting expectation' as
'the most cruel adversary of all honourable doings'.[6] In *Astrophel
and Stella* 21, Sidney writes of the friend – perhaps Greville but
possibly Languet – who tells him that

> to my birth I owe
> Nobler desires, least else that friendly foe,
> Great expectation, wear a train of shame.
> For since mad March great promise made of me,
> If now the May of my years much decline,
> What can be hoped my harvest time will be?

That 'friendly foe' remained with Sidney until the year of his
death: in 1586 Molyneux refers to him as 'a gentleman of great
hope, and exceeding expectation. . .if his good fortune. . .answer
his noble deserts and worthiness, he is most like to prove a famous,
great, and rare personage for the service of his country and commonwealth'.[7]

That 'great hope' took the shape that Sidney would play an active role in the political and religious affairs of England by heading a Protestant League in Europe. For this role his tutor was Hubert Languet, a leading Protestant scholar, and ambassador of the Elector of Saxony at Paris and later at Vienna. His ambitions for Sidney are summed up by James Osborn in his recent biography, *Young Philip Sidney 1572–1577*:

Besides admiring Sidney's charm and fresh intelligence, Languet saw him as the messiah who could lead the much-desired unification of the Protestants of Europe. Languet hoped to bring together the Lutherans, the Calvinists, and the Anglicans of England, and by this means to resist the forces of Catholicism, which seemed neither to slumber nor to sleep. To this purpose Languet felt his greatest contribution could be to guide, train, and even create the future champion of the Protestant cause.[8]

The possibility of such a league raised apocalyptic hopes. After exhorting Sidney to express his virtues in action, Languet observes that 'Satan is beginning to gnash the teeth, because he sees that his throne is tottering.' Public preferment for Sidney meant more – or even other – than service to his Queen and country: it meant that he would serve God's will.

From 1575 to 1577 he could expect that such preferment would be given him. In 1577 he was appointed the Queen's ambassador to visit Germany, ostensibly to offer her condolences to the Emperor on the death of his father but really, according to Greville who accompanied him, 'to salute such German Princes as were interested in the cause of our religion or their own native liberty'.[9] In a letter to the Landgrave of Hesse on May 13th of that year, Sidney expresses Elizabeth's desire to have a Protestant League set up in Europe:

One of these matters is how you may together repulse the designs of the Bishop of Rome who seeks with all his might to destroy those who have cast off the yoke he had laid upon the necks of our forefathers, and who now maintain themselves in such liberty as enables them rightly and devoutly to worship God and to work out their own salvation. To achieve these ends, however, the Pope is attempting to join such Kings and Princes as are still bound in his tyranny in alliances that are to destroy us in concert. This, in their view, will be easy unless we also join together, to repel the harm they will try to inflict on us.[10]

His pride in his position is shown by the tablet which hung under his arms wherever he lodged:

Illustrissimi & Generosissimi Viri
Philippi Sidnaei Angli,
Pro-regis Hiberniae filii, Comitum Warwici
Et Leicestriae Nepotis, Serenissimi
Reginae Angliae ad Caesarem Legati.[11]
(The most illustrious and noble Englishman, Philip Sidney, son of the
Deputy of Ireland, nephew of the Earls of Warwick and Leicester, and
ambassador of the great English Queen to the Emperor.)

After completing his official mission, Sidney met William of
Orange, as a result of which he was commissioned to offer a union
of Holland and Zeeland with England. William proposed that the
union be marked by marriage between his daughter and Sidney.
If the union and that marriage had taken place, it would have
established Sidney as a major Protestant ruler in Europe. Later
William reported that 'her Majesty had one of the ripest and
greatest counsellors of estate in Sir Philip Sidney, that at this day
lived in Europe'.[12] That embassy was a personal triumph for
Sidney, and when he returned to England in June 1577, Edward
Waterhouse told Sir Henry how his son had returned 'with great
good acceptance of his service at her Majesty's hands; allowed of
by all the Lords to have been handled with great judgement and
discretion, and hath been honoured abroad in all the princes'
courts with much extraordinary favour'.[13] Walsingham wrote to
him in the same terms:

The gentleman hath given no small arguments of great hope, the fruits
whereof I doubt not but your lordship shall reap, as the benefits of the
good parts which are in him, and whereof he hath given some taste in
this voyage, is to redound to more than your lordship and himself. There
hath not been any gentleman, I am sure these many years, that hath
gone through so honourable a charge with as great commendations as
he.[14]

At this moment when the great expectations held out for Sidney
gave every promise of being fulfilled, he wrote *The Lady of May*,
his first and only work as a courtier–poet.

'THE LADY OF MAY'

The Lady of May belongs to this first stage of Sidney's career
as the work of a courtier–poet who entertains his Queen by grace-
fully praising her. Its opening words in the 1598 folio edition,

'Her most excellent Majesty walking in Wanstead Garden', suggest that it is a dramatic 'happening':[15] it records what happened to the Queen on a certain May-day. Yet it may be regarded as a masque written for the Queen: as audience and participant, she becomes the device upon which the formal argument turns, and praise of her provides the climax.

That May-day when the Queen visited Sidney's uncle, the Earl of Leicester, and walked in his garden may have been either in 1578 or in 1579. The earlier date is preferred by Ringler because the names of two of the shepherds appear in the *Old Arcadia* which had not 'completely taken form' in 1578.[16] Yet that reason serves equally well for the later date because the *Old Arcadia* was not completed, so far as one knows, until 1580. The later date is preferred by Robertson because the reference to Master Robert of Wanstead (clearly Leicester) as 'foully commaculated with the papistical enormity' would be more appropriate to 1579 when Catholics attacked Leicester for opposing the Queen's renewed negotiations to marry Alençon.[17] Yet such doubtful topical allusion would destroy the witty climax of the work. In the concluding address to the Queen, Leicester, a known opponent of Rome, is accused of a Popish practice: he uses a rosary. Slander of Leicester changes into praise of the Queen when it is revealed that the object of his prayers is not the Virgin Mary but the Virgin Queen. In the absence of evidence, I prefer the earlier date. By 1579 Sidney was becoming more estranged from the court, imaginatively if not physically. There was never, of course, any clean break with the court, and he continued to take part in tilts, tournaments, and triumphs throughout his life. By 1579, however, he would surely have been deeply engaged in writing the *Old Arcadia*.

The Lady of May is interesting historically since it stands 'at the head of all the English masques of the sixteenth century' and is 'the earliest example in English of conventionalized pastoral drama'.[18] It has literary interest as Sidney's first work, and, in itself, as a pastoral work with a complex and ambivalent argument.

While the Queen is walking in Wanstead Garden, she is confronted by a mother who begs her to end a bloody controversy over her daughter who has been chosen the Lady of May. She

need not turn out of her way, the mother explains, for 'your own
way guides you to the place where they [the suitors] encumber
her'. After this device, which serves as a formal prologue, a song
praises the Queen's powers. Then follows a spectacle which expresses the Lady of May's divided state: she appears pulled between six shepherds and six foresters. (The 6:1:6 grouping is
traditional in a masque to represent the conflict within a woman
in love.) A Master Rombus who tries to end the strife is buffeted.
The Queen's powers are illustrated when her mere presence stills
the strife: all stop to gaze in wonder upon her. The antimasque,
which her presence routs, leads to a formal masque when she is
asked to judge the quarrel. The two suitors engage in a singing-
match so that she may judge which is more worthy to possess the
Lady. Before she can deliver her judgment, however, a second
quarrel breaks out between the shepherds and the foresters. The
two sides engage in a formal debate so that she may judge which
is the more worthy life. At the end she judges between the two
suitors but not between the two lives.[19] The work is rounded out,
and fulfils the purpose for which it was written, by praise of the
Queen. At the beginning she is addressed as 'most fair lady'; at
the end the Lady of May recognizes her as the true Lady of May,
wishing that 'as hitherto it hath excellently done, so henceforward
the flourishing of May, may long remain in you and with you'.
A coda to the work, preserved in the Helmingham Hall MS, adds
to such pastoral praise the courtly cult of the Queen: Master
Rombus reveals that Master Robert adds 'and Elizabeth' to his
paternoster and prays to her on his rosary as his Virgin.

As *The Lady of May* is a literary masque, its spectacle is
largely verbal. For example, it balances prose styles in a very
witty manner, playing off one against the other. At the beginning
the mother states her daughter's problem simply and realistically:
'other women think they may be unhappily cumbered with one
master husband; my poor daughter is oppressed with two, both
loving her, both equally liked of her, both striving to deserve her'.
When the old shepherd, Lalus, tries to express this problem, he
fails to get beyond its opening terms: 'a certain she-creature,
which we shepherds call a woman, of a minsical countenance...
hath disanulled the brain-pan of two of our featious young men'.
In the verbal fireworks that follow, the pedant schoolmaster,

Master Rombus, like Shakespeare's Armado, 'draweth out the thread of his verbosity finer than the staple of his argument': 'a certain *pulchra puella profectò*, elected and constituted by the integrated determination of all this topographical region, as the sovereign lady of this, Dame Maia's month, hath been *quodammodo* hunted, as you would say, pursued by two, a brace, a couple, a cast of young men, to whom the crafty coward Cupid had *inquam* delivered his dire doleful digging dignifying dart'. As in *Love's Labour's Lost*, which it clearly anticipates, the joyful playing with words heralds the birth of a major poet.[20]

Since the work is a masque, its verbal spectacle conveys an argument. The Queen is asked to choose between the Lady of May's two suitors, 'whether the many deserts and many faults of Therion, or the very small deserts and no faults of Espilus be to be preferred'. The choice between them is not clear-cut. As his name suggests, the forester, Therion, is a 'wild beast': although he serves the Lady in lively fashion, she complains that 'withal he grows to such rages, that sometimes he strikes me, sometimes he rails at me'. The shepherd Espilus, the 'woolly one', is richer than Therion and gentler but a dull lover, so she complains: 'as his fortune hath not been to do me great service, so hath he never done me any wrong'. As the Lady has good reason to like both but love neither, choice between them is difficult.

Choice is to be made on the basis of their songs:

Espilus: Two thousand sheep I have as white as milk,
              Though not so white as is thy lovely face;
              The pasture rich, the wool as soft as silk,
              All this I give, let me possess thy grace:
                  But still take heed, lest thou thyself submit
                  To one that hath no wealth, and wants his wit.

Therion: Two thousand deer in wildest woods I have,
              Them can I take, but you I cannot hold:
              He is not poor, who can his freedom save,
              Bound but to you, no wealth but you I would:
                  But take this beast, if beasts you fear to miss,
                  For of his beasts the greatest beast he is.

The love that each offers the Lady reflects his own state: Espilus compares her to a sheep, Therion to a wild animal. Espilus's 'possess' reveals that he values her as he does his sheep: while she is richer than they are, she is to be kept, as Therion notes, 'among his flock'. Yet Therion hunts the Lady as he does the deer, and his charge that his rival is 'the greatest beast' turns against himself. The merits of the two suitors are balanced in each particular by their faults. Espilus offers the Lady all his wealth yet seeks to possess her as his wealth. Therion may well claim that the Lady is all his wealth, for he has none, and his life of freedom may prove to be freedom to starve. Life with the placid Espilus as a substitute sheep would be drab but more secure than with the irascible Therion who strikes the Lady as if he were hunting a beast. While the Queen is expected to choose between the suitors, the courtly audience with her (and later readers) cannot, any more than can the Lady of May. However she may choose, the audience is expected to debate her choice without ever agreeing.

When the suitors kneel before the Queen, the masque seems near its end: with the Queen's judgment and some speech in her praise, the work would fulfil its purpose. Surprisingly, as all wait in silence for her judgment, a second controversy develops from the first, a debate between the two parties for the Lady, 'whether the estate of shepherds or foresters were the more worshipful'. The old shepherd, Dorcas, argues that his contemplative life is to be preferred: there is 'no envy, but all obedience' when one may contemplate the works of nature 'neither subject to violent oppression, nor servile flattery'. The young forester, Rixus, answers that his active life goes beyond the shepherd's life because it 'doth both strengthen the body, and raise up the mind with this gallant sort of activity'. The Lady of May must extend her suit to the Queen: 'in judging me, you judge more than me in it'. Yet on that May-day the Queen was prepared only to judge that the shepherd Espilus deserved the Lady of May; just why we are not told: 'what words, what reasons she used for it, this paper, which carrieth so base names, is not worthy to contain'. Her choice of the shepherd may suggest that she would judge 'the estate of shepherds. . .the more worshipful' but in fact she did not judge between the two lives.

The Queen may have found that the argument is too complex for simple choice, and that it equivocates in its treatment of the two lives in relation to the courtier's life. For in this second part of the masque, Sidney goes beyond the courtier–poet's role of entertaining the Queen by employing the figure that characterizes his role. In his *Art of English Poesy*, Puttenham observes that the poet who entertains the Queen must 'dissemble his conceits as well as his countenances, so as he never speak as he thinks, or think as he speaks, and that in any matter of importance his words and his meaning very seldom meet; for so as I remember it was concluded by us setting forth the figure *Allegoria*, which therefore not impertinently we call the Courtier or figure of fair semblant'.[21]

Dorcas claims that the shepherd's life has its 'honest using', for the eye is 'busied in considering the works of nature, and the heart quietly rejoiced in the honest using them'. Rixus answers that the foresters 'have no hopes, but we may quickly go about them, and going about them, we soon obtain them'. In opposition to such aggressive striving to satisfy desire, Dorcas upholds the shepherd's life as one in which 'it is lawful for a man to be good if he list, and hath no outward cause to withdraw him from it'. Their argument extends a debate initiated in the Renaissance by Tasso's *Aminta*, which defines the Golden Age by the law, '*s'ei piace, ei lice*' (if it pleases, it is lawful). Since such a law, applied to man's life after the Fall, leads to the libertine motto, 'doing as one likes', or to the anarchic claim that what one desires is lawful, Guarini replies to Tasso by positing the law, '*piaccia se lice*' (it is pleasing if it is permitted).[22] In the *Faerie Queene*, Spenser is even more negative: in the Golden Age 'each unto his lust did make a law, / From all forbidden things his liking to withdraw.'[23] Sidney is more negative still. The plain inference from Dorcas's claim is that in society it is not possible for man to be good even if he wishes to be: he must retire from society to lead a good life.

Both parties in the debate apply this criticism of society to life at the court. Dorcas contrasts the quiet life of shepherds with the life of 'violent oppression' and 'servile flattery' suffered by courtiers under their mistresses. He alludes covertly to the Queen when he says that he has heard 'one name sound in many mouths [of courtiers]. . .making our vales witnesses of their doleful agonies'. So does Rixus when he contrasts the satisfied life of foresters with 'those that, having long followed one (in truth) most excellent chase, do now at length perceive she could never be taken; but that if she stayed at any time near her pursuers, it was never meant to tarry with them, but only to take breath to fly further from them'. It is difficult to allow that the Queen would interpret such covert allusion simply as flattery, particularly in a context which rejects the courtly life.[24] Sidney's dissimulation amounts to duplicity when 'servile flattery', rejected by Dorcas, is illustrated in the epilogue which tells how Master Robert idolizes the Queen as though she were the Virgin Mary and a fourth member of the Trinity. The Queen may have decided not to choose between the lives of the shepherd and the forester because choice of either implied a condemnation of the courtly life.

The criticism of courtly life in *The Lady of May* reflects Sidney's position at court at that time. After his return from the embassy in June 1577, he stood not only at the height of expectations but also at the height of fulfilment. His success proved his undoing. The Queen was resolved not to become entangled in Europe and, above all, not to provoke conflict with Spain; instead, England was to hold a balance of power in Europe as the tongue of the scales between France and Spain.[25] At most she would encourage other countries, chiefly the Low Countries and Germany, to form a Protestant League. Since these other countries were unable to agree among themselves, Sidney's embassy failed. In 1578 the Queen charged him with the mission to inform Prince Casimir, the chief proponent of the League, that he could not hope for English aid. Leicester wrote that he had rather Sidney 'perished in the sea than that he should be the instrument of it'.[26] Although that mission was cancelled, there was little prospect for any Protestant front, and in March Sidney wrote to Languet: 'unless God powerfully counteract it, I seem to myself to see our cause withering away'.[27]

From 1577 to 1579 Sidney became increasingly alienated from the court. He assumed no active role except as a minor attendant to swell a progress. At most there were rumours that he would be given service against Spain in the Netherlands as deputy under Leicester, or joint commander with Casimir, or vice-admiral of a fleet under William of Orange; these rumours, being unfounded, would have left him increasingly frustrated. His *Discourse on Irish Affairs* in October 1577, a bold defence of his father's deputyship, associated him with his father's disfavour at court. The policy which he advocated, using 'severe means' to make the Irish 'find the sweetness of due subjection',[28] again called for an aggressive and expensive policy that was contrary to the Queen's desire. His bitter quarrel with the Earl of Oxford in August 1579 only served to remind him that he was no more than an untitled gentleman. His rash letter to the Queen in November or December 1579[29] opposing her proposed marriage to Alençon, the French Catholic Duke of Anjou, may have led to his absence from the court for most of 1580.

The humanist code which required a man to serve his country recognized that he might not be as effective as he would like because he must obey his sovereign. The code is expressed in More's *Utopia*: in response to the claim by the idealist Hythloday that total reform would be the price for his service to a ruler, More replies that if a counsellor cannot persuade his ruler, he does not forsake the commonwealth or persist in fruitless effort but 'must with a crafty wile and a subtle train study and endeavour yourself, as much as in you lieth, to handle the matter wittily and handsomely for the purpose; and that which you cannot turn to good, so to order it that it be not very bad'.[30] That same code lies behind Languet's letter in January 1580 when he learned that Sidney had withdrawn from court because of his objections to the Queen's marriage:

I admire your courage in freely admonishing the Queen and your countrymen of that which is to the state's advantage. But you must take care not to go so far that the unpopularity of your conduct be more than you can bear....I advise you to persevere as long as you can do anything that may benefit your country; but when you find that your opposition only draws on you dislike and aversion, and that neither your country, your friends, nor yourself derive any advantage from it, I advise you to give way to necessity.[31]

Some eight months later he wrote again on the matter because he had observed a cloud over Sidney's fortunes:

Consider well, I entreat you, how far it is honourable to you to lurk where you are, whilst your country is imploring the aid and support of her sons. If the advice which you offered, believing it to be good for England, was not received as it deserved, you must not therefore be angry with your country; for good citizens ought to pardon her every wrong, and not for any such reason desist from working for her preservation.[32]

Languet belonged, as did Sir Henry, to the older generation of humanists who held that a man must serve his ruler to the utmost of his abilities. Yet Sidney would know what the fruits of such service were by his father's disfavour, particularly in 1578. Edmund Molyneux notes that Sir Henry's service 'was subject to the ear, and not object to the eye, by means whereof his noble virtues and deserts were many times suppressed, and seldom or never seen, but his faults often told and willingly heard'.[33]

Instead of being content to serve the Queen's will, Sidney sought to impose his will – or what he saw as God's will – upon her. Inevitably, he lost her favour and was left to languish or retire from the court. His skill in public affairs seems limited to that of a diplomat, a role in which he could present the views of another persuasively without needing to modify them. He lacked political cunning, the ability to survive by being able to compromise, temporize, and dissemble. He proved unfit for public office through a characteristic which Wallace finds dominant in him, high-mindedness.[34] In his idealism, he ought to belong to what Anthony Esler describes as 'the aspiring mind of the Elizabethan younger generation': the 'natural, passionate idealism' of the generation of the 1560s led it to reject 'the cautious negativism and apparent hypocrisy of a spiritually burned-out older generation'. But the fact is that he does not belong, and lacks entirely 'the deeper spiritual alienation of the younger generation from the ideals of their elders'.[35] Instead of looking forward with a Marlovian aspiring mind, he looks back to the antique age, as Greville notes when he praises him for 'restoring amongst us the ancient majesty of noble and true dealing'.[36]

Sidney's failure to be employed during these years marks the first major crisis in his life. Not to exercise his virtue in some worthy cause for his country frustrated the end to which his whole life had been directed. The pressure upon him to act is shown in Languet's letter to him in June 1574: 'God has bestowed mental powers on you which I do not believe have fallen to anyone else I know, and he has done so not for you to abuse them in exploring vanities at great risk [Sidney had said that he wanted to visit Rome while in Italy], but for you to put them in the service of your country, and of all good men; since you are only the steward of this gift, you will wrong Him who conferred such a great benefit on you if you prove to have abused it.'[37] That the parable of the talents haunted Sidney becomes clear in *Astrophel and Stella* 18:

> With what sharp checks I in myself am shent,
>   When into reason's audit I do go:
>   And by just counts myself a bankrupt know
> Of all those goods, which heav'n to me hath lent:
> Unable quite to pay even nature's rent,
>   Which unto it by birthright I do owe:
>   And which is worse, no good excuse can show,
> But that my wealth I have most idly spent.
>   My youth doth waste, my knowledge brings forth toys.

The compulsion to act was given the utmost urgency through the belief, which Sidney expressed to Languet in June 1574, that 'the Almighty is ordering Christendom with a wonderful providence in these our days'.[38] Since everything in his life encouraged him to expect some high office in which to exercise his virtues, idleness drove him to despair. In a letter to Languet in March 1578, he complains: 'I have not as yet done any thing worthy of me.'[39]

Idleness was particularly dangerous to him because he was tempted by it. By nature he was subject to melancholy which made him withdrawn and studious. As a young boy he was cautioned by his father to 'give yourself to be merry';[40] Greville comments on his early love of learning;[41] and Moffet notes the absence in him of a 'combative spirit', and how he preferred to withdraw from court to 'read and dispute somewhere in an inn with a few University men'.[42] Idleness allowed him to cultivate his enormous interest in all the arts and sciences, from discussing proportion in drawing with Nicholas Hilliard to studying chemistry under John Dee. In a Latin poem dated 14 January 1579, Daniel Rogers records Sidney's discussion with Dyer and Greville on law, religion, and moral philosophy.[43] A natural impulse to retreat was abetted by a delicate, even sickly, constitution: he seems never to have enjoyed good health. In a letter to him in January 1574, Languet notes: 'I am very much troubled by the letter in which you write that you are not in very good health, and are even more melancholy than usual',[44] and Sidney replied: 'I readily confess that I am often more melancholy than either my age or my activities demand; but I have fully proved by experience that I am never less liable to moods of melancholy than while I am pitting my weak mental powers against some difficult challenge.'[45]

Idleness only fed his melancholy, causing him to waver between extremes of withdrawal and rash action on his own. His mood became more violent as time passed. In November 1577 Languet remarks that 'desire of fame and glory makes your present inactivity irksome to you'.[46] In March 1578, Sidney replies to Languet's charge that he is slothful by admitting that his once active mind 'is now beginning, by reason of my indolent ease, imperceptibly to lose its strength, and to relax without any reluctance'.[47] In July of that year, Languet rejoices at news that Sidney had been employed by the Queen for he feared that 'the ardour of youth might suggest to you some rash project, and your destiny snatch you from your country and your friends by an inglorious end'. Now that his 'new honours' tie him to his country, 'you must henceforth consult its advantage rather than your own inclination'.[48] Yet that news proved false and Sidney remained free to consult his own inclination to retire.

Languet's most comprehensive letter on Sidney's life was written in September 1580.[49] Since it discusses Sidney's life particularly after 1575, it supplements Sidney's own account up to that date given through Philisides in the *Old Arcadia*. At that time Sidney had retired from the court: a month before he had noted bitterly to Leicester that he keeps from court because of a cold: 'my only service is speech and that is stopped', and goes on to complain in a wry pun that although the Queen may ask how he is, 'so long as she sees a silk doublet upon me, her Highness will think me in good case'.[50]

In his letter Languet chides Sidney for the pleasure he finds in his long retirement. Friends suspect 'that you are tired of that toilsome path which leads to virtue, which you formerly pursued with so much earnestness', and fear that 'the sweetness of your lengthened retirements may somewhat relax the vigorous energy with which you used to rise to noble undertakings, and a love of ease, which you once despised, creep by degrees over your spirit'. Yet he himself hopes that if Sidney is granted long life 'your country would find no small assistance in dangers from your virtue' and notes the gifts showered upon him, such as 'mental endowments, splendour of birth, majesty of person, the expectation of great wealth, the authority and influence of your relations in your country'. However, he fears that modesty and lack of ambition could lead Sidney to seek a life of ease:

You used sometimes to say that you were by nature entirely averse to the excitement and the fascinations of a court, and that when you returned home [in 1575 from his tour], nothing would delight you more than to pass your life with your friends in dignified ease, if ever such a lot should be granted to you.

After his return from the embassy to Germany in 1577, the Queen had expressed her high esteem for him, and his father and friends were delighted 'when they saw everything turn out so prosperously for you, in your very probation at court'. Now only three years later, upon coming to England to rejoice in Sidney's success, Languet laments that 'I found a sort of cloud over your fortunes, which turned the pleasure which I already enjoyed by anticipation, into sorrow'. He concludes his review of Sidney's life by asking him to consider 'how far it is honourable to you to lurk where you are [i.e. at Wilton], whist your country is imploring the aid and support of her sons'. For Languet, a man of Sidney's talents must lead an active life. His last extant letter, a month later, reminds Sidney that 'however pleasant it may be to enjoy familiar intercourse with his family. . .his first duty is to his country'.[51] For him, Sidney's only alternative to the active life was a life of ignoble ease, either with his family or, as he most feared, at court where he 'should be brought to take pleasure in pursuits which only enervate the mind'.[52]

By 1580 Sidney had found another life: neither a life of action, such as Languet would understand, nor a life of ease, nor a contemplative life. Instead, it was the life of a writer:

> Although to write be lesser than to do,
> It is the next deed, and a great one too.[53]

During this year he completed the extended labour of writing the *Old Arcadia*. In his correspondence with Languet, the only clue to this life is found in a letter of 1 March 1578, written at the very time when he was about to undertake his new role. He laments his state of 'indolent ease' in which even his mind begins to relax: 'for to what purpose should our thoughts be directed to various kinds of knowledge, unless room be afforded for putting it into practice, so that public advantage may be the result, which in a corrupt age we cannot hope for'.[54] In his letter to Edward Denny of May 1580, he complains that 'the unnoble constitution of our time doth keep us from fit employments'.[55] His point is

Aristotle's, that man's end is not knowing but doing. Since it is not possible to practise virtue because the age is corrupt, the alternative would seem to be a life of contemplation to cultivate the mind. Yet he rejects this life: 'for while the mind is thus, as it were, drawn out of itself, it cannot turn its powers inward for thorough self-examination; to which employment no labour that men can undertake, is any way to be compared'. He concludes this part of his letter by remarking that he is 'cleverly playing the stoic', and may become a cynic unless Languet reclaims him. He was more serious than he wished Languet to know, for he had found in writing a means by which the mind could 'turn its powers inward for thorough self-examination'. Although writing was not a life of action, it prepared for it. Later, in the *Defence*, he justifies poetry on the grounds that it best achieves the end of knowledge, which is virtuous action, through 'knowledge of a man's self, in the ethic and politic consideration'.[56] In fact, it becomes clear from his argument in this work that 'well-doing' is possible only through 'well-knowing': only through self-knowledge may man practise virtue. As a consequence, all his later writings illustrate the Platonic injunction: 'know thyself'.

THE 'OLD ARCADIA'

Its relation to Sidney

The *Old Arcadia* is a product of Sidney's enforced leisure. According to his father's secretary, Edmund Molyneux, he started it after his embassy to Germany in 1577, and before he was appointed governor of Flushing in 1585: 'not long after his return from that journey, and before his further employment by her majesty, at his vacant and spare times of leisure (for he could endure at no time to be idle and void of action), he made his book which he named *Arcadia*'.[57] Sidney is known to have spent 'times of leisure' at Wilton with his sister Mary, the Countess of Pembroke, from August to December 1577, during the winter of 1579, and from March to August 1580. It seems reasonable to assume that the *Arcadia* was planned in the earlier years and written in 1580. One manuscript is dated 1580, and in October of that year Sidney wrote to his brother Robert that 'my toyful book [or

'books', referring to its five books or acts] I will send with God's
help by February'.[58] (Presumably four months were needed not to
complete the work but to transcribe it.) David Hume of Godscroft
records that Sidney read parts of the work to the Earl of Angus,
known to be in England in 1581–2: 'he was then in travail, or had
brought forth rather (though not polished and refined as now it is)
that his so beautiful and universally accepted birth, his *Arcadia*'.[59]
In his *Devises* (1581), Thomas Howell complains, in a poem
'Written to a most excellent book, full of rare invention', that
Sidney 'all too long...hid'st so perfect work'.[60] The only other
evidence for dating the completion of the *Old Arcadia* in 1580
is Greville's letter of November 1586 in which he refers to Sidney's
'old Arcadia' and to 'a correction of that old one done four or five
years since which he left in trust with me'.[61] The date 1581 or
1582 would refer to its latest revision. Further, while there is no
evidence that Sidney was influenced by Spenser, they were 'in
some use of familiarity'[62] in 1579, and it can hardly be a coinci-
dence that Spenser began *The Faerie Queene* at the same time
that Sidney began its prose equivalent.

While *The Lady of May* is a public work, requested by Leicester
and written for the Queen to be performed in her presence, the
Old Arcadia is a private work, requested by Sidney's sister and
written for her, mostly in her presence. In his dedicatory letter to
her, he writes:

You desired me to do it, and your desire to my heart is an absolute commandment. Now it is done only for you, only to you....Your dear self can
best witness the manner, being done in loose sheets of paper, most of it in
your presence, the rest by sheets sent unto you as fast as they were done.

As the work is a product of his idle times, he refers to it as 'this
idle work' to be read in her 'idle times'. Fittingly, it tells a story
of idle times: of what happens when a ruler retreats for a year
through fear of misfortune prophesied for him, and of what
happens as a consequence when two princes abandon the active
life for his retreat in order to woo his daughters. As in *The Lady
of May*, the pastoral life is opposed to the active life, and the work
concludes with a prince's judgment. In the masque, the lives of
both shepherd and forester are contented: the one is free from
'violent oppression' and the other from any hopes that may not
be quickly satisfied. In the pastoral romance, however, the two

princes suffer 'violent oppression' through love, and entertain hopes which cannot be lawfully satisfied. Unlike the shepherds, it is not possible for them to be good: subject to love's law, which drives them to satisfy desire, they commit actions for which they are justly condemned to death; indeed, their violence goes far beyond that of the forester whose worthiness to have the Lady of May is judged by the Queen. While the worthiness of the two princes to marry their ladies is also judged, the work transcends such considerations. In the masque, the best that may be said for the shepherd's life is (to use Sidney's words in his letter to Languet) that the mind becomes 'drawn out of itself' by the works of Nature, and for the forester's life that it 'raise[s] up the mind' through activity. In the romance, the experience of loving forces the princes to turn the powers of the mind 'inward for thorough self-examination'. Through their story, the reader gains 'knowledge of a man's self, in the ethic and politic consideration', and comes to understand human nature, and therefore his own nature, both its capacity for corruption and its potential greatness.

Sidney's relation to the *Old Arcadia* is suggested by his correspondence with Languet.[63] In October 1578 Languet had written to him: 'I am especially sorry to hear you say that you are weary of the life to which I have no doubt God has called you, and desire to fly from the light of your court and betake yourself to the privacy of secluded places to escape the tempest of affairs by which statesmen are generally harassed.'[64] From Languet's remarks it is clear that Sidney had described as his own state the device that opens the romance: Basilius flees his court to the privacy of secluded places in order to escape the tempest of affairs threatened by the oracle. Further, just as Sidney had proven his worth by his embassy and was expected to fulfil his promise, so, too, his princes at the beginning have proven their worth by heroic adventures and are expected to crown their careers on their return home. So one may discern parallels between Languet's frequent exhortations to Sidney not to retire from active life and Musidorus's remonstrations against Pyrocles's decision to enter Arcadia. Musidorus marks in his friend 'not. . .an alteration, but a relenting, truly, and slacking of the main career you had so notably begun and almost performed' (13), and urges him to examine himself:

See with yourself how fit it will be for you in this your tender youth (born so great a prince, of so rare, not only expectation, but proof, desired of your old father, and wanted of your native country, now so near your home) to divert your thoughts from the way of goodness to lose, nay to abuse, your time. (19)

He speaks with the very accents of Languet:

. . .reflect how grievously you would be sinning against your excellent father, who has placed all his hopes in you, and. . .expects to see the full harvest of all those virtues, which your character promises so largely to produce.[65]

Rudenstine has concluded rightly that the *Old Arcadia* served Sidney 'as an imaginative means of illuminating, exploring, and distancing problems which engrossed him'.[66] Fiction becomes the means by which his mind may 'turn its powers inward for thorough self-examination'.

Sidney relates himself to his story through the character Philisides, a transparent adaptation of his own name. Among the shepherds in Arcadia are 'divers strangers, as well of great as of mean houses, especially such whom inward melancholies made weary of the world's eyes' (56); and among these strangers is Philisides, a solitary knight disguised as a young shepherd, prostrate 'with so deep a melancholy that his senses carried to his mind no delight' (71). He enters the action of the story on only one crucial occasion, to fight the rebels who threaten the lives of his main characters. In the eclogues to Book iii he tells a fable taught him by his mentor, 'old Languet',[67] and finally is persuaded in the eclogues to Book iv to reveal why he is melancholy. He tells the story of his (i.e. Sidney's) life up to his return in 1575 from his European tour. After his return he continues to enjoy 'the benefits of a quiet mind', for he is 'even in the secret of my soul bent on honesty' (i.e. chastity) until 'a most true event', love, brings a change 'much in state but more in mind'. He reviews his early state in verse and goes on to tell how he came to love Mira. Earlier, when he was content,

> Far from my thoughts was aught whereto their minds aspire
> Who under courtly pomps do hatch a base desire.
> Free all my powers were from those captiving snares
> Which heav'nly purest gifts defile in muddy cares.

In this quiet state he studies nature, straining his mind 'the depths of things to find'. Suddenly he sees a vision of Venus and Diana

attended by a maid, Mira. When he prefers Mira to the two god-
desses, he is three times cursed. Venus gives Mira beauty that will
kindle burning fire in him; Diana gives her chastity that will make
him live in despair; and together they declare: 'thou. . .shalt see
such beams shine in her face / That thou shalt never dare seek
help of wretched case.' When he awakens, the dream proves true:
he meets Mira and the curses take effect. He has spent his youth
pursuing her, 'sometimes with some measure of favour, sometimes with unkind interpretations of my most kind thoughts', until
he resolves 'by perpetual absence to choke mine own ill fortunes'
by retiring into Arcadia. Since Philisides is Sidney, what he
singles out as 'a most true event' could only be taken by his sister
and her circle of friends as a personal confession. No evidence
survives, however, to corroborate such an event.

Philisides's role as the melancholy lover retired in disguise is
traditional: it is, for example, the role of Sincero, Sannazaro's
self-portrait in his *Arcadia*. As such, he provides the norm by
which one may measure the actions of the two princes. Kalstone
writes that 'the fall of Philisides, emblematic as well of the fate of
Pyrocles and Musidorus, can be taken as a key to the *Arcadia*'
for his dream 'dramatizes a fall away from the straightforward
growth and positive values of the active life'.[68] Yet Philisides's
earlier state, in which he strained his mind 'the depth of things
to find', is what Sidney describes to Languet as the contemplative
state in which the mind is 'drawn out of itself'. It is not falling
in love that may bring him into that higher state in which the
mind may 'turn its powers inward for thorough self-examination'.
Since he is cursed not to prosecute his love, he may only languish
in despair. His state is entirely contrary to that of the two princes:
he leaves his love to retire into Arcadia in disguise while they enter
Arcadia in disguise to gain their loves. While he remains unchanged, they are forced by love to turn the powers of the mind
'inward for thorough self-examination'. In disguise, they reveal
their princely natures, their shame turns to glory, and by the end
they may put off disguise to become themselves, now fulfilled by
love.

The story Sidney tells his sister is essentially simple: how two
young men woo two young ladies. It becomes complicated because
the men must shamefully disguise themselves, one as an Amazon

and the other as a shepherd, when they are denied access to their ladies.[69] Their disguise is all the more shameful as they are princes, and as their earlier heroism has almost perfected them in virtue. Their wooing becomes a delightful comedy: as an Amazon, Pyrocles cannot reveal his love to Philoclea; yet he is loved by her father, Basilius, and also by her mother, Gynecia, who penetrates his disguise. As a shepherd, Musidorus is rejected by Pamela, and must woo her by wooing Mopsa, the daughter of the clownish herdsman, Dametas. Their wooing is all too successful: Pyrocles seduces Philoclea, and Musidorus, having persuaded Pamela to elope, is only prevented from raping her by the arrival of some rebels. Their lust changes comedy into tragedy: Basilius is found 'dead', apparently poisoned by Gynecia who, having confessed in her anguish over her lust to his murder, is condemned to be buried alive; the two princes are condemned to death; Philoclea is to be confined to a nunnery for life; and Pamela is deprived of succession to the throne. Then tragedy changes to tragicomedy when Basilius, who had been drugged and not poisoned, awakens to pardon them all.

Sidney relates himself to this story by his role as narrator. He remains throughout a presence directing and determining the reader's response. As narrator, his tone is complex, both mocking and sympathetic, bemused and indulgent, asking us to believe, but not to believe wholly, in the story.[70] To Ariosto's playfulness as story-teller in *Orlando Furioso*, he adds Chaucer's keen sympathy for his lovers in *Troilus and Criseyde*. At points where the story itself invites moral judgment, he expresses his amusement. For example, when Pyrocles declares that he will disguise himself as an Amazon, Musidorus condemns him: 'this effeminate love of a woman doth so womanize a man that, if you yield to it, it will not only make you a famous Amazon, but a launder, a distaff-spinner, or whatsoever other vile occupation their idle heads can imagine and their weak hands perform' (20). However, when Pyrocles appears as the Amazon Cleophila, the narrator intrudes to say that he will use this new name, 'for I myself feel such compassion of his passion that I find even part of his fear lest his name should be uttered before fit time were for it; which you, fair ladies that vouchsafe to read this, I doubt not will account excusable' (27). When 'her' song, 'Transformed in show, but more transformed in mind', confirms Musidorus's worst fears and invites moral condemnation, Sidney adds:

I might entertain you, fair ladies, a great while, if I should make as many interruptions in the repeating as she did in the singing. For no verse did pass out of her mouth but that it was waited on with such abundance of sighs, and, as it were, witnessed with her flowing tears, that, though the words were few, yet the time was long she employed in uttering them; although her pauses chose so fit times that they rather strengthened a sweeter passion than hindered the harmony. (29)

Even Musidorus who overhears the song is won over, 'more moved to pity by the manner of Cleophila's singing than with anything he had ever seen – so lively an action doth the mind, truly touched, bring forth'. As a moral spokesman, he is undercut when love transforms him into a shepherd. He tells his story to Pyrocles 'with such passionate dilating', the narrator adds, 'that, for my part, I have not a feeling insight enough into the matter to be able lively to express it' (42). In place of moral judgment, the narrator seeks to awaken sympathy that will lead the reader to understand the lovers' plight.

The lovers gain our sympathy chiefly through the delight they provide. Being so outstanding, they stand outside judgment: whatever they do may be excused. Love becomes wonderful in them because of its extravagance. 'Thus in this one lodge was lodged each sort of grievous passions, while in the other the worthy Dorus was no less tormented, even with the extremest anguish that love at any time can plague the mind withal' (98): we believe this to be so because the lovers do. When Pyrocles reveals himself to Philoclea, he declares that he is 'a living image and a present story of the best pattern love hath ever showed of his workmanship' (120). No reader would be churlish enough to contradict him, or even want to. Surprisingly, our sympathy extends even to the adulterous Basilius and Gynecia. His shameful lust for an Amazon becomes foolish doting, since he seeks a man for his bed, and in an octogenarian – Sidney thought Elizabeth ripe for death when she was only 42 – such vigour assumes heroic proportions. We may not condemn Gynecia because she condemns herself more strongly than her harshest critic:

Forlorn creature that I am, I would I might be freely wicked, since wickedness doth prevail; but the footsteps of my overtrodden virtue lie still as bitter accusations unto me. I am divided in myself; how can I stand? I am overthrown in myself; who shall raise me? Vice is but a nurse of new agonies, and the virtue I am divorced from makes the hateful comparison the more manifest. No, no, virtue; either I never had but a shadow of thee, or thou thyself art but a shadow, for how is my soul abandoned! How are all my powers laid waste! My desire is pained, because it cannot hope; and if hope came, his best should be but mischief. (183)

When she goes on to complain: 'O strange mixture of human minds: only so much good left as to make us languish in our own evils', she involves the sympathy of all but Pharisees in her plight.

As narrator, Sidney similarly involves the reader – and the example is typical of his technique – when he tells how Gynecia believes that Cleophila loves her rather than her daughter: 'Gynecia [was] already half persuaded in herself (O weakness of human conceit!) that Cleophila's affection was turned towards her. For such, alas, are we all! In such a mould are we cast that, with the too much love we bear ourselves being first our own flatterers, we are easily hooked with others' flattery, we are easily persuaded of others' love' (206). Certainly none of the 'fair ladies' addressed by the narrator would fail to understand Gynecia's plight, or fail to sympathize with her. The repeated 'we' includes the narrator, too, and invites all readers to share his sympathetic understanding.

Even when the princes' love turns to lust, the narrator refuses to condemn them. When Musidorus goes to rape the sleeping Pamela, despite his oath to preserve her chastity, he goes to her 'overmastered with the fury of delight' (202): 'of delight' because the narrator shares the passion – and so then the reader – by feeling it with Musidorus. When Pyrocles lays Philoclea on her bed, he recalls a song sung by Philisides about the beauties of his mistress. The narrator assures the 'fair ladies' that Pyrocles does not have leisure to recall the whole song because he is too busy overcoming her weak resistance, and adds: 'he gives me occasion to leave him in so happy a plight, lest my pen might seem to grudge at the due bliss of these poor lovers whose loyalty had but small respite of their fiery agonies' (243). 'So happy a plight. . .due bliss': these are brave and challenging words to describe an act of fornication.

In the two final books, the narrator drops his address to his audience and allows the story to take over. When moral judgment is finally invoked against the lovers, the reader is left deeply divided. The third book ends with the narrator rejoicing in the happiness of Pyrocles and Philoclea; the fourth begins with God's judgment pronounced against them:

The everlasting justice (using ourselves to be the punishers of our faults, and making our own actions the beginning of our chastisement, that our shame may be the more manifest, and our repentance follow the sooner) took Dametas at this present (by whose folly the others' wisdom might receive the greater overthrow) to be the instrument of revealing the secretest cunning – so evil a ground doth evil stand upon, and so manifest it is that nothing remains strongly but that which hath the good foundation of goodness. (265)

As Pyrocles is exposed by 'everlasting justice', so too is Musidorus; vagabonds prevent the rape, 'guided by the everlasting justice to be chastisers of [his] broken vow' (307).

This justice is administered by Evarchus, the father of Pyrocles and uncle of Musidorus.[71] Not knowing who they are, he judges them worthy of death according to the laws of Arcadia, and upholds his verdict even when he learns who they are. All those present at the trial are amazed by what happens – even the hostile Philanax is moved to pity: 'most of them, examining the matter by their own passions, thought Evarchus (as often extraordinary excellencies, not being rightly conceived, do rather offend than please) an obstinate-hearted man, and such a one, who being pitiless, his dominion must needs be insupportable' (414). Yet Evarchus upholds justice absolutely: 'never, never, let sacred rightfulness fall. It is immortal, and immortally ought to be preserved. If rightly I have judged, then rightly have I judged mine own children, unless the name of a child should have force to change the never-changing justice' (411). By their actions the princes are worthy only of death, and nothing qualifies his verdict against them: 'your vices have degraded you from being princes, and have disannulled your birthright' (412). Yet by their worth the princes are worthy only of life, as their conduct in prison and during the trial confirms. Not the narrator, but Musidorus says:

We have lived, and have lived to be good to ourselves and others. Our souls (which are put into the stirring earth of our bodies) have achieved the causes of their hither coming. They have known, and honoured with knowledge, the cause of their creation. And to many men (for in this time, place, and fortune, it is lawful for us to speak gloriously) it hath been behoveful that we should live. (371)[72]

Nothing qualifies that verdict either. The reader is divided between these two verdicts, caught in the clash between justice and equity, justice and mercy, and between what must be and what should be. Sidney rescues him from his dilemma by manipulating the story: Basilius awakens before the sentences are carried out. Yet the dilemma of the trial is not resolved but only forgotten.

If one wonders why Sidney chose to write such a story, one may only speculate – since biographical evidence is lacking – that he was exorcizing his private nightmare. By his mid-twenties he must have feared that he would not fulfil the great expectations held out for him. In writing the *Old Arcadia*, he follows Languet's injunction cited above: 'reflect how grievously you would be sinning against your excellent father, who has placed all his hopes in you, and who being now in the flower of life, expects to see the full harvest of all those virtues'. His natural inclination to retire, his long enforced idleness, and perhaps 'a most true event' of falling in love would lead 'that friendly foe, / Great expectation [to] wear a train of shame',[73] and he might hear his father declare: 'your vices have degraded you from being a prince and have disannulled your birthright'. It is noteworthy, then, that in the revised *Arcadia*, which reveals the earlier history of the chief characters, Evarchus is said to be 'about fifty years' when the princes assumed their disguise.[74] That was Sir Henry's age in 1579 when Sidney was writing the *Old Arcadia*.

As for the genesis of the story there is only Sidney's remark to Mary in dedicating the work to her: 'you desired me to do it, and your desire to my heart is an absolute commandment'. Again one may only speculate, but now with more assurance, that in their 'idle times' together they read romances.[75] Since these would have been chiefly foreign, a concern for English letters may have led her to suggest that he write a romance in English. He may call the work a 'trifle' for several reasons: because it is a romance or fiction and he anticipates the response of 'severer eyes', or because he writes in the vernacular.[76] Paradoxically, his use of the term may indicate that he regards it seriously. His pose of studied nonchalance is nicely spelled out by Greville:

...a new counsel rose up in me, to take away all opinion of seriousness from these perplexed pedigrees; and to this end carelessly cast them into that hypocritical figure *Ironia*, wherein men commonly (to keep above their works) seem to make toys of the utmost they can do.[77]

Accordingly, when Sidney goes on to speak of his 'trifle' as 'triflingly handled' – using the rhetorical term for the disposition or arrangement of the parts of a work – he notes (even with some pride) its careful, deliberate craftsmanship in design and execution.

In the *Defence*, he urges poets to use 'art, imitation, and exercise'. By 'art' he means the 'artificial rules' through which a work acquires fitting artifice; by 'imitation', the 'imitative patterns' or literary models which a poet must use to give his work form; and by 'exercise', the methods by which poets should 'exercise to know' rather than 'exercise as having known'.[78] In the *Old Arcadia*, he shows what he urges others to do, particularly through his careful use of sources.[79]

Sources

The chief sources of the *Old Arcadia* were cited by John Hoskyns, about 1599, in referring to the revised 1590 *Arcadia*: 'for the web, as it were, of his story, he followed three: Heliodorus in Greek, Sannazarius's *Arcadia* in Italian, and *Diana* [by] de Montemayor in Spanish'.[80] In 1607 Gervase Markham defended his earlier claim that Sidney drew 'both from Heliodorus, and *Diana*' by arguing that 'judicial reading. . .first brought it [his mind] to perfection' as 'his contemplative labour first brought him to active worthiness'.[81] To these three sources, William Vaughn Moody, in 1894, added a fourth: *Amadis of Gaul*.[82] Montemayor's work may be ignored here: while it may have suggested to Sidney a pattern of narrative interspersed with songs in a pastoral setting, it influences the structure only of the *New Arcadia*. The *Old Arcadia* openly proclaims its three sources: its setting, reflected in its title, declares its kinship with Sannazaro's *Arcadia*; its involved central plot is extracted chiefly from *Amadis of Gaul* Book XI, and the concluding trial scene is modelled upon that in Heliodorus's *Æthiopian history*. These sources provide the 'imitative patterns' upon which Sidney structures the beginning, middle, and end of his work. Such a conjunction of sources in one work is startling: a third-century Greek romance, a medieval 'French' book of chivalry, and an early sixteenth-century Italian pastoral. It confirms his remark on reading in his letter to Edward Denny of May 1580: 'variety rather delights me, than confounds me'.[83] Clearly he sought to make his work comprehensive in its origins, drawing upon the best works available to him in the classical, medieval, and modern periods.

Sannazaro and the concept of Arcadia   Sidney's *Defence* suggests why he should write a work entitled 'Arcadia', why he opens with a description of that Greek province, and why he begins his action by having Pyrocles yearn to enter such a 'heavenly dwelling':

Do you not see how everything conspires together to make this place a heavenly dwelling? Do you not see the grass, how in colour they excel the emeralds, everyone striving to pass his fellow – and yet they are all kept in an equal height? And see you not the rest of all these beautiful flowers, each of which would require a man's wit to know, and his life to express? Do not these stately trees seem to maintain their flourishing old age with the only happiness of their seat, being clothed with a continual spring because no beauty here should ever fade? (15)

In just these terms he defends the work of the 'right poet' who makes things better than Nature:

Nature never set forth the earth in so rich tapestry as divers poets have done; neither with so pleasant rivers, fruitful trees, sweet-smelling flowers, nor whatsoever else may make the too much loved earth more lovely. Her world is brazen, the poets only deliver a golden.[84]

The difference between the poet's golden world and Nature's brazen one is that between Sidney's Arcadia and the barren, harsh region of the Peloponnesus, and that between the idealized Virgilian Arcadia, which Panofsky characterizes as a place of 'luxuriant vegetation, eternal spring, and inexhaustible leisure for love' and the realistic Ovidian Arcadia which affords only a savage life fit for beasts.[85]

It was inevitable that Sidney should turn to Sannazaro's *Arcadia* as a model to imitate. As C. S. Lewis notes, 'it creates for the singing shepherds a landscape, a social structure, a whole world; a new image, only hinted by previous pastoralists, has come into existence – the image of Arcadia itself'.[86] Yet that ideal world is alien to man: its harmony exposes his own inner discord, and its innocent happiness intensifies the suffering of his fallen state. More than any other work of the Renaissance, Sannazaro's *Arcadia* shows man's alienation from Nature in his isolated and divided state. The opening eclogue expresses this theme: 'Spring and her days do not return for me, / nor do I find herbs or flowers that profit me; / but only thorns and splinters that lacerate the heart.'[87] As the shepherds penetrate more deeply into Arcadia, they expose more clearly man's afflicted state. They enter a retreat guarded by a fearful waterfall where they gather at the tomb of a shepherd whose death caused the woodland deities to abandon the fields, and here they lament the loss of the Golden Age. The hero, Sincero, tells his story of unhappy love, which leads him to lament his presence 'among these Arcadian solitudes in which. . .I can hardly believe that the beasts of the woodlands can dwell with any pleasure, to say nothing of young men nurtured in noble cities'.[88] He is not consoled by a shepherd's love story: its happy ending is impossible to him for his love is dead. To purge another shepherd driven mad by love, the company enters a sacred wood that leads to 'a very deep ravine, bounded on every side by solitary and echoing forests of an unheard-of wildness; so beautiful, so marvellous and strange, that at first sight it strikes with unwonted terror the minds of those that enter there'.[89] Their final way lies through a place of darkness at the source of a 'most terrible river'. The journey to the mysterious centre of the wood inhabited by gods provides a fitting climax to the 1502 version. In the two added sections of the 1504 edition, Sincero is led out of Arcadia by a fearful under-water journey to learn that his lady is dead. Then he yearns for death and curses the hour he left Arcadia.

For Sidney the importance of Sannazaro's work lay in its concept of Arcadia. His praise of the poet's golden world which contains all that 'may make the too much loved earth more lovely' is equivocal, since Nature's brazen world is already 'too much loved'.[90] Accordingly, our response to Arcadia becomes strongly ambivalent: that golden world awakens the happy memory of the Garden of Eden but also the nostalgic awareness that man's life within it has been irretrievably lost. In its innocent life, it is man's true home; but it is also a forbidden place of death. For this reason, Sidney places at its centre a cave in which

Pyrocles, fearful as though he 'had been ready to tread upon a deadly stinging adder' is seized by a passionate Queen.[91] As the analogy with Eden leads one to expect, her lust causes him to be condemned to death by his father. Sidney's Arcadia is closer to Spenser's Bower of Bliss than it is to Eden. Sannazaro does not develop the concept beyond that of Pyrocles's state of mind when he wishes to abandon the active life in order to woo Philoclea. In Sannazaro, the eclogues express this state of mind while the prose provides their setting; in Sidney, the eclogues, placed as detached epilogues to the Books, only comment upon the action. Once the landscape initiates the action, it is used only at certain key points.

Sidney shows how entirely man is alienated from the idyllic world of Arcadia. While the Arcadians are noted 'principally for the moderate and well tempered minds of the people' who have found 'contentation. . .by following the course of nature' (4), the courtly figures who enter their world become hopelessly divided within themselves. The princes, shamefully transformed, yield to lust; Basilius is reduced to a comic mock Duke who commits adultery with his own wife and drinks the potion that brings his 'death'; Gynecia is guilty of lust; and the princesses are caught up in their lovers' guilt. All the major characters invert the Arcadian norm.[92]

'Amadis of Gaul' and chivalric romance   The plot of Sidney's *Arcadia* begins when Pyrocles, in love, despairs of being able to enter Basilius's Arcadian retreat until 'love, the refiner of invention, put in his head a way how to come to the sight of his Philoclea' (12) by disguising himself as an Amazon. This way, and some of its consequences, are taken from *Amadis of Gaul* Book VIII, which tells how Amadis of Greece, having seen the picture of a sequestered princess, disguises himself as an Amazon to woo her, only to be frustrated when he is wooed by her aged father. So, too, Musidorus's device to woo Pamela derives from *Amadis* Book IX, which tells how Florisel disguises himself as a shepherd to woo his lady. Sidney's use of *Amadis* as a source for his plot was compounded when he came to Book XI, in which four scattered chapters treat the adventures of Prince Agesilan and his cousin Don Arlanges after they see a picture of the princess Diane. When the Prince falls in love with her, he

disguises himself as an Amazon, and, in the company of Arlanges disguised as a damsel, journeys to where she lives in forced retirement with the Queen. After they are accepted into service, Arlanges falls in love with Cléophile. Much later in the same Book, and in another story, several chapters relate the adventures of the Prince after he leaves. No longer disguised, he is shipwrecked off the coast of Galdap. While he is talking to the Queen, he is confronted by the jealous King: to escape suspicion, he declares that he is a maid. As a result, the King loves him to the point of madness and the Queen locks him up until he agrees to yield to her. Sidney needed only to combine these stories to yield his main plot. More important than the stories, however, is their context in *Amadis of Gaul* which introduces the values of chivalry into pastoral romance.

In chivalric romance, the claims of chivalry and love upon the hero are one: inspired by love, the knight is ready to undertake any heroic adventure to prove himself worthy of his mistress. Only when Amadis is scorned by Oriana does he retire to a hermitage; but when she declares her love for him he becomes the Knight of the Green Helmet. In this new role he becomes more famous than he was as Amadis, and is rewarded by having Oriana take him to bed for eight days 'in joys dearer to him than even Paradise'.[93] The central chivalric formula by which he lives is expressed by Spenser: 'love does always bring forth bounteous [i.e. virtuous] deeds'.[94] It is promised of Amadis, and the promise is amply fulfilled, that 'such deeds shall he do as none would think could be begun nor ended by body of man. . . .He shall be the knight in the world who most loyally maintains his love, and he shall love one answerable to his high prowess.'[95]

Sidney inverts the chivalric formula. To gain their mistresses' favour, Pyrocles and Musidorus abandon heroic adventure and assume shameful disguise. In their roles as Amazon and shepherd, they are mocked, abused, and humiliated. Pyrocles reveals himself to Philoclea as 'a miserable miracle of affection. . .whom you only have brought to this fall of fortune and unused [i.e. unusual] metamorphosis; whom you only have made neglect his country, forget his father, and lastly forsake himself' (120). When his friend reveals his plan to elope with Pamela, he sums up his career in these despairing terms:

There came straight before her mind, made tender with woes, the images of her own fortune; her tedious longings; her causes to despair; the cumbersome folly of Basilius; the enraged jealousy of Gynecia; herself a prince without retinue, a man annoyed with the troubles of womankind, loathsomely loved, and dangerously loving; and now, for the perfecting of all, her friend to be taken away by himself, to make the loss the greater by the unkindness. (174)

Although the one elopes with Pamela and the other seduces Philoclea, both are captured and justly condemned to death. While love sustains Amadis in all heroic endeavour, it puts Sidney's heroes to shame. Chivalric values measure not their achievement but their decline.

Heliodorus and heroic romance   The superiority of Heliodorus's *Æthiopian history* to *Amadis* is upheld by its translator, Underdowne, who defends the work as 'the most honest (as I take this to be) history of love': 'If I shall compare it with other of like argument, I think none cometh near it. *Morte Darthur, Arthur of little Britain*, yea, and *Amadis of Gaul*, etc. accompt violent murder, or murder for no cause, manhood: and fornication and all unlawful lust, friendly love.'[96] While Sidney may have shared the contempt of pious humanists for the 'open manslaughter and bold bawdry' of medieval romance,[97] in the *Defence* he praises *Amadis* in qualified terms: 'Truly, I have known men that even with reading *Amadis de Gaule* (which God knoweth wanteth much of a perfect poesy) have found their hearts moved to the exercise of courtesy, liberality, and especially courage.'[98] Yet he agrees with Underdowne in his praise of Heliodorus's 'sugared invention of that picture of love in Theagenes and Chariclea'. Since Heliodorus invented 'so true a lover as Theagenes', transcending what Nature may produce, he has written 'an absolute heroical poem'.[99]

In seeking 'imitative patterns' for his *Arcadia*, Sidney would be attracted by the strange, violent, and erotic world of Greek romance, and particularly by Heliodorus, because of the exemplary nature of his characters and his variety of wonder-evoking episodes which test the characters' inner worth. More particularly, he would be interested in the structure of the *Æthiopian history*, for Scaliger had recommended that the epic poet read Heliodorus very carefully and set his work before him as a most excellent model.[100] As his close imitation shows, Sidney was attracted by its concluding trial-scene with its dazzling dilemmas.

After heroic adventures in which they miraculously preserve their chastity – they are betrothed but their marriage is not confirmed – Theagenes and Chariclea prove worthy to be sacrificed to the gods. He proves himself chaste by the ordeal of putting his foot in fire: 'there was great wondering, both for that he being so tall and beautiful, as also because he was so young and lusty, and had never to do with any woman'. She proves herself even more chaste by standing in fire: 'thereat was every man amazed, . . .and wondered beside all other things, that she being more beautiful than any mortal woman, and in her best youth had not lost her virginity'.[101] Not knowing who she is, her father, Hydaspes, condemns them to death. When he learns who she is, he is overcome by joy but also by wonder; as an Ethiopian, he is amazed that she is white, until his wife explains to his satisfaction (if not to ours) that she was gazing at a picture of the white body of Andromeda when Chariclea was conceived. However, Hydaspes upholds his verdict: for the sake of justice, his own child must die.

Sidney inverts his source, so that his two heroes are not proved chaste but found guilty of lust:

> . . .he that terms himself Timopyrus [Pyrocles's assumed name] denies not he offered violence to the lady Philoclea, an act punished by all the Grecian laws with being thrown down from a high tower to the earth. . . .And since the wickedness of lust is by our decrees punished by death, though both consent, much more is he whose wickedness so overflows as he will compel another to be wicked. The other young man confesseth he persuaded the princess Pamela to fly her country, and accompanied her in it – without all question a ravishment no less than the other; for, although he ravished her not from herself, yet he ravished her from him that owned her, which was her father. This kind is chastised by the loss of the head, as a most execrable theft. (405–6)

Yet the trial which proves their guilt proves their worth. Their inward state is displayed outwardly when they appear in attire which strikes beholders with 'the more violence of magnanimity, and so to conquer the expectation of the lookers with an extraordinary virtue' (377). During the trial they take the guilt upon themselves in order to exonerate the princesses. After the trial Pyrocles humbly submits himself to his father's verdict and begs pardon only for his friend. Then Musidorus begs for Pyrocles's pardon, 'each employing his wit how to show himself most worthy to die, to. . .an admiration of all the beholders' (414). In their moment of greatest shame they achieve the height of heroic virtue.

While the trial vindicates the princes in their magnanimity, it also vindicates Evarchus in his justice. Here Sidney follows Heliodorus closely. Evarchus says to the princes, 'I prefer you much before my life, but I prefer justice as far before you' (411) and Hydaspes says to the people: 'so will I make more account of your weal public than mine own private commodity'.[102] Each uses much the same language in urging his child to accept his verdict: 'if ever thou didst show thyself to be of stout courage and princely mind, now pluck up thy heart'. . .'if there be anything left in you of princely virtue, show it in constant suffering'.[103] Both judges pass the supreme test of preferring justice before the closest human bonds.

The trial scene shows that Sidney regarded his *Old Arcadia* as an heroical poem: in the *Defence* he argues that this kind of poem 'maketh magnanimity and justice shine through all misty fearfulness and foggy desires'.[104] Yet where magnanimity (the highest private virtue) and justice (the highest public virtue) conflict, as they do in the trial-scene, some device is needed to provide a happy ending. In Heliodorus the device is simple and sufficient: since justice is based on the people's custom, the people force Hydaspes to pardon his daughter. When the priest persuades him that the gods no longer want human sacrifice, he may also pardon her lover, 'seeing that these things be thus appointed by the will and pleasure of the gods'.[105] In Sidney, the device is simpler: Basilius revives to pardon them all. Yet this is not sufficient once justice is conceived as 'sacred rightfulness'; then the 'never-changing justice' can only be forgotten in the general rejoicing. The crimes of the princes, their 'so many foul breaches of hospitality, civility, and virtue' (411) remain 'both abominable and inexcusable' (407–8). Yet finally Basilius may claim, as does Hydaspes, that 'all had fallen out by the highest providence' (416) for the princes' deeds confirm the oracle.

In revising the *Old Arcadia*, Sidney changed the oracle, to have the princes guilty only of the murder of Basilius. It would follow,

then, that when Basilius revived, they could be freed without
ignoring Evarchus's solemn charge: 'never, never, let sacred rightfulness fall'. Ringler suggests that Sidney 'apparently became
aware of the ethical ambiguity of this scene' and eliminated it
by revising the oracle.[106] It is more likely, however, that he was
aware of the ambiguity from the beginning. It is just possible that
the work grew as he wrote, so that what began as a light-hearted
pastoral romance developed in the two final books into a serious
heroic poem. Yet it remains carefully designed in relation to its
sources, as Sidney had first planned. Robertson notes rightly that
'it is clear from the words of the oracle at the very beginning
that Sidney had planned his five-act drama with extreme care;
and he triumphantly carried out his intentions with unflagging
execution right through to the final scene'.[107] The *peripeteia*
achieved by Basilius's revival is essential to the happy ending
needed for a tragicomedy. That Sidney revised the *Old Arcadia*
may, but need not, imply that he was in some way dissatisfied
with it. However that may be, the revised oracle belongs to a
different work, about which we cannot speculate because its ending remains unknown. In the *Old Arcadia* as it stands, the ethical
ambiguity of the trial scene is essential to its whole argument.

Argument

The argument of the *Old Arcadia* may be epitomized simply as
'Love under judgment'. The five Books or Acts provide an anatomy
of love: its nature, its working within man, its power both to debase
and ennoble, and its conflict with morality and public order.[108]

Act I Pyrocles need see only the picture of Philoclea, to be
overcome by 'that wonderful passion which to be defined is impossible, by reason no words reach near to the strange nature of it.
They only know it which inwardly feel it. It is called love' (11–12).
That claim stands as a formal prologue to a work which seeks to
define 'that wonderful passion' through its plot.

Love's 'strange nature' is expressed in the two opposed views of
love in the debate between the two princes. Musidorus denounces
love because it takes man from 'the true exercise of virtue' (18) by
permitting the passions to conquer reason:

This bastard love (for, indeed, the name of love is unworthily applied to so hateful a humour as it is, engendered betwixt lust and idleness), as the matter it works upon is nothing but a certain base weakness, which some gentle fools call a gentle heart; as his adjoined companions be unquietness, longings, fond comforts, faint discomforts, hopes, jealousies, ungrounded rages, causeless yieldings; so is the highest end it aspires unto a little pleasure, with much pain before, and great repentance after. (19–20)

Pyrocles defends love indirectly by defending woman as being capable of virtue: since man should love virtue, he may love virtue in a beautiful woman. He defends love directly as it belongs to 'the highest power of the mind', which he links with man's love of virtue. Since love works in the virtuous heart, 'if we love virtue, in whom shall we love it but in virtuous creatures? – Without your meaning be I should love this word of virtue when I see it written in a book' (22). Finally he defends the state of loving itself, which is directed to virtuous creatures in order to prepare man for heavenly love. These opposed views on the nature and working of love provide the framework for the plot. By the end both are proven true.

Act I shows love's triumph over each of the major characters. Musidorus yields to love once he sees Pamela: 'O thou celestial, or infernal, spirit of love. . .or what other heavenly or hellish title thou list to have, for both those effects I find in myself' (42). When Pyrocles appears as the Amazon, Basilius dotes on him, Philoclea delights in his presence, and 'a new wonderful passionate love' overwhelms Gynecia: 'it reduced her whole mind to an extreme and unfortunate slavery – pitifully, truly, considering her beauty and estate; but for a perfect mark of the triumph of love who could in one moment overthrow the heart of a wise lady, so that neither honour long maintained, nor love of husband and children, could withstand it' (48).

Love's triumph is expressed emblematically in the concluding scene. The disguised princes and the three ladies enter an enclosed Arcadian retreat in which Pyrocles's wooing of Philoclea and Musidorus's attentions to Pamela are interrupted by a lion and a bear. These beasts attack the princesses but are slain by their suitors. While Musidorus comforts the swooning Pamela with kisses, Pyrocles runs after the frightened Philoclea to present her with the lion's head. When Gynecia joins the chase, the narrator comments: 'it was a new sight fortune had prepared to those woods, to see these three great personages thus run one after the other, each carried away with the violence of an inward evil' (48). As the violence in the princes is embodied in the beasts, their slaying of them reveals their heroism[109] even in their transformed state, as David's slaying of the lion and bear, which endangered the sheep, proved him worthy to meet Goliath.[110] The chase itself becomes an emblem of love's violence, as it does in the chase in which Basilius joins to attend the wounded Pyrocles: 'it seemed that love had purposed to make in those solitary woods a perfect demonstration of his unresistible force, to show that no desert place can avoid his dart. He must fly from himself that will shun his evil' (49). The narrator observes that the passion which rules Gynecia and Basilius is 'so wonderful and in effect incredible' that no words can describe its power, and he appeals to the experience of his audience: 'but you, worthy ladies, that have at any time feelingly known what it means, will easily believe the possibility of it. Let the ignorant sort of people give credit to them that have passed the doleful passage, and daily find that quickly is the infection gotten which in long time is hardly cured' (49).

Act II shows the working of love: 'the cup of poison, which was deeply tasted of all this noble company, had left no sinew of theirs without mortally searching into it' (91). What Sidney calls 'a very stage-play of love' (54) is acted out in the laments of the lovers, beginning and ending with Gynecia because love works most intensely in her. In her 'violent passion', Gynecia laments that she has become 'a plague to myself, and a shame to womankind' (92). She is interrupted by Pyrocles who laments the inward evil that he suffers through love, and both are interrupted by Basilius's 'doting love' (97). Philoclea is shown suffering 'strange unwonted motions in herself' through a 'burning affection' for the Amazon (97). Musidorus is shown suffering 'the extremest anguish that love at any time can plague the mind withal' (98). When Pamela realizes who he is, 'every passion he expressed had his mutual working in her. Full well she found the lively image of a vehement desire in herself' (106).

After this catalogue of love's variety, which extends to Mopsa's 'certain smackering' (100) towards Musidorus, the second half of the Act shows love in its two extreme states: innocent love in

Philoclea and guilty lust in Gynecia. The narrator points to the importance of Philoclea, whose name indicates that she is 'famed for love', when he turns to consider her suffering: 'But alas, sweet Philoclea, how hath my pen forgotten thee, since to thy memory principally all this long matter is intended' (108).[111] Her transition from innocent love when she responds to Pyrocles as an Amazon, to stirrings of desire when she wishes him to be a man, to fullness of love when she yields to him knowing him to be a man, is subtly and poignantly rendered. While her falling in love is a fall from innocence into experience, she remains innocent. Because Gynecia is totally fallen, it is given to her to interrupt her daughter's confession of virtuous love for Pyrocles. Her 'inflaming agonies of affection' (122) are displayed as guilty lust and jealousy. But when she is about to display her 'deadly desires', she is interrupted by rebels who come to kill the royal party. As with the attack of the beasts in Book i, this attack provides a concluding emblem for the Book. Social chaos reflects the inner chaos of the royal party and offers an occasion for the princes to reveal their heroic valour even in their transformed states.[112]

Act III presents the love-game comedy that follows when the princes are determined to satisfy desire. When Musidorus becomes a slave to desire, he is determined to elope with Pamela. When Pyrocles is confronted by the lustful Gynecia who is determined to satisfy her desire, he must act: 'there was no way but to yield to the violence of their desires, since striving did the more chafe them; and that following their own current, at length of itself it would bring her to the other side of her burning desires' (185). In effect, their motto is: 'what dare not love undertake, armed with the night and provoked with lust?' (224). Musidorus elopes with Pamela, but is prevented from raping her when rebels interrupt him. Pyrocles arranges to have Basilius and Gynecia go separately to a cave where each expects to join him, and while the Duke commits adultery with his own wife in the darkness, Pyrocles goes to seduce Philoclea. As he goes, he reviews his present state of mind: 'all the great estate of his father seemed unto him but a trifling pomp, whose good stands in other men's conceit, in comparison of the true comfort he found in the depth of his mind; and the knowledge of any misery that might ensue this joyous adventure was recked of but as a slight purchase of possessing the top of happiness' (228–9). His state of 'all for love', which is also Musidorus's, brings final judgment against them.

Act IV shows the immediate consequences of love's actions. Basilius takes the poison which causes his 'death', leaving Gynecia in her guilt ready to confess his murder; the despairing Pyrocles, knowing that Philoclea will be condemned to death for fornication, tries to take his own life; Musidorus and Pamela are seized by the rebels and returned to Arcadia; and Arcadia is reduced to chaos, 'all the whole multitude fallen into confused and dangerous divisions' (320).

In *Act V* the lovers, and through them love itself, are brought to judgment before Evarchus. Gynecia need not be tried because she is ready to confess that she murdered Basilius, 'brought first by the violence of that ill-answered passion [her lust for Pyrocles], and then by the despairing conceit she took of the judgement of God in her husband's death' (384). In contrast, the princes glory in their love despite their open shame. Pyrocles says to Musidorus: 'for my part (and so dare I answer for you) I call all the gods to witness, I am so far from that [repenting his love] no shame, no torment, no death, would make me forgo the least part of the inward honour, essential pleasure, and living life I have enjoyed in the presence of the faultless Philoclea' (372). In his defence Pyrocles claims that he was 'inflamed with love (a passion far more easily reprehended than refrained)' (392): although he offered force to Philoclea, 'love offered more force to me' (394). Musidorus also pleads 'love's force' to excuse his elopement with Pamela: 'manlike courages that by experience know how subject the virtuous minds are to love a most virtuous creature...will deem it a venial trespass to seek the satisfaction of honourable desires' (402).

Evarchus judges Pyrocles guilty because he has confessed that he offered violence to Philoclea: 'nothing can be imagined more unnatural than by force to take that which, being holily used, is the root of humanity, the beginning and maintaining of living creatures, whereof the confusion must needs be a general ruin' (405–6). He also judges Musidorus guilty of ravishment because he confessed that he persuaded Pamela to elope. In opposition to the 'unbridled desire' which led the two princes to their sinful acts, he defines love as 'that sweet and heavenly uniting of the

minds, which. . .hath no other knot but virtue; and therefore if
it be a right love, it can never slide into any action that is not
virtuous' (407). Since the princes have committed offences that
are 'both abominable and inexcusable', on behalf of justice and
in accord with the laws of Arcadia, he condemns them to death.
Even when he learns who they are, he upholds his judgment: 'if
rightly I have judged, then rightly have I judged mine own children, unless the name of a child should have force to change the
never-changing justice' (411). Accordingly, he is swayed neither
by personal grief, nor by Musidorus's scorn of his tyranny, nor by
Pyrocles's appeal that Musidorus be pardoned because his own
death would satisfy justice, nor by the sympathy of the people for
the princes.

Yet the dilemma brought by his judgment challenges that
judgment and even justice itself.[113] Evarchus claims that he
reached his judgment by weighing the evidence presented at the
trial 'with my most unpartial and furthest reach of reason', and
that his judgment must stand 'if rightly I have judged' (411). Yet
the act of judging itself has been challenged earlier by Gynecia
when she warns Philanax that 'it may be truth doth make thee
deal untruly, and love of justice frames unjustice in thee' (381).
When Evarchus first appears he warns the Arcadians that, being
a man, he is 'a creature whose reason is often darkened with error'
(365). His judgment becomes suspect when he condemns Gynecia
to death for a crime she did not commit. When he agrees to pre-
side at the trial of his own children, the narrator observes that
'the strange and secret working of justice had brought [him] to be
the judge over them – in such a shadow or rather pit of darkness
the wormish mankind lives that neither they know how to foresee
nor what to fear, and are but like tennis balls tossed by the racket
of the higher powers' (385–6). Evarchus judges in this pit of darkness, and the working of justice is more 'strange and secret' than
he sees. Accordingly, when Pyrocles submits himself to his judgment, declaring that it has pleased the 'unsearchable wisdoms' of
the 'almighty gods' to shame him before his father, those wisdoms
prove more 'unsearchable' than either knows. His actions, and
Musidorus's, which so offend justice, fulfil the oracle. Evarchus
claims that true love 'can never slide into any action that is not
virtuous'; yet the oracle declares that Pyrocles and Philoclea shall

love with Nature's blessing. At the end Basilius may well declare
that 'all had fallen out by the highest providence' and the narrator note (though in another matter) how 'uncertain are mortal
judgements' (416).

What most challenges justice, or rather, the absolute justice upheld by Evarchus, is its denial of equity: the strict application of
the letter of the law fails to take into account both the circumstances of the acts being judged and the worth of the actors. While
the princes have always been worthy to live, at that moment when
each pleads that he may die so that the other may live, 'each employing his wit how to show himself most worthy to die' (414),
both prove themselves worthy only to live. Evarchus is rightly
warned by Pyrocles not to seek 'too precise a course of justice'
(414); for, in disobeying the Biblical injunction, 'Be not thou just
overmuch',[114] he becomes unjust.

The dilemmas of the trial-scene are not meant to be resolved
by Basilius's revival. The response of all readers, particularly the
response of the 'fair ladies' whom Sidney addresses, must remain
divided. Only another Evarchus could uphold his judgment without wavering. The work as a whole demands a divided response:
the delight it affords constantly wars with its instruction in order
to invite the reader's participation. For example, when Pyrocles is
trapped in Philoclea's room, 'he saw the weak judgement of man
would condemn that as a death-deserving vice in her which had
in truth never broken the bands of a true living virtue' (290). So
Evarchus would have judged her if he had known that she willingly yielded to him; but the reader, who does know, is left with
the contradiction that Philoclea is both guilty of 'a death-deserving vice' and that she has never broken 'the bands of a true living
virtue'. When love is finally brought to judgment in the trial-
scene, delight and instruction stand opposed. Basilius's revival
may be designed for the frailty of the reader who is unable to
face the reality brought to life by 'sacred rightfulness' and who
desires a happy ending whatever the cost. It is also the poet's
defiant assertion of what must be and should be.

Sidney observes to his audience at one point that 'it is better to
know by imagination than experience' (227) and later in the Defence argues that it is better to learn by the poet's 'feigned example'
than by a true one.[115] Whatever reasons may have prompted him

to write the *Old Arcadia*, through it he prepares for life by imaginatively projecting the conflicting demands of living and loving
upon a young man. Rudenstine claims that the work 'reveals itself
. . .as a fictional extension of Sidney's letters in defense of relaxa-
tion, reflection, and a life of dignified ease'.[116] Yet it is an attack,
not a defence, for it shows the conflict between man's private and
public lives, and his successful efforts to resolve the pressures from
within and the demands from without. It poses the fundamental
question: how may man fulfil his nature? Must he do so through
action in the world, gaining worldly honour at the expense of his
own nature which requires him to love and, in loving, seek to
satisfy desire? In his opening debate with Basilius, Philanax upholds the life of virtuous action, and the disasters that follow
Basilius's retreat from that life confirm all that he says. At the beginning the princes, too, uphold that life, and believe that they
give it up when they yield to love. The oracle shows, however,
that a power greater than they know controls their lives. By retiring, Basilius seeks to prevent the oracle being fulfilled; yet by
doing so he creates the circumstances through which it may be fulfilled. By following him, the princes give themselves up to shame;
by yielding to shame, however, they fulfil themselves in virtue.

This story is Sidney's own in the ways noted earlier: the presence of Philisides, the narrator's control over his reader's response,
and the implicit fear that instead of fulfilling his father's high
expectations, finally his father would condemn him. The work
supports Greville's claim that in it he presents 'delicate (though
inferior) pictures of himself'.[117] Yet that story is in no way pecu-
liarly his own but extends to every man. As a consequence, it is
serious though never solemn; it is characterized by the quality,
which C. S. Lewis notes in its author, a 'joyful seriousness'.[118]
Robertson concludes soundly that Sidney's treatment of the role
of fortune and divine providence 'does not mean that he was
trying to turn his often light-hearted tale into a Calvinistic
treatise'.[119]

The first – and almost final – fact about the work is that Sidney
began to write it as a young man of 24 for his favourite sister, who
was 17. He was prepared to call it 'a trifle' because the delight it
affords the reader is deeply serious.

Sidney's 'unelected vocation'

In the *Defence of poetry* Sidney refers to the work as 'the defence of that my unelected vocation', explaining that 'I know not by what mischance in these my not old years and idlest times [I have]. . .slipped into the title of a poet'.[1] The studied nonchalance behind this modest disclaimer suggests that poetry has become his elected vocation. For if the *Defence* was written in 1579–80, he must be referring to the three poems in *The Lady of May*, the 'gallant variety, both in matter and form'[2] of the verse in the *Old Arcadia* (the 51 poems in the text and the set of eclogues placed after each of the first four Books), perhaps thirty of the 32 *Certain sonnets*, and possibly his translation of 43 psalms.[3] The extent and variety of these early poems suggests that Sidney would include himself among those who are said in the *Defence* to be 'inclinable' to poetry, that is, those to whom that 'divine gift' is given.[4] The radical experimenting in this early work – in metre, verse form, internal structuring, and relationships between poems – reveals his concern to cultivate his gift. Yet there is scant contemporary evidence of his interest in writing poetry. In 1587 Lodowick Bryskett recorded that he and Sidney scaled the Apennines during their European tour 'still with the Muses sporting'.[5] After his German embassy, Sidney was addressed by Paul Schede as 'Sydnee Musarum inclite cultibus'.[6] Fortunately, Sidney adds an appendix to the *Defence* in which he discusses the current state of English poetry and his relationship to it.

In the first part of the *Defence* Sidney defends the art of poetry itself by describing its 'right use both of matter and manner' (119). He shows in detail how the 'right poet' may be 'lifted up with the vigour of his own invention. . .freely ranging only within the zodiac of his own wit'. In the second part, he describes the right use of that art in England by showing how English poets have failed to employ their own invention and wit. For the real enemies of poetry are not the poet-haters, who reject the art itself, but the poet-apes who abuse it: base men with servile wits publish their verse with the result that the true poets 'suppress the outflowings of their wit' in order not to be included among them. By writing poetry himself, Sidney has learned why the art of poetry is abused in England:

But I that, before ever I durst aspire unto the dignity, am admitted into the company of the paper-blurrers, do find the very true cause of our wanting estimation is want of desert – taking upon us to be poets in despite of Pallas. Now, wherein we want desert were a thankworthy labour to express; but if I knew, I should have mended myself. But I, as I never desired the title, so have I neglected the means to come by it. Only, overmastered by some thoughts, I yielded an inky tribute unto them. (111)

His argument in this part of the *Defence* is expressed in its proposition: 'Marry, they that delight in poesy itself should seek to know what they do, and how they do; and especially look themselves in an unflattering glass of reason, if they be inclinable unto it.' He considers first how the matter of poetry may be given form by the three means of 'art, imitation, and exercise'. From the right use of matter, he turns to the right use of manner – from poetry as an art of dialectic to poetry as an art of rhetoric – by treating the chief means by which diction may become eloquent. He concludes his digression with the same modest disclaimer with which he began, and adds that writing poetry has taught him its art:

I think this digression will make my meaning receive the fuller understanding: which is not to take upon me to teach poets how they should do, but only, finding myself sick among the rest, to show some one or two spots of the common infection grown among the most part of writers, that, acknowledging ourselves somewhat awry, we may bend to the right use both of matter and manner. (119)

He goes on to praise the English language as 'being indeed capable of any excellent exercising of it': 'for the uttering sweetly and properly the conceits of the mind (which is the end of speech), that hath it equally with any other tongue in the world'. Before concluding with a peroration to the whole work, he appends a note on the practice of two kinds of verse, quantitative and accentual.

From the manner in which Sidney presents his argument in this part of the *Defence*, it becomes clear that he tried to show in his early poetry how the 'divine gift' should be cultivated if English poets were to show that their language is 'indeed capable of any excellent exercising of it'. Ringler concludes that in the *Defence* he 'taught his countrymen that a poet should be...an accomplished craftsman, and in his own poetry he provided both technical models to be followed and examples of excellence. He introduced new techniques of rhythm and rhyme, new stanzaic patterns, and new examples of poetic kinds. What he taught his countrymen in the 1580s, many of them were practising in the 1590s.'[7] In his earlier poetry, however, his more immediate purpose was to teach himself the craft of writing. Not modesty alone led him to remark that he had neglected the means to come by the title of a poet but recognition that his gift must be assiduously cultivated if ever he was to achieve a style worthy of an English poet. In writing his early poetry, he could not know, as we now do, that he would display such a style in *Astrophel and Stella*.

QUANTITATIVE VERSE

Sidney's experimenting is most noticeable in his one failure, the effort to adapt classical quantitative verse to English in place of accentual verse. In October 1579 Spenser wrote to Harvey that Sidney and Dyer 'have proclaimed in their ἀρείῳ πάγῳ, a general surceasing and silence of bald rhymers, and also of the very best too; instead whereof, they have by authority of their whole senate, prescribed certain laws and rules of quantities of English syllables for English verse, having had thereof already great practice'.[8] As Spenser implies, one purpose in writing quantitative verse was to make poetry learned, as opposed to the vulgar rhyming of those whom Sidney terms the 'poet-apes'. Its chief purpose was not to make English verse classical but to allow it to rival the classics, as Spenser reveals in his outburst to Harvey: 'for, why a God's name, may not we, as else the Greeks, have the kingdom of our own language, and measure our accents by the sound, reserving the quantity to the verse'.[9] Behind the experiment was an effort to prove a claim that Sidney makes in the *Defence*, that 'it is not rhyming and versing that maketh a poet': 'verse [is] but an ornament and no cause to poetry, since there have been many most excellent poets that never versified, and now swarm many versifiers that need never answer to the name of poets' (81). More positively, he wanted to show how the poet may order his words.

The case for quantitative verse is made in the 'First Eclogues' of the *Old Arcadia* by Dicus in his debate with Lalus on the relation of poetry to music. He argues that properly measured words may give poetry its own 'secret music': 'since by the measure one may perceive some verses running with a high note fit for great matters, some with a light foot fit for no greater than amorous conceits' (89). Further, quantitative metre may avoid the monotony and plainness of accentual verse. His argument may be illustrated by Musidorus's lament, which is introduced as 'elegiac verse' with the metre

$$- - - - - \cup \cup - \cup \cup - \cup \cup - -$$
$$- - - \cup \cup - - \cup \cup - \cup \cup -$$

Fortune, Nature, Love, long have contended about me,
    Which should most miseries cast on a worm that I am.
Fortune thus gan say: 'Misery and misfortune is all one,
    And of misfortune, Fortune hath only the gift.
With strong foes on land, on seas with contrary tempests,
    Still do I cross this wretch, what so he taketh in hand.'
'Tush, tush', said Nature, 'this is all but a trifle, a man's self
    Give haps or mishaps, e'en as he ord'reth his heart.
But so his humour I frame, in a mould of choler adusted,
    That the delights of life shall be to him dolorous.'
Love smiled, and thus said: 'Want joined to desire is unhappy.
    But if he naught do desire, what can Heraclitus ail?
None but I works by desire; by desire have I kindled in his soul
    Infernal agonies unto a beauty divine,
Where thou, poor Nature, left'st all thy due glory to Fortune.
    Her virtue is sovereign, Fortune a vassal of hers.'
Nature abashed went back; Fortune blushed, yet she replied thus:
    'And e'en in that love shall I reserve him a spite.'
Thus, thus, alas! woeful in nature, unhappy by fortune,
    But most wretched I am now love awakes my desire. (79–80)

Even with the rules that Sidney appends to the lament, the lines are difficult to scan for the reasons that Ringler offers: 'the rules themselves incongruously yoke contradictory principles. The quantities of syllables are determined first by their position, otherwise by their natural sound; but the Latin rule of position is not valid for determining the length of English syllables, and its mechanical application results in patterns of scansion that continually clash with Elizabethan pronunciation.'[10] The lines are difficult to scan for the further reason that Dicus offers: we lack the music by which 'a poet should straight know how every word should be measured' (89). Yet despite the difficulty in scanning the lines, and even because of it, the words in their placing acquire a disturbing rhythm which gives them a power and weight of meaning far beyond what accentual rhymed verse or prose could provide in the 1570s.

One may compare, for example, Pyrocles's lament which begins:

> Transformed in show, but more transformed in mind,
> I cease to strive, with double conquest foiled;
> For (woe is me) my powers all I find
> With outward force and inward treason spoiled. (28)

Or his lament with Musidorus:

Alas! What further evil hath fortune reserved for us, or what shall be the end of this our tragical pilgrimage? Shipwracks, daily dangers, absence from our country, have at length brought forth this captiving of us within ourselves which hath transformed the one in sex, and the other in state, as much as the uttermost work of changeable fortune can be extended unto. (43)

In place of rhetoric, the measured verse has a dialectic: it produces a poetry of statement which argues the case of Fortune against Nature and Love. The conclusion to which that argument inevitably leads in the two final lines becomes persuasive chiefly because the measured verse has forced the reader to attend to its logic. In the *Defence* 119–20, Sidney refers to 'the low or lofty sound of the well-weighed syllable' in quantitative verse. Sound reinforces sense to give the verse its 'secret music', which it would not have if the concluding line, for example, read:

> But I most wretched am now love awakes desire.

Sound and sense together produce a metrical line in which words are significantly ordered.

In reply to Dicus's arguments for measured verse, Lalus claims that poetry goes beyond music, for it appeals to the mind as well as the ear. To the measure of music the poet may add rhyme and accent to beautify his words: 'he that rhymes observes something the measure but much the rhyme, whereas the other attends only measure without all respect of rhyme; besides the accent which the rhymer regardeth, of which the former hath little or none' (90). The history of English poetry shows that Lalus wins the debate. Quantitative verse failed because the English language is strongly and stubbornly stressed, as Sidney himself recognized: 'though we do not observe quantity, yet we observe the accent very precisely'.[11]

The debate over the two kinds of verse is moderated by Basilius who claims that 'in both kinds he wrote well that wrote wisely'. For Sidney, to write wisely requires the poet to weigh his words. Quantity was one way to do this, and therefore he experimented with it in a dozen of some 300 poems. In the *Defence* he praises poetry because it considers each word, 'not only (as a man may say) by his most forcible quality, but by his best measured quantity, carrying even in themselves a harmony' (100). Such union of the two kinds of verse is illustrated in Pyrocles's lament in the eclogues to Book II: 'as if her long-restrained conceits did now burst out of prison, she thus. . .threw down the burden of her mind in Anacreon's kind of verses':

> ⏑ – ⏑ – ⏑ – –
> My muse what ails this ardour
> To blaze my only secrets?
> Alas, it is no glory
> To sing my own decayed state.
> Alas, it is no comfort
> To speak without an answer.
> Alas, it is no wisdom
> To show the wound without cure. (163)

Here rhyme added to short lines, which seek to convey overwhelming grief, would render them simply rhetorical, expressing emotion but little substance. As each line stands independently, the monosyllables in the first part allow the stress to fall upon the concluding words which convey the meaning. Through such simplicity, the lament becomes gradually more complex. The lover's repeated challenge to the Muse to tell why she forces him to reveal his love may then be dramatically interrupted: the Muse applies the lover's claim that 'the singer is the song's theme' to himself. She is himself, suffering love as he does and finding inspiration in love. The wit deepens in the concluding lines:

> My muse, I yield, my muse sing,
> But all thy song herein knit:

> The life we lead is all love,
> The love we hold is all death,
> Nor aught I crave to feed life,
> Nor aught I seek to shun death,
> But only that my goddess
> My life, my death, do count hers. (164)

Accent enforces quantity to stress the paradoxes – that life is all love and that love is all death – which are acted out in the story of the *Old Arcadia*. The poetry is close to simple statement, in contrast to the lines cited above in which Pyrocles reveals his overwhelming grief. Accent and quantity give the poem in its plainness a music which the poet uses to convey meaning simply and movingly.

Although Sidney experimented with quantitative verse in other ways, such as adding to measure both accent and rhyme, he did not need to continue: he had proved his claim for the work of the 'right poets' that 'it is not rhyming...that maketh a poet'. Further, his defence of the 'well-weighed syllable' in measured verse could be extended into a defence of verse, whether measured or rhyming, as the 'fittest raiment' for the poet's matter: 'not speaking (table-talk fashion or like men in a dream) words as they chanceably fall from the mouth, but peising [weighing] each syllable of each word by just proportion according to the dignity of the subject' (82).

The argument for structuring syllables to produce a metrical line of verse could be extended into an argument for structuring verses in a poem. In reviewing English poetry, Sidney found few poems with 'poetical sinews': one verse produced the next 'without ordering at the first what should be at the last' with the result that a poem became 'a confused mass of words, with a tingling sound of rhyme, barely accompanied with reason'.[12] We know now, as the original audience of the *Defence* would not have known, that he refers only to published poems and excludes the unpublished *Old Arcadia*, where he experiments radically with ways of structuring poems both internally and in relation to other poems.

VERSE IN THE 'OLD ARCADIA'

Eclogues

The singing-match between Lalus and Dorus, which begins the First Eclogues after a song announces the theme, illustrates how Sidney attempted to give 'poetical sinews' both to separate poems and to poems in relation to each other. The match consists of seven pairs of poems in which the second poem of a pair replies to the first by applying what had been said in an increasingly elaborate and intricate manner. The complex interweaving of the separate poems into one larger poem is described by Ringler: 'Lalus begins in terza rima with three-syllable rhyme, but is not able to keep up the pace and descends to feminine and then to masculine rhyme. In an effort to outdistance Dorus, who has easily followed him, he shifts to an intricate system of medial rhyme in which the final syllable of one line is made to rhyme with the fourth syllable of the following line. When Dorus follows him in this device also, in a final desperate effort he changes to an intricate five-line stanza rhyming $a^5b^3c^5c^3b^5$; but Dorus surpasses him by beginning his reply with the last line of Lalus's stanza and then repeating the same form. The roles are now reversed, for Lalus is forced to reply to Dorus by beginning with his last line. He manages to do so for one stanza, but when Dorus again successfully caps his effort, he returns to the terza rima with which he had begun and acknowledges defeat.'[13] Such craftsmanship is designed to contrast the plain style of the shepherd and the ornate style of the prince. Both styles become more intricate as the singing-match develops but, by the end, more simple as both rest in a final line that sums up the lover's state: 'O wretched state of man in self-division'. When Dorus graciously yields the laurels to Lalus, he returns to his opening address to the Muse in order to fix his own plight:

> But ah, my muse, I would thou hadst facility
> To work my goddess so by thy invention
> On me to cast those eyes, where shine nobility:
> Seen and unknown; heard, but without attention.

John Thompson rightly points to the metrical achievement of that concluding line: 'it has the ring of speech. Word for word, however, it does fit the metrical pattern, even the exact iambic pattern',[14] and Rudenstine adds that 'its monosyllables do indeed create speech rhythms which break up the iambic norm, but those rhythms themselves are. . .highly patterned'.[15]

Such technical accomplishment is used to reveal the lover's dilemma: the line, 'Seen and unknown; heard, but without attention', serves as Musidorus's motto. In addressing it to Pamela, he creates an emblem of his state as a lover, his suit unrecognized because he is. Beyond this, there is his dilemma as a prince. In his love Lalus remains at the sheepish level of Espilus in *The Lady of May*:

> Disdain me not, although I be not fair.
> Who is an heir of many hundred sheep
> Doth beauties keep, which never sun can burn,
> Nor storms do turn: fairness serves oft to wealth.

Musidorus's complaints 'come forth from dungeon of my mind'. As Kalstone says, 'he transforms Lalus' offerings one by one into an inner landscape of despair'.[16] He resembles Therion in that his only wealth is his lady:

> I have no shows of wealth: my wealth is you,
> My beauty's hue your beams, my health your deeds;
> My mind for weeds your virtue's liv'ry wears.

Yet as a prince he can neither give all for love nor enjoy the simplicity of life and loving allowed to shepherds. As the exchange between shepherd and prince continues, their songs merge into a powerful, single statement of man's plight since his fall from Eden.

Sidney gives 'poetical sinews' to the four sets of eclogues by relating them to each other and to the Book that each follows. Their carefully integrated structure has been described by Ringler: 'each of the four groups develops a situation and explores a theme: the first presents the pangs of unrequited love, the second the struggle between reason and passion, the third the ideals of married love, the fourth the sorrows of lovers and the sorrows of death'. He notes further their internal structure: 'the first two sets of eclogues each contain eight poems arranged in precisely parallel order. In each of the two sets the first poem announces the theme with which all the following poems are concerned, the second begins the development of the theme, the third is a comic interlude satirizing the theme, the fourth returns to the theme, the fifth deals with Philisides and his love, and the last three, recited by the disguised princes Pyrocles and Musidorus, exemplify the application of the theme.' In the third set, the five poems are linked in that they celebrate the marriage of the shepherds Lalus and Kala. The fourth set consists of six paired poems which 'exploit the double nature of the renaissance elegy as a song of the sufferings of lovers or a lament for the dead'.[17] Such elaborate structuring suggests that Sidney endeavoured to show his contemporaries how poems could be given form, internally and in relation to each other, by 'ordering at the first what should be at the last'.

The relation of the eclogues to the main plot has been described by Davis: 'while they divide the plot book by book into themes of love, suffering, marriage, and death, they also generalize the plot and relate this particular action of two Greek princes to the timeless themes of man's life on earth. They draw events into a general thematic unity, and thus provide a framework for all of the incidental episodes Sidney used to amplify his plot.'[18] The relation may be illustrated by the rustic marriage of Lalus and Kala, which is celebrated in the Third Eclogues. We are told that he wooed her 'with a true and simple making her know he loved her; not forcing himself beyond his reach to buy her affection, but giving her such pretty presents as neither could weary him with the giving nor shame her for the taking' (244), and that she yielded to him after gaining the consent of both parents. Davis comments: 'the very first sentence takes a slant look at those [the two princes] who do feign, in their pride, and force themselves beyond their reach, and the implicit contrast between such pastoral humility and courtly pride continues throughout the description of their wooing'.[19] While the contrast is there, praise of the marriage of shepherds does more than reprove the princes. Love and marriage are simple for shepherds, for Kala's parents readily offer their consent. Since Pamela is a princess and heir to a throne, her father denies access to all suitors. If anything, the joyous marriage of the shepherds deepens our sympathy for the princes. This counterpoint between the eclogue and the Book suggests that the relation between the pastoral and the courtly worlds becomes as subtle and complex as that in Shakespeare's early romantic comedies.

Sonnets

In the 51 poems within the Books of the *Old Arcadia*, Sidney experiments with the sonnet form, learning how a sonnet may project the lover's state, how sonnets relate to each other, and chiefly, how poetry relates to prose. Although he follows Montemayor's *Diana* in mingling poetry and prose, in that work, which is essentially a Menippean romance, songs are inserted as *divertissements* to embellish the prose. The prose itself, which carries the burden of the plot, provides only the setting or occasion for the poetry. Sidney was interested rather in how the meaning of a poem is enlarged, even determined, by the prose, and how prose may culminate in poetry. In short, he was interested in the harmony of verse and prose.

In Book I there are five poems: the oracle, two comic poems on the comic characters, and paired poems on the inner transformation of the princes. Pyrocles laments that his powers are 'with outward force and inward treason spoiled' and Musidorus laments that through love he 'spoils himself of bliss'. As their transformation provides the device upon which the plot turns, it is fitting that their two poems should be highlighted. Since Book II shows the working of love in the major characters, here the poems express the lover's passion in all its variety. Poems may be paired to show how variously love works even in one person. For example, two answer-poems contrast Philoclea's state before she loves Pyrocles and after. Their prose setting enhances the meaning: Philoclea falls from innocence by falling in love, yet remains innocent because she believes Pyrocles to be an Amazon. Being free from lust, her love is pure despite her agony. Yet the prose setting makes her state pathetic, for it tells us that Pyrocles is a man determined to seduce her. Her state of innocence is defined more clearly when her mother expresses her infernal agonies of love and jealousy. With Pyrocles's lament on his agonies, the prose setting does more than enhance meaning: it supplies it.

> Loved I am, and yet complain of love;
> As loving not, accused, in love I die.
> When pity most I crave, I cruel prove;
> Still seeking love, love found as much I fly.

Burnt in myself I muse at others' fire;
What I call wrong, I do the same, and more;
Barred of my will, I have beyond desire;
I wail for want, and yet am choked with store. (114)

He concludes with the triumphant paradox: 'Let me be loved, or else not loved be.' Out of context, such heaping of contraries would seem to express the lover's usual paradoxical state, though here mysteriously paradoxical. In context, the contraries are witty because they are only apparent: Pyrocles cannot seek Philoclea's love because of her mother's and father's love for him.

In the concluding three Books, where the two forms mingle,[20] the poems express the significance of the prose. In Book III, for example, the songs sung in the cave express the inner agonies of the lovers in ways that show why the cave provides the symbolic centre of the retreat in Arcadia. Pyrocles's lament explains why he seeks the cave as his centre:

Since that the stormy rage of passions dark
(Of passions dark, made dark by beauty's light)
With rebel force hath closed in dungeon dark
My mind ere now led forth by reason's light;

Since all the things which give mine eyes their light
Do foster still the fruit of fancies dark,
So that the windows of my inward light
Do serve to make my inward powers dark;

Since, as I say, both mind and senses dark
Are hurt, not helped, with piercing of the light;
While that the light may show the horrors dark,
But cannot make resolved darkness light;
   I like this place where, at the least, the dark
   May keep my thoughts from thought of wonted light. (179–80)

The song offers a brief allegory of his life in its progress from light to darkness. The two rhyme words, 'light' and 'dark', express a number of paradoxes: the central paradox of Pyrocles's life, that a noble prince should become so debased; the paradox of love itself, that love should cause man's fall; and the paradox of the state of man, that 'the children of light'[21] should become creatures of darkness. His lament is intensified by Gynecia's, for her agonies of loving are such that she welcomes the cave as her grave.

For what is life to daily dying mind
Where, drawing breath, I suck the air of woe;
Where too much sight makes all the body blind,
And highest thoughts downward most headlong throw?
Thus then my form, and thus my state I find:
Death wrapped in flesh, to living grave assigned. (181)

The paradox of her state, the death-in-life which is man's fallen state, is extended in her next lament on the paradox of loving, 'Sick to the death, still loving my disease', and finally it is confirmed by Evarchus's judgment that she be assigned living to Basilius's grave. Although in the darkness Pyrocles does not know who she is, his inner darkness responds to hers. In seeking her out, he initiates the central action of the whole work; for when she seizes him, he is forced to reveal his sex and promise to satisfy her desire. Yet this action is delayed by two more laments in which she expresses her plight: 'How is my sun, whose beams are shining bright, / Become the cause of my dark ugly night?', and a correlative verse on her state of darkness. Then in prose she welcomes the darkness of the cave because it allows her to see 'the picture of my inward darkness' and universalizes her state:

Forlorn creature that I am, I would I might be freely wicked, since wickedness doth prevail; but the footsteps of my overtrodden virtue lie still as bitter accusations unto me. I am divided in myself; how can I stand? I am overthrown in myself; who shall raise me? Vice is but a nurse of new agonies, and the virtue I am divorced from makes the hateful comparison the more manifest. . . .O strange mixture of human minds: only so much good left as to make us languish in our own evils!

Verse and prose work together to express the dilemma of man's fallen state, in which 'our erected wit maketh us know what perfection is, and yet our infected will keepeth us from reaching unto it'.[22] In her inner darkness, expressed by the cave's darkness, Gynecia provides an emblem of man's fallen state, which Sidney refers to later as the 'pit of darkness' in which 'the wormish mankind lives' (385).

In Book iv there is only one poem by a major character: Basilius praises night for the adulterous pleasures he has enjoyed with Gynecia. His song confirms his commitment to darkness, and also that of the others (except Philoclea) in their state of sin. Then it is triumphantly countered by the one poem in Book v,

Musidorus's song in which he dismisses the fear of death. It shows that man may escape darkness and find the light:

> Our owly eyes, which dimmed with passions be,
> And scarce discern the dawn of coming day,
> Let them be cleared, and now begin to see
> Our life is but a step in dusty way.
>   Then let us hold the bliss of peaceful mind,
>   Since this we feel, great loss we cannot find. (373–4)

His song answers Gynecia's in Book III, resolving the action which she initiated. As her song led her to dedicate herself to the infernal furies in order to 'assuage the sweltering of my hellish longing' (183), his expresses his release, and Pyrocles's, from subjection to life, as the prose confirms: 'thus did they, like quiet swans, sing their own obsequies, and virtuously enable their minds against all extremities which they did think would fall upon them' (374). His song signals their release from inner darkness, which is expressed outwardly by the prison. In proving their virtue, it answers all the previous songs, which project the lovers' subjection to passion, by showing their victory over life and death.

TRANSLATION OF THE PSALMS

It is not known whether Sidney, together with his sister, translated the Psalms early or late in his career. (He translated the first 43 psalms, and his sister the rest.) Stylistic development is difficult to trace, particularly in a translation. His tutor, Moffet, says that he began working on the Psalms after he had written *Astrophel and Stella* and the *Arcadia*; however, he lumps all Sidney's writings together as juvenilia in order to praise him for turning to serious matters in his maturity.[23] Duncan-Jones places the translations late: 'Sidney's short poetical career satisfyingly shows the traditional progress from secular to sacred verse.'[24] Clearly this dating depends upon what one finds satisfying; and, for Sidney, any such 'traditional progress' would need to ignore the fact that his only two religious sonnets, *Certain sonnets* 31 and 32, were written before *Astrophel and Stella*. Ringler concludes that the translation was 'not an early work of experimentation, but a later exhibition of virtuosity';[25] however, since Sidney died before he had stopped experimenting, one may equally conclude that it was not a later work of experimentation but an early exhibition of virtuosity.

In his poem, 'Upon the translation of the Psalms by Sir Philip Sidney, and the Countess of Pembroke his sister',[26] Donne explains why they translated the Psalms. He refers to the Psalms in their original language as 'the highest matter in the noblest form'. Yet in English – in the popular Sternhold-Hopkins version – they were 'more hoarse, more harsh than any other'. Since the Church may not be reformed until the translations are reformed, he welcomes the 'sweet learned labours' of Sidney and his sister: 'They shew us islanders our joy, our King, / They tell us *why*, and teach us *how* to sing.' St James tells us why we should sing Psalms: 'Is any among you. . .merry? let him sing psalms.'[27] A poet may best tell us how to sing because his art best fulfils the end of speech, which is 'the uttering sweetly and properly the conceits of the mind'.[28] That Sidney and his sister attempted to show others how to sing is indicated by the title-page of one of the manuscripts: 'The Psalms of David translated into divers and sundry kinds of verse, more rare and excellent for the method and variety than ever yet hath been done in English'. In a dedicatory poem the Countess tells how together they produced their translations:

> That heaven's King may deign his own transform'd
>   in substance no, but superficial tire
>   by thee put on; to praise, not to aspire
> To those high tones, so in themselves adorn'd,
>   which angels sing in their celestial choir,
>   and all of tongues with soul and voice admire
> These sacred hymns thy kingly prophet form'd.

Sidney's technical experimenting is shown by his rendering each psalm in a different stanzaic form. Hallett Smith concludes that Sidney compiled 'what might be regarded as a School of English Versification'.[29] Yet he attempted much more; within the limits of producing a metaphrase, he sought to render each psalm as a song in which a human voice may be heard singing God's praise. Louis L. Martz concludes that he brought the art of the Elizabethan lyric into the service of psalmody 'in a way that makes the psalm an intimate, personal cry of the soul to God'.[30]

In the *Defence* 77, Sidney argues that the Psalms are a divine poem on several grounds: etymology – the name signifies 'songs'; form – they are written in metre; and the poetical handling of prophecy – 'for what else is the awaking his musical instruments, the often and free changing of persons, his notable *prosopopoeias*, when he maketh you, as it were, see God coming in His majesty, his telling of the beasts' joyfulness and hills leaping, but a heavenly poesy'. This description of 'heavenly poesy' suggests Psalm 29, which he translates as follows:

1 Ascribe unto the lord of light,
    Ye men of pow'r even by birthright,
    Ascribe all glory and all might.

2 Ascribe due glory to his name,
    And in his ever glorious frame
    Of sanctuary do the same.

3 His voice is on the waters found,
    His voice doth threat'ning thunders sound,
    Yea, through the waters doth resound.

4 The voice of that Lord ruling us
    Is strong though he be gracious,
    And ever, ever glorious.

5 By voice of high Jehovah we
    The highest cedars broken see,
    Ev'n cedars, which on Leban be;

6 Nay, like young calves in leaps are borne,
    And Leban' self with nature's scorn,
    And Sirion like young unicorn.

7 His voice doth flashing flames divide,
8   His voice have trembling deserts tried,
    Ev'n deserts where the Arabs bide.

9 His voice makes hinds their calves to cast,
    His voice makes bald the forest waste;
    But in his church his fame is plac'd.

10 His justice seat the world sustains,
    Of furious floods he holds the reins,
    And this his rule for aye remains.
    God to his people strength shall give,
    That they in peace shall blessed live.

What Sidney seeks to accomplish in his translation becomes clear if we compare the Hopkins translation, for example, verses 3–4:

    His voice doth rule the waters all,
      even as himself doth please:
    He doth prepare the thunderclaps,
      and governs all the seas.
    The voice of God is of great force,
      and wondrous excellent:
    It is most mighty in effect,
      and most magnificent.[31]

He seeks first of all to follow the Geneva version as closely as possible:

> The voice of the Lord is upon the waters: the God of glory
>   maketh it to thunder: the Lord is upon the great waters.
> The voice of the Lord is mighty: the voice of the Lord is
>   glorious.[32]

Sidney's word 'threat'ning', in verse 3, is suggested by the Geneva footnote: 'the thunderclaps, that are heard out of the clouds, ought to make the wicked tremble for fear of God's anger'. At the same time, he gives a sense of God's presence rather than simply His power: he 'maketh you, as it were, see God coming in His majesty'. By invoking God's presence, he wants to show the prophetic element in the Psalms, how David 'almost. . .showeth himself a passionate lover of that unspeakable and everlasting beauty to be seen by the eyes of the mind, only cleared by faith'. His word 'gracious', in verse 4, is not suggested by the Geneva version: in its line it counters 'strong', which is all that Hopkins conveys. Then by rhyme, and the repetition of 'ever' to create suspense, the verse ends triumphantly: 'And ever, ever glorious' notes God's goodness, which deserves man's love. Stress upon God's goodness leads Sidney to add to Geneva the first line in verse 10: 'His justice seat the world sustains'. Ringler notes that he turned to Beza's *Paraphrasis*: '*Dieu préside comme Juge*'. Yet Sidney adds to Beza the phrase, 'the world sustains', because he wishes his reader to share David's love of God.[33]

'CERTAIN SONNETS'

Between 1577 and 1581 when he was writing the *Old Arcadia*, Sidney wrote a number of poems which he gathered under the title, *Certain sonnets*.

The first fact about them is that they are a miscellany of kinds, *rime sparse*, though not simply miscellaneous in their arrangement. Fewer than half are regular sonnets – that is, quatorzains; eight are 'sonets' – that is, songs composed for tunes, and five more are to be set to music; five are translations; and five (some of which are songs) use the quantitative metre. Since one poem is included in the *New Arcadia*, Sidney may have intended at one time to collect poems for later use. At some time, however, he saw that the love poems gave the collection a separate identity. He grouped certain kinds of poems, for example, songs with the same tune (*CS* 3–4), translations (*CS* 12–14), and translations from the same author (*CS* 28–9). He arranged short sequences: for example, after *CS* 7, which praises the heaven in his lady's face, he adds four poems which lament the smallpox stains on her face. Either by writing or arrangement, he connected separate sonnets: for example, *CS* 6 expands the conceit of Desire as a babe who cries to suck the lady's breast and *CS* 9 contracts that conceit into one line: 'Her milken breasts the nurse of child-like love'. (His care for these poems is indicated by the fact that he transcribed *CS* 6 at the end of Jean Bouchet's *Les annuales d'Aquitaine* [Poitiers 1557] and later revised it.)[34] The love poems hang together, as they treat a love which mars the lover's mind. Finally, he unified the miscellany by placing at the beginning two poems which treat the *innamoramento*, the moment of first falling in love, and balanced them at the end by two concluding sonnets which bid love farewell.

The second fact about the *Certain sonnets* is that they are appended to three manuscripts of the *Old Arcadia*, which is also their place in the 1598 folio.[35] That work concludes with the hope that another will tell 'the poor hopes of the poor Philisides in the pursuit of his affections'. Since the *Certain sonnets* tell, in effect, the story of Philisides's love, it may be regarded as its appendix or coda.

Unlike the conventional Petrarchan lover who suffers because he is rejected by a cruel, chaste mistress, Philisides suffers because he once enjoyed his mistress but through some fault made her angry with him. As that love is singled out as 'a most true event', it has the complications of 'fact' which convention usually simplifies. Although the nature of his fault is not told, one infers from the poem sent to her what may have happened: after responding to his love, she refused him; in anger he sought some revenge, either by resorting to force or, like Astrophel, too explicitly craving 'the thing which ever she denies'.[36]

> Well, but faulty I was; reason to my passion yielded,
>   passion unto my rage, rage to a hasty revenge.
> But what's this for a fault, for which such faith be
>   abolished,
>   such faith, so stainless, inviolate, violent. (343)

That same violence of love's rage, which led to 'rage's events', marks Therion, of whom the Lady of May complains that 'he grows to such rages, that sometimes he strikes me, sometimes he rails at me'. It also marks the two princes in the *Old Arcadia*: Pyrocles admits that he offered violence to Philoclea but explains that 'love offered more force to me', adding that the 'violence' of his love 'wrought violent effects in me' (394–5). Similarly, Musidorus offers 'love's force' (402) as an excuse for his flight with Pamela.

The lover in *Certain sonnets* experiences Philisides's love. His lament, 'where be now those joys, that I lately tasted?' (*CS* 5), and recognition that 'former bliss adds to present pain, / While remembrance doth both states contain' (*CS* 24), reveal Philisides's agony in 'the remembrance what sweet joys I had once, and what a place I did hold' (*OA* 343). He suffers under Philisides's three-fold curse: not only has his mistress's beauty overwhelmed him but her virtue is such that 'reason's light, / For all his strife can only bondage gain' (*CS* 2). As Philisides 'shalt never dare seek help of wretched case', the lover in *Certain sonnets* finds himself 'longing to have, having no wit to wish' (*CS* 2). His lady enters 'chaste and cruel' (*CS* 3), leaving him burning in desire. His desire for her, expressed in *CS* 4, leads to the passionate appeal, 'Give me my kisses' in *CS* 5, and is personified in *CS* 6 as a babe who cries for the breast. Yet her virtue is such that he cannot seek to satisfy desire, and confounds his reason by separating love from desire. As a result, his mind soars through fancy only to fall (*CS* 15), become infected (*CS* 18), and divided:

> If I could think how these my thoughts to leave,
> Or thinking still my thoughts might have good end:
> If rebel sense would reason's law receive;
> Or reason foiled would not in vain contend;
> Then might I think what thoughts were best to think:
> Then might I wisely swim or gladly sink. (*CS* 19)

The climax of this theme comes in *CS* 21: he is determined to leave her, finding love 'to mar my mind'. The 'strife of thought' that only 'mars the mind' had first led him to yield to love in the opening sonnet; now it becomes his reason to leave love. By so doing, the story of his love continues the story of Philisides's love.

As that story continues, the contradictions in love emerge more clearly, and, with these, the determination to leave love. Even in the loose order of a miscellany, the rejection of love in the two concluding sonnets is seen to be inevitable. The theme of *CS* 19, 'If I could think how these my thoughts to leave', allows such thoughts even while denying them. *CS* 20, significantly entitled 'A Farewell', finds separation worse than death but the next poem finds their union no better. The recognition in *CS* 21 that love mars his mind introduces a lengthy review of his plight in *CS* 22. After analysing the contradictions in love which destroy him, he considers his 'fault' which led his lady to reject him:

> My ship, desire, with wind of lust long tossed,
> Brake on fair cleeves of constant chastity;
> Where plagu'd for rash attempt, gives up his ghost,
> So deep in seas of virtue beauties lie.
>   But of his death flies up a purest love,
>   Which seeming less, yet nobler life doth move.

The consequence of his apparent attempt to force her to yield to him divides love and desire. Love, which has moved him to seek to satisfy desire, dies; out of its ashes there arises, phoenix-like, a 'purest love' which may move the lover to 'nobler life'. Yet the flight of such love must be steadily upward to what the two concluding sonnets call 'higher things'. The farewell to earthly love becomes steadily more explicit: in *CS* 23, 'He ever dies that wasteth / In love, his chiefest part'; in *CS* 24, he flies upward as flames burn his desire; in *CS* 25, he is burned by her light; in *CS* 26, the double negative in the refrain, 'No, no, no, no, I cannot hate my foe,' implies the affirmative; in *CS* 27, he rejects her although her sorrow causes him regret; and in *CS* 30 he celebrates love's death:

> From so ungrateful fancy,
> From such a female franzy,
> From them that use men thus,
> Good Lord deliver us.

The witty turn in the concluding stanza in which he rejects his own fancy for condemning love implies, with a more witty turn, that he rejects love as fancy. The miscellany moves inevitably to its two concluding sonnets which reject both desire and love.

The third fact about the *Certain sonnets* is the bibliographical evidence[37] which suggests that the two opening sonnets were

added to the collection after the others had been written.
These sonnets balance the two concluding sonnets: *CS* 1 tells how
desire forces him to yield to love and *CS* 2 tells the consequences
of yielding. In *CS* 31 he is determined to subdue desire, and in
CS 32 he forsakes earthly love, that 'loathed yoke' of the opening
sonnet, for the 'sweet yoke' offered to man by Christ (Matt.
11:30), 'whose service is perfect freedom' (BCP). The opening
sonnet supplies an apt commentary on the kind of love shown
in the later poems in its list of the nine contradictions in his state
which determine him to yield to love, summed up in the paradox:
'strife of thought but mars the mind'. He yields to love on condition that she will be grateful to him. If she should treat him
harshly, he will free himself from love's 'loathed yoke':

> I yield, O Love, unto thy loathed yoke,
> Yet craving law of arms, whose rule doth teach,
> That hardly used, whoever prison broke,
> In justice quit, of honour made no breach:
>   Whereas, if I a grateful guardian have,
>   Thou art my lord, and I thy vowed slave.

Since she does not prove grateful, he breaks out of prison and
turns to 'eternal love'.

The fourth and crucial fact about the *Certain sonnets* is that
love may be rejected. The lover loves his lady for better, not for
worse, and he is love's slave by 'free choice' (*CS* 17). The reasons
given in *CS* 1 to yield to love serve equally to reject love: resistance to love 'but mars the mind'; but so does yielding, as *CS* 21
records: 'finding those beams, which I must ever love, / To mar
my mind'. Accordingly, he concludes: 'Desire, desire, I have too
dearly bought, / With price of mangled mind thy worthless ware'
(*CS* 31). The third and final curse upon Philisides, that he shall
'never dare seek help of wretched case', finally becomes a curse
upon him. As *CS* 2 announces, there is no escape from his
dilemma in loving: the lady's beauty overpowers his passion and
her virtue binds his reason, so that he remains 'longing to have,
having no wit to wish'. On the one hand, she will not satisfy his
desire; on the other, he loves her on condition that he may
persuade her to satisfy his desire. His purpose becomes suspect,
leading him to mock his craft:

> Are poets then the only lovers true,
>   Whose hearts are set on measuring a verse:
>   Who think themselves well blessed, if they renew
>   Some good old dump, that Chaucer's mistress knew,
>   And use but you for matters to rehearse? (*CS* 17)

For such a lover, the only course is action. In *CS* 16, at the mid-point of the collection,[38] he compares himself, as one who expresses his love in words, to the satyr who fled in fear of the horn which he had blown:

> Even thus might I, for doubts which I conceive
> Of mine own words, my own good hap betray,
> And thus might I, for fear of may be, leave
> The sweet pursuit of my desired prey.

Such doubts about his intent are confirmed by the story implicit in the collection, that he had offended her either by some violent act or when he 'once said what I conceived' (*CS* 7). Where speech faulted, he offers amends in songs of praise:

> This you hear is not my tongue,
> Which once said what I conceived,
> For it was of use bereaved,
> With a cruel answer stung,
> No, though tongue to roof be cleaved,
> Fearing lest he chastised be,
> Heart and soul do sing in me.

Yet his rhetorical purpose is defeated when she remains 'chaste and cruel'. Since she rejects desire, he rejects love.

'ASTROPHEL AND STELLA'

In his major sonnet sequence, Sidney treats a love that may be neither satisfied nor rejected. At the end Astrophel cannot command (or pray), 'Leave me O love, which reachest but to dust': instead of killing desire in order to turn to eternal love 'which breaks the clouds and opens forth the light', he still seeks his 'only light' in her while he remains hopelessly bound in the 'dark furnace' of unsatisfied desire.

In the *Defence* Sidney admonishes lovers who write 'that lyrical kind of songs and sonnets' for he is not persuaded that they truly love:

But truly many of such writings as come under the banner of unresistible love, if I were a mistress, would never persuade me they were in love: so coldly they apply fiery speeches, as men that had rather read lovers' writings – and so caught up certain swelling phrases which hang together like a man that once told my father that the wind was at north-west and by south, because he would be sure to name winds enough – than that in truth they feel those passions, which easily (as I think) may be bewrayed [revealed] by that same forcibleness or *energia* (as the Greeks call it) of the writer. (116–17)

As in response to this criticism, Astrophel persuades the reader that he truly loves right from the opening sonnet:

> Loving in truth, and fain in verse my love to show,
> That she (dear she) might take some pleasure of my pain:
> Pleasure might cause her read, reading might make her know,
> Knowledge might pity win, and pity grace obtain,
>   I sought fit words to paint the blackest face of woe,
> Studying inventions fine, her wits to entertain:
> Oft turning others' leaves, to see if thence would flow
> Some fresh and fruitful showers upon my sun-burn'd brain.
>   But words came halting forth, wanting invention's stay,
> Invention, nature's child, fled stepdame study's blows,
> And others' feet still seem'd but strangers in my way.
> Thus great with child to speak, and helpless in my throes,
>   Biting my truant pen, beating myself for spite,
>   'Fool,' said my muse to me, 'look in thy heart and write'.[39]

As one 'loving in truth', the lover plans so to entertain his lady by his sonnets that she will yield to him.[40] The argument of the sonnet is that he may write not because he reads what other lovers have written but because he truly loves. The forcibleness of his passion is shown in the dynamic clash of verbs: 'loving. . .studying . . .turning', rising to the intensity of 'Biting. . .beating' and ending with the simple, double imperative, 'look. . .write'. The sonnets promise to be dominated not by swelling phrases taken from others but by the voice of a man 'great with child to speak'.

Biography in relation to fiction

Since Astrophel is presented as one 'loving in truth', many readers are persuaded that the truth in loving is biographical.[41] So many biographical facts are scattered throughout the sequence that no contemporary reader, at least no one in the secret circle in which the manuscript first circulated, could fail to identify

Astrophel as Sidney. It comes as no revelation, or even surprise, in sonnet 30, for example, that the question asked of Astrophel, 'How Ulster likes of that same golden bit, / Wherewith my father once made it half tame', refers to Sir Henry's deputyship in Ireland and specifically to the cess which he imposed on landowners. That reference comes as naturally – and inevitably? – as in the *Defence* when he refers in passing to what a man 'once told my father'. Further, no one among the select circle could fail to identify Stella as Lady Rich, particularly after the punning on her name in sonnet 24. Yet since the sequence treats Astrophel's love for Stella, how does fact relate to fiction?

What facts there are fit Sidney's life at the time one assumes he wrote the sonnets. In October 1580 he wrote to his brother Robert that he had 'given over the delight in the world',[42] which suggests that he had given up his pastoral retirement at Wilton during which he wrote the *Old Arcadia*, and was ready to resume a busy life at court. In 1581, from January to March, he attended the sessions of the House of Commons; in January, May, and November he entered major tournaments; in April and May he took active part in the festivities to celebrate the Queen's proposed marriage to Alençon; and in September he accompanied Don Antonio, the Pretender to the Portuguese throne, to Dover and Gravesend, and petitioned to return to help his father. The year was a turning-point for him because during it Leicester's heir was born, dispossessing him of his inheritance, and Languet died. Also, in January, Sidney's aunt, the Countess of Huntingdon, introduced to the court her attractive charge, Penelope Devereux, and undertook the arrangements that led to her marriage to Lord Rich on 1 November. Sidney would know Penelope, for her father, the Earl of Essex, had proposed their marriage in 1576; and at the court, before and after her marriage, he could hardly have avoided contact with her. If their 'affair' took place during the year, he would have had time to write the sonnets while he was at Wilton over Christmas and January, and during the summer of 1582 when he may have been with his father in Wales. His death-bed repentance for 'a vanity wherein I had taken delight, whereof I had not rid myself. It was my Lady Rich', would seem to allude to his failure to reject that love in *Astrophel and Stella*. His only reference to his own poetry – 'overmastered by some thoughts, I yielded an inky tribute unto them' – suggests the immediate pressure of personal experience behind the sonnets.[43]

The biographical matter in *Astrophel and Stella* is ignored by C. S. Lewis on general grounds: 'the first thing to grasp about the sonnet sequence is that it is not a way of telling a story. It is a form which exists for the sake of prolonged lyrical meditation, chiefly on love but relieved from time to time by excursions into public affairs, literary criticism, compliment, or what you will. External events – a quarrel, a parting, an illness, a stolen kiss – are every now and then mentioned to provide themes for the meditation. . . . The sonnet sequence does not exist to tell a real, or even a feigned, story.'[44] Yet Sidney's sequence does tell a story: real, as the story of Sidney's love for Lady Rich, and feigned, as the story of Astrophel's love for Stella. Each sonnet treats Sidney's / Astrophel's love for Lady Rich / Stella at some stage from their first meeting to their final separation. Together the sonnets record the stages of a courtship from the lover's first woe when he falls in love, to his joy when he believes that his love is shared, to his final despair when his love is rejected. In opposition to Lewis, Ringler argues that 'we cannot avoid the biography'. He identifies Sidney with Astrophel and Lady Rich with Stella so completely that, at one point, he refers to Sidney's love for 'Stella'. For him, the 'substance' of *Astrophel and Stella* is autobiographical; and he allows that 'mere fact was made subservient to the requirements of art' only to the extent that the sequence is not a diary which includes all of Sidney's interests and activities at the time of writing.[45]

A compromise between the opposing claims of fiction and fact is suggested by Northrop Frye's comment on the nature of experience for a Renaissance poet: 'the Renaissance poet was not expected to drift through life gaining "experience" and writing it up in poetry. He was expected to turn his mind into an emotional laboratory and gain his experience there under high pressure and close observation. Literature provided him with a convention, and the convention supplied the literary categories and forms into which his amorphous emotions were to be poured. . . .Poetry is not reporting on experience, and love is not an uncultivated experience; in both poetry and love, reality is what is created, not the raw material for the creation.'[46] Since Sidney is such a poet, the 'reality' of his love for Lady Rich is found not in biography but in fiction, Astrophel's love for Stella. The experience of love recorded in the sonnets is found only there and not in any separate personal experience. Fact becomes fiction, and fiction remains fact, because Sidney realizes the experience of his love for Lady Rich in the act of giving it poetic form. In him, the activities of lover and poet become one, with the result that personal experience becomes impersonal: instead of treating his love, the sonnets treat love itself.[47]

The general relation of biography to fiction may be illustrated by the 'biographical' sonnet 37:

> My mouth doth water, and my breast doth swell,
>> My tongue doth itch, my thoughts in labour be:
>> Listen then lordings with good ear to me,
> For of my life I must a riddle tell.
> Towards Aurora's court a nymph doth dwell,
>> Rich in all beauties which man's eye can see:
>> Beauties so far from reach of words, that we
> Abase her praise, saying she doth excel:
> Rich in the treasure of deserv'd renown,
> Rich in the riches of a royal heart,
> Rich in those gifts which give th'eternal crown;
>> Who though most rich in these and every part,
>> Which make the patents of true worldly bliss,
>> Hath no misfortune, but that Rich she is.

Lewis's claim that a biographical reading gains us nothing is denied by this sonnet: it gives us an answer to the riddle by alluding to Lady Rich. Ringler claims that Sidney wrote this sonnet and sonnets 24 and 35, which have the same allusion to Lady Rich, in order 'to reveal her married name'.[48] Yet after the two earlier sonnets why would Sidney need to write a third to reveal what is already known? Surely no lording who was allowed to read the one manuscript which did not omit these three sonnets would need to have the affair revealed to him.

While biography cannot be ignored, the substance of the sonnet is not autobiography. The sonnet as a whole registers the clash between what Stella should be as the object of Astrophel's love and what she is as Lady Rich. The argument of the sestet turns upon the shift from the preposition 'in' to the copula 'is', and therefore from the worth bestowed upon her by the poet to her misfortune in being married to Lord Rich. The wit in the final line is not found in the allusion to Lady Rich. The catalogue of

what Stella is 'Rich in' should lead to a final personification: one
so rich in all the gifts of fortune should be called Rich. So it does:
she is Rich. But this literary identification is cut across by historical fact: it is Stella's misfortune that she is Rich. When this
sonnet is read in its context within the sonnet sequence, rather
than as biography, the clash between fact and fiction may be
seen as a means by which Sidney uses fact to explore the nature
of love. It is necessary for many reasons that the fiction be maintained, not the least of which for him would be social. Appearing
as Philisides in the *Old Arcadia*, he is persuaded to reveal his love
for Mira; in the *New*, he loves a lady 'that was the star whereby
his course was only directed' but his motto, 'Spotted to be
known', indicates that he would be shamed if his love were
known. In the sonnets, he may declare openly that he joys in his
love 'though nations count it shame' because he speaks covertly as
Astrophel in love with Stella.

In displaying fact as fiction, the sonnets never separate the lover
who suffers the passions from the poet who describes them even
when they are most artificial, as in sonnet 9:

> Queen Virtue's court, which some call Stella's face,
> Prepar'd by Nature's chiefest furniture,
> Hath his front built of alabaster pure;
> Gold is the covering of that stately place.
> The door by which sometimes comes forth her grace,
> Red porphyr is, which lock of pearl makes sure:
> Whose porches rich (which name of cheeks endure)
> Marble mixed red and white do interlace.
> The windows now through which this heav'nly guest
> Looks o'er the world, and can find nothing such,
> Which dare claim from those lights the name of best,
> Of touch they are that without touch doth touch,
> Which Cupid's self from Beauty's mine did draw:
> Of touch they are, and poor I am their straw.

The elaborate allegorical description turns from the heavenly
guest who looks out from the windows of Stella's eyes to the
mansion filled with Nature's choicest furniture in order to explode
in the final phrase which shows the lover as a straw man attracted
and burned by her light. The wit of the sonnet – its formal cause –
lies in the shock of moving from the formal rhetorical opening to
the plain colloquial ending. High artifice is reduced to the simple,

human level: in 'poor I am their straw', the poet's wit and the lover's cry become one.

The relationship between biography and fiction through which the lover's sincerity is shown by the poet's craftsmanship is illustrated by sonnet 47:

> What, have I thus betrayed my liberty?
> Can those black beams such burning marks engrave
> In my free side? or am I born a slave,
> Whose neck becomes such yoke of tyranny?
> Or want I sense to feel my misery?
> Or sprite, disdain of such disdain to have?
> Who for long faith, though daily help I crave,
> May get no alms but scorn of beggary.
> Virtue awake, beauty but beauty is,
> I may, I must, I can, I will, I do
> Leave following that, which it is gain to miss.
> Let her go. Soft, but here she comes. Go to,
> Unkind, I love you not: O me, that eye
> Doth make my heart give to my tongue the lie.

This sonnet is dominated, as are all the sonnets, by the voice of a man, a living voice fully and yet simply human: of a man in conflict with himself because he loves, of one so fully aware of loving against himself that he persuades us he truly loves. The truth of loving is conveyed directly, immediately, and physically by the presence of Astrophel and his encounter with Stella. Only after reading the sonnet does one become aware of the poetic craftsmanship which has shaped the experience of loving into a sonnet. That experience and its expression in poetry are fused in the dramatic soliloquy: love is experienced in the act of giving it poetic form. The lover persuades us that he truly loves because the poet does, so that the fact of loving becomes 'real' through fiction.

Since fact becomes fiction, the anatomy of Sidney's love for Lady Rich recorded in the sequence becomes what C. S. Lewis terms 'an anatomy of love', or what Robert L. Montgomery more properly calls 'the anatomy of the lover's mind'.[49] As his purpose in the *Arcadia* is 'to limn out such exact pictures of every posture in the mind, that any man being forced, in the strains of this life, to pass through any straits or latitudes of good or ill fortune might (as in a glass) see how to set a good countenance upon all the discountenances of adversity, and a stay upon the exorbitant smilings of chance',[50] so his purpose in *Astrophel and Stella* is to limn out exact pictures of every posture in the mind of a man in love from his first resistance to love to his final total submission to it. All the stages of loving and of being loved – from loving in hope and anguish, to loving in expectation and anguish, to loving in despair – are so set down that any man might (as in a glass) see how to set a good countenance upon all the discountenances of adversity in love, and a stay upon the exorbitant smilings of chance. Sir John Harington calls Sidney 'our English Petrarch', and his praise of Petrarch – 'in those his sweet mourning sonnets. . .he seems to have comprehended all the passions that all men of that humour have felt' – applies to Sidney.[51] Yet he remains an English Petrarch, or, more correctly, a Protestant English Petrarch, because, for him, earthly love is not a ladder to the love of God. The way to eternal love requires man to forsake earthly love, as in the resolution to the *Certain sonnets*. Nor is there any place in his sequence for Petrarch's retrospective understanding which allows him to repent and renounce earthly love: 'loving in truth' means that he may never give up loving.[52] Since love is treated as an earthly passion, it is free from the profundity, and consequent solemnity, given it by Renaissance neo-Platonists. As a poet and lover, Sidney as Astrophel plays the game of love by remaining the courtier – cultivated and urbane, intelligent and witty – who seeks to seduce his lady. He may play the game seriously because it is a game.[53] Accordingly, the intensity of passion in the concluding sonnets signals the end of the sequence.

Structure of the sonnets

The sonnet form   Sidney's plan to write an extended poem of 108 sonnets and 11 songs required him first to master the structure of the individual sonnet as a complete poem in itself, then to link sonnets so that they may be read in sequence, and finally, to devise a structure to unify all the poems as a sonnet sequence or one larger poem. In so doing, he was responding to what K. O. Myrick aptly terms his 'deep-seated instinct for form'.[54]

His mastery of the sonnet form may be illustrated by sonnet 5:

> It is most true, that eyes are form'd to serve
> The inward light: and that the heavenly part

Ought to be king, from whose rules who do swerve,
Rebels to Nature, strive for their own smart.
　　It is most true, what we call Cupid's dart,
An image is, which for ourselves we carve;
And, fools, adore in temple of our heart,
Till that good god make Church and churchman starve.
　　True, that true beauty virtue is indeed,
Whereof this beauty can be but a shade,
Which elements with mortal mixture breed:
True, that on earth we are but pilgrims made,
　　And should in soul up to our country move:
　　True, and yet true that I must Stella love.

Against the pattern set up by the previous sonnets – an octave followed by a sestet which consists of a quatrain and couplet or two triplets – here there are two quatrains, a triplet, a couplet, and a final line divided into two parts. In thirteen lines wit tells the lover all that ought to be, and should be, according to neo-Platonic doctrine and Christian faith. The hammering repetition of 'It is most true' confirmed by 'True' is summed up in the first word of the concluding line and then refuted by the concluding four words, 'I must Stella love'. The one word 'must' in that simple, powerful statement overweighs all that has been said before, and the whole sonnet is focussed upon the ending. In so doing, it illustrates Donne's observation that 'in all metrical compositions. . .the force of the whole piece is for the most part left to the shutting up; the whole frame of the poem is a beating out of a piece of gold, but the last clause is as the impression of the stamp, and that is it that makes it current'.[55] Ideally, a Sidney sonnet seeks to exhaust itself in its final phrase. The concluding point of wit is the occasion for all that comes before, and nothing is left over. As a result, a sonnet stands complete within itself, detached and discrete. In its prescribed length and set rhyme-scheme, which turns the sonnet inward upon itself, it calls attention to itself as a technical *tour de force* and celebrates its own triumph of poetic craftsmanship.

In order to organize his sonnets into a single long poem to be read in sequence, instead of a miscellany to be read in any order, Sidney mastered the complex art of linking them. That art is illustrated particularly in the first twelve sonnets in which he establishes the basis for the whole poem.

The programme of the whole poem is announced in the opening sonnet: as one loving in truth, the lover will describe his love
in verse so that Stella will find pleasure in reading of his pain, and
coming to know his plight may be persuaded, through pity, to
satisfy his desire. Since his success as a lover depends upon his
success as a poet, he spells out the means by which he may write:
not to follow the inventions of others but to find inner inspiration
from his love of Stella. As poet and lover, he provides the subject
of his poem. Accordingly, the first six sonnets describe his poetic
method and the nature of his love.

The opening two sonnets are carefully balanced: the first describes the stages of knowledge, feeling, and action by which Stella
may be brought to love him and the second describes the similar
stages by which he was brought to love her. As she may take
pleasure in his pain, he tries to make himself believe 'that all is
well' while, as he says, 'I paint my hell'. Usually the moment of
falling in love, the *innamoramento*, is a sudden ecstasy, as in Mar-
lowe's 'Who ever lov'd, that lov'd not at first sight?'. Astrophel's
reluctant yielding shows how he literally 'falls in love': an internal fall that leaves him divided against his better self. Instead
of simply showing his love to Stella, as he plans in the opening
sonnet, he will need to convince himself that he should love her.[56]

Sonnet 3 elaborates the 'inventions fine' of the opening sonnet
into four methods of writing love poetry which differ from his
own. While he seeks 'fit words', other poets are content with
'phrases fine'. Since he needs only to look in his heart to write of
his love, he mocks them for needing to call upon all the Muses to
write of their fancies. In the opening sonnet he turns from the inventions of others to find inspiration within himself: here he
opposes what others read in poetic manuals to what he reads in
Stella's face. In effect, he turns from art to Nature. His method of
copying the love and beauty that Nature writes in Stella's face
deserves the praise given Petrarch by Gabriel Harvey: his invention is not wit but 'pure Love itself' for he 'exercise[s] his fairest
gifts in a fair subject, and teacheth wit to be enamoured upon
Beauty...to make art more excellent by contemplation of excel-
lentest Nature'.[57] From Love which Nature writes in Stella's face,
Astrophel turns in sonnet 4 to 'vain love' in himself. His love for
her clashes with his virtue. What this sonnet calls the 'bate be-

tween my will and wit' is illustrated in sonnet 5. Significantly, there is no resolution: will and wit remain irreconcilable throughout the poem.

Sonnet 6 rounds out the opening group of sonnets – it uses the twelve-syllable line of sonnet 1 – by treating the poet as lover. Astrophel contrasts the extravagant posturings of other lovers with his simple feelings, and their indirections and artifice with his 'trembling voice'. His mockery of others becomes self-mockery when he uses the extravagance he mocks, as in the phrase 'powdered with golden rain'. Earlier professions of love – 'Loving in truth', 'I loved, but. . .', 'Virtue, thou thyself shalt be in love', and 'I must Stella love' – culminate in the simple final confession: 'I do Stella love'.

The next six sonnets divide into two groups of three: the first treats Stella and the second Astrophel. The three central concepts in the Petrarchan love sonnet are, in order, Beauty, Love, and Virtue. The lady's beauty arouses love which her virtue then opposes. Accordingly, Stella's beauty is displayed in sonnet 7, her relation to love in sonnet 8, and her virtue in sonnet 9. As opening exercises on conventional themes, these sonnets use, in order, the three methods outlined in sonnet 6: oxymoron, mythology, and personification. Their confident and sophisticated handling affords a witty answer to the 'trembling voice' which is all the lover claims to have in sonnet 6.

Since Stella is a star, sonnet 7 describes her beauty as residing in her eyes whose beams shine as stars from a black sky. Since Lady Rich's eyes were in fact black, the highly conventional conceit becomes literal, which may be its witty point of departure. In sonnet 6 Astrophel had mocked poets who merely state a paradox, such as 'heav'nly beams, infusing hellish pain'; here he argues a paradox to its logical conclusion. Stella's bright beams are dressed in black, for that colour is Love's mourning weed worn to honour her lovers' deaths. This reference to Love leads in sonnet 8 to a story of how cold Love responded to Stella's beauty: since she is a star whose light gives no heat, he was forced to flee to the lover's heart which now he kindles with love. The mythology is more than decorative – a use which Sidney mocks in sonnet 6: the story of the runaway Cupid alludes to Turkish invasions, such as the invasion of Cyprus in 1573, and England's long peace in Elizabeth's reign. Further, it provides a witty comparison between 'that Turkish hardened heart' and Stella's coldness, both causing Cupid to flee, in contrast to the lover's burning heart. In sonnet 9, love, aroused by beauty, conflicts with virtue. While Stella's beauty is the work of Nature, and the love that responds to her beauty is born in Greece, her virtue, whose setting is her beauty, is a 'heav'nly guest'. The formal praise of Stella's beauty as a setting for her virtue belongs at just this point in the sequence. The sonnet provides a fitting climax to the praise of the beauty in her eyes: her eyes, which are Nature's chief work (sonnet 7) but provide light without the heat that 'needs in nature grow' (sonnet 8), are now praised as windows through which Virtue gazes upon the lover.

In these three sonnets of praise, the lover provides only the concluding point of wit: he bleeds, his heart is kindled by love, and he is drawn by love to Stella and burned. In sonnets 10–12, though Stella's eyes are mentioned, the subject is the lover himself as he confronts her beauty, his love for her, and her virtue.

The witty play of reason on sensual love, which characterizes Sidney's sonnets, is exemplified in sonnet 10. Reason should move upward in stages: climbing the Muses' hill, reaching there for Nature's best fruit, seeking heaven, and finally, seeing into heaven. These are also the stages through which a poet may move from the lower poetic kinds to heroic and divine poetry. Such, too, are the stages through which a lover may move from earthly love to virtuous and heroic love and finally to divine love. In sonnet 10, as generally in Sidney's sonnets, Reason chooses instead to move downward to earthly matters of love and sense. 'Still / Would'st brabbling be with sense and love in me' shows how low Reason has been brought: it is reduced finally to defending sensual love by proving 'good reason her to love'. Love itself is treated in sonnet 11: it is content to look upon Stella's outward beauty until reason urges: 'fool, seek'st not to get into her heart'. While Love may be offered reason to love Stella for more than her outward beauty, sonnet 12 shows why the lover cannot get into her heart: 'her heart is such a citadel, / So fortified with wit, stor'd with disdain, / That to win it, is all the skill and pain'. As in the previous group, Stella's beauty is extended: here from her eyes (sonnet 10), to her cheek and breast (sonnet 11), to the catalogue of her beauty in sonnet 12.

The opening twelve sonnets provide a comprehensive introduction to the sonnet sequence. Stella's beauty, which arouses love, leaves Astrophel divided within himself; and her virtue determines that his desire will remain unsatisfied. The cruel, chaste lady and the despairing lover are traditional counters for the Petrarchan poet: the two exist on different levels in a fixed relationship, as she is the heavenly idol whom he worships from afar. What binds the lover, however, frees the poet: the lady, isolated in her virtue, is his security that his desire to write sonnets will not be frustrated.[58] She must never yield to him, so that, like Shakespeare's Armado, he may 'turn sonnet', forever writing and polishing his complaints at being frustrated. As the example of Petrarch shows, she may have only a ghostly existence, and he may write about her after her death. But the love anatomized in *Astrophel and Stella* is, like Donne's, 'not so pure, and abstract, as they use / To say, which have no mistress but their muse'. Sidney introduces elements that upset any fixed Petrarchan stance. The image of Stella as the star is too extreme to be maintained for long, and praise of her 'clear voice' in sonnet 12 deliberately prepares for a role quite different from that of the distant, disdainful mistress. Further, the image of Astrophel as the lover of the star is at odds with the strong presence of a man 'loving in truth'. His direct, speaking voice with its intimate, cajoling tone conveys an easy, familiar manner towards his mistress and indicates that his desire will demand to be satisfied. Even his act of writing assumes that her virtue may be overcome. Her heart, though 'fortified with wit, stor'd with disdain' (sonnet 12), is assumed to be vulnerable to witty persuasion. Some change and development in their relationship must follow.

Since the sonnets in *Astrophel and Stella* are carefully structured to form a sequence, each must be interpreted in the context of the whole poem. In his preface to the first quarto edition, Nashe speaks of the work as 'the tragicomedy of love...performed by starlight': 'the argument cruel chastity, the prologue hope, the epilogue despair'.[59] Clearly the opening sonnet provides a prologue in which the lover announces his purpose to persuade the lady to yield to him; the hope that she will do so is finally abandoned in the concluding sonnet, providing an epilogue in which he despairs. The difficulty is to see how the intervening sonnets provide a middle. Ringler finds a three-part structure and concludes that the poem is 'more carefully structured than that of any other Elizabethan sonnet collection'.[60] Others find different three-part structures, for the poem's comprehensiveness invites different perspectives.[61] Yet preliminary to all these structures, and basic to the argument of the work, is a three-part structure which traces the progress of love from its first awakening, to strong hopes for fulfilment, to final frustration. Probably Sidney took this structure from Chaucer's *Troilus and Criseyde*, which was, according to Gabriel Harvey, 'one of Astrophil's cordials',[62] for he tells a similar story in the 'double sorwe' of Astrophel: 'in loving, how his aventures fellen / Fro wo to wele, and after out of joy'.

Sonnets 1–35   Sonnets 1–12 provide the formal introduction to the sequence, with an appendix in sonnet 13 which offers an extravagant compliment to Stella, associating her with Lady Rich by alluding to the Devereux arms.[63] In the succeeding sonnets, Astrophel becomes increasingly withdrawn from those around him until he remains alone in physical and spiritual darkness. In sonnet 14 he strives to defend his sinful state even while he allows that desire 'doth plunge my well-form'd soul even in the mire / Of sinful thoughts, which do in ruin end'. Yet the agony of loving becomes more intense and internal. Linked sonnets show him poisoned (16), pierced with Love's arrows (17), bankrupt (18), and fallen (19). With Stella's dramatic entrance in sonnet 20, her heavenly eye wounds him mortally. Being marred both in mind and fortune as one 'whom Love doth windlass [i.e. ambush] so' (21), he becomes pensive (23), jealous (24), frustrated (25), abstracted (27), enslaved (29), and separated from the pressing life about him (30). By the end of this group of sonnets, his isolation seems complete.

In displaying the lover's increasing isolation, the sonnets are variously linked. One sonnet may prompt the next; so sonnet 15 advises poets to 'Stella behold' and sonnet 16 reveals what happened when he 'beheld / Stella'. In sonnet 21 he asks, 'Hath this world aught so fair as Stella is?' and answers that question in sonnet 22 by explaining why the sun burns other ladies but only kisses her. Sonnets may be formally organized into a catalogue: Astrophel addresses his friends (20), his special friend (21), curious wits (23), rich fools (24), the wisest scholar (25), dusty wits (26), idle gossips (27), curious readers (28), and busy wits (30). Or they may be subtly organized by appearing to be casually linked. Sonnet 29 provides an elaborate and extravagant fiction of Cupid as a foreign aggressor who has conquered Stella's body, which is described as the coast upon which the lover looks. Sonnet 30 turns abruptly from this puzzling fiction to brute fact, the topical matter of Turkish aggression which threatened Europe at the time: 'Whether the Turkish new moon minded be / To fill his horns this year on Christian coast'. Some sonnets are linked in that they clash violently being juxtaposed. Sonnet 22 celebrates the triumphant victory of Stella's beauty over the sun. In sonnet 23 Astrophel dismisses as fools those curious wits who do not realize that his thoughts dwell only on Stella's eyes and her heart. Then sonnet 24 treats the filthy heart of that rich fool who possesses Stella, and counters sonnet 22 in its revelation of Stella handled, enjoyed, and her beauty blotted with foul abuse.

Sonnets 30–5 mark the first turning-point in the sequence. Their structuring is too deliberate not to have been planned and yet too significant to have been merely planned. In sonnet 30 Astrophel appears as Sidney himself without the anonymity conferred previously by his use of a persona:

> Whether the Turkish new moon minded be
>   To fill his horns this year on Christian coast;
>   How Poles' right king means, without leave of host,
> To warm with ill-made fire cold Muscovy;
> If French can yet three parts in one agree;
>   What now the Dutch in their full diets boast;
>   How Holland hearts, now so good towns be lost,
> Trust in the shade of pleasing Orange tree;
>   How Ulster likes of that same golden bit,
> Wherewith my father once made it half tame;
> If in the Scottish court be welt'ring yet;
>   These questions busy wits to me do frame;
>   I, cumbered with good manners, answer do,
>   But know not how, for still I think of you.

Modern readers are so distracted by attempting to unravel the seven political matters which exercised the 'busy wits' in 1582 that the poem loses its force. Contemporary readers would have been shocked that such matters should be dismissed by one who was expected to play a major role in England's foreign affairs.[64] Languet would have been horrified; and Sidney could hardly have written this sonnet while he was alive. Clearly the sonnet is meant to shock: it is one thing for an anonymous lover to declare that he is ready to give up the world for love, but a different thing for Sidney to explicitly identify himself and reject a political career. This sonnet marks a turning-point in the sequence because it marks a turning-point in Sidney's life.

In speaking directly about himself for the first time, Sidney directly addresses Stella for the first time: he dismisses any thought of political concern 'for still I think of you'. His meditation upon her is illustrated in the famous sonnet 31, 'With how sad steps, O moon, thou climb'st the skies'. Sonnet 32 is a companion poem: while he communes with the moon, he is led to dream. The colloquial address of 'ev'n of fellowship, O moon, tell me' is paralleled in the address to Morpheus: 'Vouchsafe of all acquaintance this to tell'. In sleep, he projects Stella's image in his heart, the 'ivory, rubies, pearl and gold' which 'show her skin, lips, teeth and head so well'. The lover's dream that Morpheus stole Stella's image from him prompts the memory when he awakens of how Stella was in fact stolen from him. The highly conventional image of Stella is violently juxtaposed against sonnet 33 on her identity as Lady Rich:

> I might, unhappy word, O me, I might,
> And then would not, or could not see my bliss:
> Till now, wrapped in a most infernal night,
> I find how heav'nly day wretch I did miss.
> Heart rend thyself, thou dost thyself but right,
> No lovely Paris made thy Helen his:
> No force, no fraud, robbed thee of thy delight,
> Nor Fortune of thy fortune author is:
> But to myself myself did give the blow,
> While too much wit (forsooth) so troubled me,
> That I respects for both our sakes must show:
> And yet could not by rising morn foresee
> How fair a day was near, O punished eyes,
> That I had been more foolish or more wise.

To understand this sonnet one must know that marriage had once been proposed between Sidney, when he was almost twenty-two, and the thirteen-year-old Penelope Devereux. Even with such biographical knowledge, however, the sonnet remains puzzling: lines 9–11 seem to allude to matters too personal to be made public.[65]

The sudden irruption of biographical matter in sonnets 30 and 33 separates fiction from fact, the lover's golden world which he creates as a poet from the real world in which he lives. In sonnet 30 Sidney forsakes the world for Stella only to find by sonnet 33 that he has forsaken life for a mere fiction. Worse than ever Pygmalion was, he is left with Stella's image while another enjoys the reality. With the loss of his 'heav'nly day', he remains 'wrapped in a most infernal night'. The shock of this moment, now first realized, leads to sonnets 34 and 35 which challenge in a fundamental way his reasons for writing the sonnet sequence. The first relates to himself as a lover: 'How can words ease?', and the second to himself as a poet: 'What may words say?'.

At the beginning Astrophel had assumed that if he found fit words to express his grief in verse he would persuade Stella to pity him. In sonnet 34 he recognizes that words serve no purpose:

> Come let me write, 'And to what end?' To ease
> A burdened heart. 'How can words ease, which are
> The glasses of thy daily vexing care?'
> Oft cruel fights well pictured forth do please.
> 'Art not asham'd to publish thy disease?'
> Nay, that may breed my fame, it is so rare:
> 'But will not wise men think thy words fond ware?'
> Then be they close, and so none shall displease.
> 'What idler thing, than speak and not be heard?'
> What harder thing than smart, and not to speak?
> Peace, foolish wit, with wit my wit is marred.
> Thus write I while I doubt to write, and wreak
> My harms on ink's poor loss, perhaps some find
> Stella's great powers, that so confuse my mind.

A traditional function of verse is to provide 'solace through utterance': grief may be controlled by imposing poetic form upon it. In 'The Triple Fool' Donne writes: 'I thought, if I could draw my pains, / Through rhyme's vexation, I should them allay, / Grief brought to numbers cannot be so fierce, / For, he tames it, that fetters it in verse.'[66] Sidney challenges this function and also one inference from it which Donne draws, that publishing verse only releases and renews grief. Yet the effort needed to persuade himself to write, and the doubts about the sense of writing that follow his belated recognition that he failed to act when he should, show that he cannot continue his role as a lover who is content to express his grief.

At the beginning he had also assumed that he would be able to reveal himself as one 'loving in truth'. In sonnet 35 he realizes that his truth may seem only empty useless flattery:

> What may words say, or what may words not say,
> Where truth itself must speak like flattery?
> Within what bounds can one his liking stay,
> Where nature doth with infinite agree?
>   What Nestor's counsel can my flames allay,
> Since reason's self doth blow the coal in me?
> And ah what hope, that hope should once see day,
> Where Cupid is sworn page to chastity?
> Honour is honour'd, that thou dost possess
>   Him as thy slave, and now long needy fame
>   Doth even grow rich, naming my Stella's name.
> Wit learns in thee perfection to express,
>   Not thou by praise, but praise in thee is raised:
>   It is a praise to praise, when thou art praised.

Since words cannot measure either Stella's perfection or his boundless love, he is reduced to the posture, which he mocks in the *Arcadia*, of uttering 'those immoderate praises which the foolish lover ever thinks short of his mistress, although they reach far beyond the heavens'.[67] The dilemma of language makes manifest his dilemma in loving Stella: his boundless love cannot be revealed in words, nor restrained by reason, nor ever be satisfied. Instead of narrowing the sonnet in the sestet to a final witty point, he catalogues 'Stella's great pow'rs' by addressing her directly and naming her explicitly as Lady Rich. As the play on 'praise' in the final line suggests, the sonnet fulfils the function of the lyric as a poem of praise; accordingly, it provides a fitting conclusion to the first part of the sequence.

Sonnets 36–71   The second part begins with sonnet 36 which records Stella's fresh 'assault' upon Astrophel by her singing. For the first time he addresses her by name:

> Stella, whence doth this new assault arise,
> A conquered, yelden, ransacked heart to win?
> Whereto long since, through my long battered eyes,
> Whole armies of thy beauties entered in.
>   And there long since, Love thy lieutenant lies,

My forces razed, thy banners rais'd within:
Of conquest, do not these effects suffice,
But wilt new war upon thine own begin?
　With so sweet voice, and by sweet nature so,
In sweetest strength, so sweetly skill'd withal,
In all sweet stratagems sweet art can show,
That not my soul, which at thy foot did fall,
　　Long since forc'd by thy beams, but stone nor tree
　　By sense's privilege, can 'scape from thee.

Until now she has assaulted him with the bright beams from her eyes; now she assaults him with the sound of her voice. Her eyes have been praised as Nature's chief work, as in sonnet 7; now to Nature her voice adds art, and their combined powers totally overwhelm him. Now when he sleeps, as he complains in sonnet 38, her image 'not only shines but sings'. Three songs, whether they belong to this part of the sequence or later, testify to their new relationship: song iii tells how men's ears and eyes are charmed when 'Stella singeth' and 'Stella shineth'; song vi debates whether her voice or face takes precedence; and its companion, song vii, praises her eyes as 'life-giving lights' but laments the effect of her 'soul-invading voice'. As the second highest sense, hearing is associated with the soul because music has the power to separate the soul from the body;[68] for neo-Platonists, it is the spiritual sense through which love enters man. Accordingly, in the opening song the lover praises Stella 'who hath the voice, which soul from senses sunders'.

　That the lover hears Stella's voice shows that she is an immediate, physical presence: not only one whom he hears but one who may hear him. Her proximity arouses desires which destroy him; or, in terms of the central star-imagery, her eyes offer light which he sees and heat which burns him. When he praises her eyes in sonnet 42, he notes their malignant effect: through seeing her 'my life forgets to nourish languished sprites'. In this, and sonnets 40 and 45, he refers to himself as love's 'wrack'. Their new relationship leads to his counter-assault, which he declares in sonnet 61: 'I Stella's eyes assail, invade her ears'. His visual assault is seen in his shifting disguises from humble suppliant to demanding lover. His verbal assault is heard in his shifts of tone. His voice varies from humble supplication to witty, sarcastic attack: it is both personal and public, solemn and gay, self-effacing and aggressive. Only in

this section does he appeal directly to her for grace, as in sonnet
40, rather than indirectly by entertaining her. His tone becomes
ever more strident, insistent, even threatening. While he may sup-
plicate as in sonnet 42, more often he speaks to her familiarly as
'my dear' (45) or simply 'dear' (46); or sarcastically in 'Dear, why
make you more of a dog than me ?' (59), which implies that she is
a perverse, even perverted, woman; or insolently, as in sonnet 63
where he addresses her as 'my young dove' from whom he 'crav'd
the thing which ever she denies'. Although he opens sonnet 48
with the humble appeal, 'Soul's joy, bend not those morning stars
from me', he does so in order to conclude with the witty address,
'Dear killer'. In this part of the poem he most deserves Sir John
Davies's praise as one 'whose supple muse chameleon-like doth
change / Into all forms of excellent device'.[69]

Some links between the sonnets show the immediate, personal
relationship between the lovers. Astrophel's involvement in the
experience of loving may be revealed in the dramatic unfolding
of a theme, such as his charge that Stella is unkind, that is 'unnatural'. In sonnet 44 he wonders why she fails to pity him even
though she hears his grief: 'what cause is there so overthwart, /
That nobleness itself makes thus unkind?'. He allows that she may
be unkind not because she is of 'tiger's kind' but because of her
'heav'nly nature'. In sonnet 47 he addresses her directly as unkind: 'Go to, / Unkind, I love you not'. He notes in sonnet 57 how
she prepares to be unkind in his presence, recalls in sonnet 62 how
'Late tir'd [i.e. savaged] with woe, even ready for to pine / With
rage of love, I call'd my love unkind', and in sonnet 65 concludes
that 'Love by sure proof I may call thee unkind'.

Alternatively, apparently casual links between sonnets may
create a sense of his involvement as both lover and poet in the
experience of loving. In sonnet 39 he woos sleep – apparently in
vain, for sonnet 40 begins: 'As good to write as for to lie and
groan'. He invokes her as one who looks down upon him 'from
the height of virtue's throne'; in sonnet 41 she looks down upon
him from the lists and her beams guide his lance true; in sonnet
42 she looks down from her heaven and he praises her eyes as
stars 'whose beams be joys'; their beauty, joy, and virtue, which
he praises, are distributed in the next sonnet in praise of her 'fair
eyes, sweet lips, dear heart'; and in sonnet 44 he addresses her

heart in particular. Other apparently casual links may suggest his involvement in his various roles. As a poet he complains in sonnet 50 of the weak power of words to express Stella's figure; as a courtier he is confronted in sonnet 51 by the 'unsuited speech' of the courtly gossiper who hinders his meditation upon Stella; as a lover in sonnet 52 his suit is again stayed, this time by a quarrel between virtue and love; as a knight in sonnet 53, his martial race is stayed when Stella's glance causes his heart to quake; and as a lover in sonnet 54 he alludes to himself as among 'dumb swans' – playing on his name, Fr. *cygne* – who 'lovers prove' and defends those 'who quake to say they love'.[70]

Their new relationship frustrates him as poet and lover both when she rejects him and later when she accepts him. His plan had been that in reading his sonnets she would take such pleasure in his pain that through pity she would yield to him. It turns out that she takes pleasure in his pain but no more than that. In sonnet 44 she hears his complaints but does not pity him: 'the sobs of mine annoys / Are metamorphos'd straight to tunes of joys' because of her heavenly nature. In sonnet 45 she does not pity him even though she pities an unhappy lover in a story that she hears, and he is tempted to abandon his role of 'loving in truth' to substitute a more moving fiction of himself: 'I am not I, pity the tale of me'. In sonnet 57 when she sings his verse, he himself takes pleasure in his pain, and in sonnet 58 when she reads his verse, her voice and face are such that 'most ravishing delight / Even those sad words even in sad me did breed'. In sonnet 59 when she prefers her dog to him, he threatens to stop loving her; in her perversity, she responds with 'fierce love and lovely hate' (sonnet 60). Yet in accepting his love, she frustrates him more, for she rejects his desire, as he complains in sonnets 61 and 62. At this point the sonnets read as a commentary upon their developing intimacy. His success as a suitor frustrates him not only as a lover but also as a poet:

> My muse may well grudge at my heav'nly joy,
> If still I force her in sad rhymes to creep:
> She oft hath drunk my tears, now hopes to enjoy
> Nectar of mirth, since I Jove's cup do keep.
>   Sonnets be not bound prentice to annoy:
> Trebles sing high, as well as basses deep:
> Grief but love's winter livery is, the boy

Hath cheeks to smile, as well as eyes to weep.
  Come then my muse, show thou height of delight
In well raised notes, my pen the best it may
Shall paint out joy, though but in black and white.
Cease eager muse, peace pen, for my sake stay.
  I give you here my hand for truth of this,
  Wise silence is best music unto bliss. (sonnet 70)

His crisis shows why any sonneteer – Dante, Petrarch, and all their tribe – selects a cruel, chaste mistress: sonnets are, in fact, 'bound prentice to annoy', and a poet hopeful of success must stop writing because he must act.[71]

Sonnets 71 and 72 mark the second turning-point in the sequence. In his mounting joy, the lover reaches a crucial stage: either he must move to higher love or descend into lust. In sonnet 71 he imitates Petrarch's transcendent vision of Laura:

Who will in fairest book of nature know,
  How virtue may best lodg'd in beauty be,
  Let him but learn of love to read in thee,
Stella, those fair lines, which true goodness show.
There shall he find all vices' overthrow,
  Not by rude force, but sweetest sovereignty
  Of reason, from whose light those night-birds flee;
That inward sun in thine eyes shineth so.
  And not content to be perfection's heir
Thyself, dost strive all minds that way to move,
Who mark in thee what is in thee most fair.
So while thy beauty draws the heart to love,
  As fast thy virtue bends that love to good:
But ah, desire still cries, 'Give me some food'.[72]

He cannot accept that vision of perfection because it denies the demands of the flesh. Yet she insists that desire be separated from love and banished, as sonnet 72 makes clear in its first thirteen and a half lines:

Desire, though thou my old companion art,
  And oft so clings to my pure love, that I
  One from the other scarcely can descry,
While each doth blow the fire of my heart;
Now from thy fellowship I needs must part,
  Venus is taught with Dian's wings to fly:
  I must no more in thy sweet passions lie;
Virtue's gold now must head my Cupid's dart.
  Service and honour, wonder with delight,
Fear to offend, will worthy to appear,

> Care shining in mine eyes, faith in my sprite,
> These things are left me by my only dear;
>   But thou desire, because thou wouldst have all,
>   Now banish'd art, but yet alas how shall?

That final question, rhetorical yet puzzled, seems to leave him paralysed. Its tone contrasts sharply with the witty banter and cajolery of the previous sonnets, particularly with the naughty ending of sonnet 68, the arch, gloating anticipation of sonnet 69, the sententious ending of sonnet 70, and the naked cry of sonnet 71. Since he is unable to distinguish desire from love, spiritualize it or forsake it, he has no choice but to yield to it. The third part of the sequence shows what happens when desire 'wouldst have all'.

Song ii – sonnet 108   The third part of the sequence begins when Astrophel steals a kiss. The stolen kiss is described in song ii and analysed in sonnet 73, and the kissing that follows is commented upon in an extended sequence. Thus the movement of the three parts is from sight to hearing to touch: sight awakens love, hearing arouses desire, and now touch seeks to satisfy desire. The sequence employs the traditional formula: *Mulier visa, audita, tacta.* To the lust of the eye and the lust of the ear is added the lust of the flesh. This movement is described in Castiglione's *Courtier*, where Pietro Bembo explains that when the lover sees a beautiful woman, his eyes will snatch the image of her beauty and carry it to his heart. There his soul 'beginneth to behold it with pleasure, and feeleth within herself the influence that stirreth her'. If the lover represses the heat of lust, he will see beauty as 'an heavenly shining beam' and satisfy desire with 'the virtue of seeing'. Accordingly, Bembo exhorts him to 'lay aside therefore the blind judgement of the sense, and enjoy with his eyes the brightness, the comeliness, the loving sparkles, laughters, gestures, and all the other pleasant furnitures of beauty: especially with hearing the sweetness of her voice, the tunableness of her words, the melody of her singing'. He cautions him to be satisfied with 'the sight and the hearing...the looks of her eyes, the image of her countenance, and the voice of her words, that pierce into the lover's heart'.[73] Only the reasonable lover may proceed as far as the kiss; for the sensual lover, the kiss will lead to the knitting of bodies.

In sonnet 81, Astrophel allows that the kiss 'even souls together ties / By links of love', but what he goes on to say confirms Bembo's restriction upon the sensual lover:

> But my heart burns, I cannot silent be.
> Then since (dear life) you fain would have me peace,
> And I, mad with delight, want wit to cease,
> Stop you my mouth with still still kissing me.

The twelve poems from song ii to sonnet 83, most of them on the kiss, constitute the erotic centre of the sequence.[74] They move from the lyricism of the song and dramatic action of sonnet 73 to the mock encomium of sonnet 75 (its bawdy ending suggests that Edward IV was willing to risk syphilis for the sake of his whore), the naughtiness of sonnet 76, the coy wittiness of sonnet 77, the invitation to adultery in sonnet 78, and the three traditional *baiser* sonnets, 79–81, in the first of which he turns from the poet's praise and prayer to the lover's preying: 'Cease we to praise, now pray we for a kiss'. The erotic climax comes in sonnet 82 with its image of plucking fruit from Stella's cherry tree. The harshly cynical sonnet 83 is Astrophel's farewell to the kiss: by sonnet 85 and song x he anticipates the full banquet of the senses.

The sonnets are linked as they comment on the progress of the 'affair'. In sonnet 84 he journeys to meet her and in sonnet 85 anticipates the satisfaction of his desire; but his evident rejection by her leads to his anguish (sonnet 86) and then hers (sonnet 87). Twelve sonnets (88–99) treat his absence from her either as physical separation or banishment as a consequence of some act by which he harmed her (sonnet 93, with its effects analysed in sonnets 94–5). Four sonnets recall her beauty: in sorrow (sonnet 100), sickness (sonnets 101–2), and before his absence (sonnet 103). Four poems are 'window-songs': sonnet 104, song xi, sonnets 105–6.

Such linking becomes complicated because ten of the eleven songs are crowded into the final third of the sequence, with five (songs v–ix) awkwardly grouped after sonnet 86. Ringler notes that 'the six songs in trochaic metres narrate the more important events of the sequence' while the rest in conventional iambic metres, some of which were written much earlier, 'are little more than fillers'. He conjectures that Sidney started to write a set of detached songs in the new trochaic metre and 'not until after he had written the songs did he think of writing the sonnets and of combining them with the songs in a single sequence'.[75] Or it may be that from the outset he planned a traditional gathering of 'Songs and Sonnets' with distinctions in form and function between the *canzone* or big song and the *sonetto* or little song.[76] The resulting amalgam is confusing only if one prefers a neat narrative record of the events in a courtship.

As a record of the troubled passions of one overwhelmed by those events, the third part of the sequence gains some of the rich complexity of Shakespeare's sonnets in their ordered disorder. For example, sonnet 87 notes Stella's sadness at leaving her lover:

> I saw that tears did in her eyes appear;
> I saw that sighs her sweetest lips did part,
> And her sad words my sadded sense did hear.

Because of her tears, sighs, and words, he 'swam in joy, such love in her was seen'. In sonnet 100 the three terms are expanded into two quatrains and a triplet in order to reach the same conclusion, that 'Such tears, sighs, plaints, no sorrow is, but joy'. The later sonnet is more comprehensive in its reference and more powerful because the intervening sonnets have demonstrated the anguish, which joy now balances, and have shown how Astrophel earns the claim that his body is 'the hell where my soul fries'.

Sonnets 107 and 108 resolve the entire sequence. The demands of living and loving have conflicted throughout because loving Stella has required Astrophel to withdraw from life and give up to her all his powers. In sonnet 107 he begs for their temporary return:

> Stella since thou so right a princess art
>   Of all the powers which life bestows on me,
>   That ere by them aught undertaken be,
> They first resort unto that sovereign part;
> Sweet, for a while give respite to my heart,
>   Which pants as though it still should leap to thee:
>   And on my thoughts give thy lieutenancy
> To this great cause, which needs both use and art,
>   And as a queen, who from her presence sends
> Whom she employs, dismiss from thee my wit,
> Till it have wrought what thy own will attends.
> On servant's shame oft master's blame doth sit;
>   O let not fools in me thy works reprove,
>   And scorning say, 'See what it is to love'.

Stella does not lead him from the world to God, as Laura leads Petrarch; nor does she yield to him, having been persuaded by his powers displayed in verse; so now he asks her to release him so that he may act in the world. Instead of a final injunction, 'Leave me O love', there is only a plea for temporary respite: let me leave thee for a while. As in an epilogue to a stage-play of love, he is dismissed; but in life he cares only that his love be not shamed.

There is no escape from love, as the concluding sonnet declares:

> When sorrow (using mine own fire's might)
>   Melts down his lead into my boiling breast,
>   Through that dark furnace to my heart oppress'd,
> There shines a joy from thee my only light;
> But soon as thought of thee breeds my delight,
>   And my young soul flutters to thee his nest,
>   Most rude despair my daily unbidden guest,
> Clips straight my wings, straight wraps me in his night,
>   And makes me then bow down my head, and say,
> Ah what doth Phoebus' gold that wretch avail,
> Whom iron doors do keep from use of day?
> So strangely (alas) thy works in me prevail,
>   That in my woes for thee thou art my joy,
>   And in my joys for thee my only annoy.

The sonnet fixes his state simply and finally as Astrophel, the lover of the star, one in darkness gazing up in love at the heavenly light. This central image of the poem is given here with full intensity: it concludes the poem by defining the lover's state. Exiled from heaven and condemned to eternal darkness in which he suffers heat without light, he dwells in hell:

> The fire of Hell this strange condition hath,
> To burn, not shine (as learned *Basil* saith).[77]

Since the lady remains his only light, thought of her only breeds despair which 'wraps me in his night'. With this concluding metaphor, the end of the sequence is antithetical to that of the *Certain sonnets* where the lover turns to the light 'That doth both shine and give us light to see'.[78]

This 'ending' departs radically from the ending of any earlier sonnet sequence. In the *Rime,* the movement from earthly to heavenly love leads to a concluding hymn to the Virgin. Petrarch imitates the *Vita Nuova*, except that Dante's love of God includes love of Beatrice. At the end, Dante may transcend earthly love while Petrarch must recant his. Through Petrarch's enormous influence, the love sonnet traditionally ends with re-cantation. Such an ending is satisfying even when it is as simple as Thomas Watson's *Hekatompathia* which is advertised as 'be-ginning sweet and ending sour', or as brutal as Ronsard's *Sonnets pour Hélène* which ends in a mood of disgust. Even Donne, who is ready to flout all love conventions in his *Songs and sonnets*, ends with a traditional 'Farewell to love'. In his *Amoretti*, Spenser seems closest to Sidney when his lover finally wanders in darkness and complains in the concluding lines of the final sonnet, 'Dark is my day, whiles her fair light I miss, / And dead my life that wants such lively bliss'; but after a song, he appends his marriage hymn. While Sidney follows the conventional ending in *Certain sonnets*, in *Astrophel and Stella* he chooses not to. In sonnet 107, the farewell to love for a while is deliberately not that long fare-well at the end of *Certain sonnets*: *Splendidis longum valedico nugis*; and in sonnet 108, the lover continues to love without hope of physical satisfaction or spiritual fulfilment.

Two contradictory responses are invited by this ending. First there is the moral judgment: yielding to passion leads to despair, the state of spiritual damnation. In Petrarch's *Secretum*, Augus-tine warns the lover that earthly love will condemn 'to everlasting darkness the clearest faculties of [his] soul'.[79] Such we see in Astrophel, as his friend had warned him: 'desire / Doth plunge [your] well-form'd soul even in the mire / Of sinful thoughts, which do in ruin end'. His ending in despair has been implicit from the beginning, and inevitable from the moment when Stella urged him 'these tempests of vain love to flee, / And anchor fast myself on virtue's shore' and he was unable to do so. Our second response, however, suspends all moral judgment. If the ending warns against yielding to desire, it also shows the need to satisfy desire:

> So must pure lovers' souls descend
> T'affections, and to faculties,
> That sense may reach and apprehend,
> Else a great prince in prison lies.[80]

In loving without hope of satisfying desire, he becomes more than – even other than – an emblem of man infected by concupiscence. In his steadfastness, loving even in despair, he appears stubbornly, magnificently human.[81] He ends where he began, trying to persuade himself that 'all is well, / While with a feeling skill I paint my hell'. The only change in him is that he embodies his own metaphor: 'wrapped in a most infernal night, / I find how heav'nly day wretch I did miss' (sonnet 33). That change brings a determination not to change. The resolution of the sequence is found in his resolution to love without hope. He becomes the pattern or image of one 'loving in truth'; or, in terms of the *Defence*, 'so true a lover every way'.

4

Sidney's poetics

In his poetry Sidney shows his contemporaries how poetry should be written. In so doing, he seeks to counter its abuse by the poet-apes through whose work, as he argues in the second part of the *Defence*, England had come to despise poetry. Yet he needed to counter also the poet-haters, the μισόμουσοι, through whose influence England had come to despise the art itself. Accordingly, in the first part of the *Defence* he describes the nature and working of the 'right poets'. In showing why poets write and how their works should be read, he provides a manifesto for the major Elizabethan writers.

Sidney may have written the *Defence* between 1580 and 1582. From Spenser's letter to Harvey in October 1579 announcing that Sidney and Dyer had proclaimed 'a general surceasing and silence of bald rhymers'[1] by experimenting in quantitative verse, one infers that Sidney had reached the position, expressed in the *Defence*, that verse is 'but an ornament and no cause to poetry' but not what he goes on to say here, that verse remains its fittest raiment. The *Defence* may have been occasioned by the attack on poetry in Gosson's *School of Abuse* (1579), or by the dedication of that work to Sidney, which provoked him not to answer Gosson specifically but Plato and all after him who had spoken against poetry.[2] For all we know – and we know little – the *Defence* may also have been prompted by Spenser's lost critical treatise, 'The English Poet'. Sidney may have wanted to complement that work by treating the art of poesy itself; or even to counter its doctrine: that poetry is 'a divine gift and heavenly instinct. . .poured into the wit by a certain ἐνθουσιασμός and celestial inspiration'[3] is exactly contrary to his own doctrine that the poet is 'lifted up with the vigour of his own invention' (78). The close relationship between Sidney's creative and critical faculties suggests that the *Defence* was prompted by his own work: he came to

understand the art of poesy by practising it. The modest reference
to himself as one who 'having slipped into the title of a poet, am
provoked to say something unto you in the defence of that my
unelected vocation' shows pride in some substantial work, which
may well be *Astrophel and Stella*. The *Defence* may be dated
after that work and before the *New Arcadia*, that is, between
1580 and 1582, because it is not necessary to our understanding
of the former but illuminates our reading of the latter. While it
could be earlier,[4] a later date is likely because of its mastery of
matter and manner. To write the *Defence*, Sidney had to assimi-
late an extensive body of contemporary learning and then integrate
the major traditions of literary doctrine from Plato, Aristotle, and
Horace to the sixteenth-century Italian critics into a profound and
original argument on the idea of the 'right poet'.[5] The sustained
brilliance of its style – it is surely the best written treatise of its
kind in any language – supports a later date. A later date may
explain why Sidney should write a defence of poetry while his
friends were writing political and religious treatises.[6] (George
Buchanan's *De Jure Regni apud Scotos* and Duplessis's *Vindiciae
contra Tyrannos* appeared in 1579, the year in which Sidney
began to take a strong interest in poetry.) Evidently he had concluded that his future lay in writing rather than in politics.

The *Defence* is characterized by its style. Swift remarks scorn-
fully, though truly, that Sidney argues 'as if he really believed
himself'. Even more, Sidney convinces his readers that they, too,
should believe what he says. His persuasive intent becomes clear
if the opening of the *Defence* is compared to the opening of the
Poetices by Scaliger, his chief Italian counterpart. The latter begins
with a division of *oratio* according to its three ends, each with its
own type of expression: 'Everything that pertains to mankind may
be classed as necessary, useful, or pleasure-giving, and by an in-
herent characteristic of all these classes the power of speech was
implanted in man from the very beginning, or, as time went on,
was acquired. Since man's development depended upon learning,
he could not do without that agency which was destined to make
him the partaker of wisdom. Our speech is, as it were, the post-
man of the mind, through the services of whom civil gatherings
are announced, the arts are cultivated, and the claims of wisdom
intercede with men for man.'[7] It is clear even in translation that,

to use his own category, Scaliger's language may be classified as 'useful': he argues logically, to convince us by reason. In contrast, Sidney begins with a personal, and apparently casual, recollection of the time 'when the right virtuous Edward Wotton and I were at the Emperor's court together' (assuming that we know who that Emperor was), and relates an anecdote about a certain John Pietro Pugliano who so over-praised horses that Sidney concludes: 'if I had not been a piece of a logician before I came to him, I think he would have persuaded me to have wished myself a horse' (thus wittily alluding to his own name, Philip, *philippos*, one fond of horses), and concludes with a disarming 'disabler', apologizing for his own apology for poetry: 'if I handle [it] with more good will than good reasons, bear with me'. Anyone who continues to read will be persuaded by Sidney's 'good will' before ever he may entertain his 'good reasons'.

Sidney's style may be illustrated in the passage in which he answers the second charge against poetry, that poets are liars:

To the second. . .that they should be the principal liars, I will answer paradoxically, but truly, I think truly, that of all writers under the sun the poet is the least liar, and, though he would, as a poet can scarcely be a liar. The astronomer, with his cousin the geometrician, can hardly escape, when they take upon them to measure the height of the stars. How often, think you, do the physicians lie, when they aver things good for sicknesses, which afterwards send Charon a great number of souls drowned in a potion before they come to his ferry? And no less of the rest, which take upon them to affirm. Now, for the poet, he nothing affirms, and therefore never lieth. . .Though he recount things not true, yet because he telleth them not for true, he lieth not – without we will say that Nathan lied in his speech before-alleged to David; which as a wicked man durst scarce say, so think I none so simple would say that Aesop lied in the tales of his beasts; for who thinks that Aesop wrote it for actually true were well worthy to have his name chronicled among the beasts he writeth of. What child is there, that, coming to a play, and seeing *Thebes* written in great letters upon an old door, doth believe that it is Thebes? If then a man can arrive to that child's age to know that the poets' persons and doings are but pictures what should be, and not stories what have been, they will never give the lie to things not affirmatively but allegorically and figuratively written. (102–3)

This extended passage answers a stock charge familiar from the time of Plato: it is a re-statement, as Shepherd notes, of the Aristotelian handling of Plato's position.[8] Clearly Sidney has a purpose beyond conveying a mere argument. It is startling that he should lead so casually and humorously to the concluding sentence, which is central to the argument of the *Defence*.

The opening conveys the accents of a man speaking, and thinking as he speaks: 'I will answer paradoxically, but truly, I think truly'. 'I think' indicates hesitation as much as it does confirmation, forcing us to follow Sidney's process of thinking rather than his thoughts, so that by the end we will think as he does. Although he argues paradoxically, we agree readily that an astronomer will prove a liar if he tries to measure the distance to a star. The Renaissance reader would consider the attempt both vain and forbidden. After this persuasive example we are ready to join Sidney in mocking the medical profession. The phrase, 'How often, think you', draws us fully to his side, particularly when he continues with the witty metaphor of patients drowned in doctors' potions before they come to Charon's ferry. The charge against doctors is a commonplace, but Sidney may have taken it from Agrippa's *Of the vanity and uncertainty of arts and sciences*: 'Well near always there is more danger in the physician, and the medicine, than in the sickness itself.'[9] When the charge is so expressed, we may agree or not, as we believe it to be true or false. As expressed by Sidney, however, all will agree, being persuaded by his wit, without pausing to quibble over just how many were drowned. Only when Sidney has persuaded us does he affirm his central doctrine that 'the poet. . .nothing affirms'. He then anticipates a reader's possible protest, namely, that the poet affirms things not true, not by logical argument but by an *argumentum ad hominem*: such a reader would place himself among those worse than the wicked or among beasts, and show less percipience than a child not to allow that the poet describes things not as they are, but as they ought to be. So readers are entertained, cajoled, even tricked, into accepting the argument that 'they will never give the lie to things not affirmatively but allegorically and figuratively written'.

The *Defence* is deeply and powerfully persuasive throughout, not because its argument immediately convinces us, but because Sidney convinces us that we should believe *him*. Not to be convinced would be to place oneself among the enemy, the unnamed because unnamable μισόμουσοι whose one great spokesman, Plato, attacks only the abuse of poetry (so Sidney shows) because he honours its proper use. Sidney impresses any reader as honest, passionate, witty, civilized, and, above all, fully human. His voice speaks for the best in us and the best in human society. It is personal in that it records Sidney's own commitments, and public in that it conveys the values and aspirations of his age.[10] As a result, the *Defence* gained central authority among contemporary writers. Lewis notes that the greatness of Sidney's theory is that 'it is the form into which the actual taste and ethics and religion and poetic practice of his age and class. . .naturally fell when reflected on and harmonized'.[11] Shepherd concludes that 'the more closely the *Apology* is studied the more astonishing appears Sidney's sensitivity to contemporary intellectual development, in the arts, in religion, in politics, and in science'.[12]

The persuasiveness and authority of Sidney's style might suggest that the *Defence* is a gracious expression of the ideas of others, 'what oft was thought, but ne'er so well expressed'. Whatever Sidney took from others, however, he made his own, and his style conveys an argument that is closely reasoned and logical in all its parts.[13] Since he possessed an eclectic and synthesizing mind, that originality appears as a simple rightness and central wholeness rather than a uniquely personal judgment. One paradox of the *Defence* is that it is both personal as it is dominated by the immediate and constant presence of Sidney as narrator, and impersonal as it expresses the truth about the essential nature and working of poetry. Another paradox is that despite its central authority, it proposes a revolutionary poetic.

The argument of the *Defence* arises from a division of poets into three kinds. The first 'imitate the unconceivable excellencies of God': 'such were David in his Psalms; Solomon in his Song of Songs. . .Orpheus, Amphion, Homer in his Hymns'. The second deal with philosophical matters: 'either moral, as Tyrtaeus, Phocylides, Cato, or natural, as Lucretius and Virgil's *Georgics*; or astronomical, as Manilius and Pontanus; or historical, as Lucan'. The third are set apart as 'indeed right poets': 'they which most properly do imitate to teach and delight, and to imitate borrow nothing of what is, hath been, or shall be; but range, only reined with learned discretion, into the divine consideration of what may be and should be' (80–1).

Sidney's source is Scaliger, who divides poets into three kinds according to their subject-matter. Yet Scaliger also divides poets into kinds according to inspiration and the age in which they wrote, and allows that there are as many kinds of poets as there are subjects.[14] What is for him a convenient classification becomes in Sidney an absolute distinction. The first kind are not really poets at all but 'may justly be termed *vates*'; of the second kind he remarks: 'whether they properly be poets or no let grammarians dispute'; only the third kind are 'indeed right poets'. Thus Scaliger classifies poets differently as they are divinely inspired or aroused by strong wine,[15] while Sidney keeps the same division to describe the inspiration of the three kinds of poets. The first kind is divinely inspired; a poet of the second kind cannot be inspired because he is 'wrapped within the fold of the proposed subject, and takes not the course of his own invention' (80). Only the right poet is properly inspired, not in the Platonic sense of inspiration as that suppression of intellect by which the poet is akin to the lunatic, but in the Christian sense of 'breathing into' by which he is 'lifted up with the vigour of his own invention' (78). Thus Sidney rejects Plato's notion that the poet receives 'a very inspiring of a divine force, far above man's wit' (109), for he holds that the poet freely ranges 'only within the zodiac of his own wit' (78).[16] He was well aware of how he had transformed his source. Scaliger classifies the poets in order to claim that Lucan is a poet because he wrote verse; Sidney adds Lucan to the second kind, those who are not true poets, and goes on to claim that 'it is not rhyming and versing that maketh a poet' (81).

Sidney went behind Scaliger to the source of the critical tradition in Plato. He adopts the adroit strategy of directing Plato's attack on poetry against the first two kinds of poets, leaving the right poet free. In this way he can absorb Plato – 'whom, the wiser a man is, the more just cause he shall find to have in admiration' (109) – and go beyond him.

The first kind, the divine poet, Plato denounces for telling false things about the gods; only if he praises the gods may he be admitted into the ideal state. Sidney allows only that the divine poet may cheer the merry and console the troubled. While he honours this 'most noble sort', he is not concerned to defend him. The second kind, the poet who takes his material at second-hand from philosophical or historical matters, Plato attacks because his poetry is twice removed from reality. Sidney allows Plato's argument when he claims that such poets 'retain themselves within their subject, and receive, as it were, their being from it' (99), and when he calls them 'takers of others' (110). As Plato compares such poets to the painter whose work is a copy of a copy, Sidney compares them to 'the meaner sort of painters, who counterfeit only such faces as are set before them' (80). Plato banishes them, but Sidney questions their right even to the name of poet.

Sidney allows, as Plato does not, a third kind of poet who 'bringeth his own stuff, and. . .maketh matter for a conceit' (99), for 'all only proceedeth from their wit, being indeed makers of themselves' (110). Such poets may not be compared to the meaner sort of painter but only to 'the more excellent, who having no law but wit, bestow that in colours upon you which is fittest for the eye to see' (80). While the first two kinds of poets take their matter from nature, the right poet 'bringeth things forth surpassing her doings' (79). He imitates not by copying nature but by creating another nature; and being a maker, he may be compared to the heavenly Maker. For Plato, such a comparison explains the creative role only of the first two kinds of poets. As the Demiurge shapes the world out of pre-existing matter according to Ideas apart from him, Plato's poet struggles with matter taken from others. Lacking its Idea, he must yield himself to his subject in admiration (as the first kind) or render it sweetly (as the second kind). For Sidney, however, the comparison illuminates the right poet's creative power. As God creates *ex nihilo* according to Ideas within himself, the right poet 'with the force of a divine breath. . .bringeth things forth' (79) for he 'borrow[s] nothing of what is, hath been, or shall be' (81). Further, 'that the poet hath that *idea* [of perfect man] is manifest, by delivering them forth in such excellency as he had imagined them' (79).

Sidney's views on the nature and working of poetry are epitomized in a passage which Dorsten calls the 'most fundamental paragraph of the *Defence*':[17]

Neither let it be deemed too saucy a comparison to balance the highest point of man's wit with the efficacy of nature; but rather give right honour to the heavenly Maker of that maker, who having made man to His own likeness, set him beyond and over all the works of that second nature: which in nothing he showeth so much as in poetry, when with the force of a divine breath he bringeth things forth surpassing her doings – with no small arguments to the credulous of that first accursed fall of Adam, since our erected wit maketh us know what perfection is, and yet our infected will keepeth us from reaching unto it. But these arguments will by few be understood, and by fewer granted. (79)

This paragraph deserves to be examined closely not only because it illustrates the cogency and clarity of Sidney's argument but also because it reveals the firm Christian basis of his poetic.[18]

Sidney is supporting his claim that all arts and sciences follow Nature, and are therefore subject to her – all except the right poet, who remains free to create another nature. Since Nature is fallen, her world is brazen; but the poet's world, being unfallen, is golden. Sidney illustrates this by comparing Nature's skill and the poet's at their greatest, in producing man. As one example, he cites Cyrus: fallen Nature has never produced 'so right a prince as Xenophon's Cyrus'. He allows two objections to his placing the poet over Nature. The first is that the works of Nature are 'essential', while those of the poet are 'in imitation or fiction'. To this he replies that the skill of any artificer stands 'in that *idea* or fore-conceit of the work, and not in the work itself'. So judged, the excellence of what he creates proves that he has the idea in his mind. Again, the work of the poet is essential because he not only makes a Cyrus, which Nature may do, but 'bestow[s] a Cyrus upon the world to make many Cyruses, if they [the readers] will learn aright why and how that maker made him'. The second objection, that the poet's creative power would far exceed Nature's, is answered in the paragraph cited above. Having concluded cryptically that 'these arguments will by few be understood, and by fewer granted', he turns to 'a more ordinary opening' of the nature of poetic creation in which the truth is obvious to all.

Sidney challenges his more discerning readers to understand his arguments, and clearly he desires that of these some will grant them. The distinction between what may be understood and what may be granted seems to refer to his arguments on the nature of poetry and those on its working. Some few in the age would understand his claims for the poet's creative power in relation to Nature, but far fewer (and none in our age?) would grant his claim for the poet's creative power over his readers.

A poet may create an image of Cyrus as 'so right a prince' exceeding what Nature may create because, in making man in His image, God first 'set him beyond and over all the works of that second nature'. Sidney alludes to Hebrews 2:7: in creating man, God 'didst set him over the works of thy hands' (the Geneva text reads: 'above the works of thine hands'). His phrase, 'beyond and over' asserts that entire dominion over Nature which man enjoyed in his unfallen state when he was commanded to 'subdue' the earth (Gen. 1:28). When man fell, his relationship to Nature was inverted: he became subject to 'all the works of that second nature', by which Sidney means fallen Nature. Accordingly, the arts which imitate Nature 'become actors and players, as it were, of what nature will have set forth'. Sidney's case against the arts and sciences is that they serve only to confirm man in his fallen state. The right poet alone claims man's former dominion over Nature by creating a golden world, which is the first, or unfallen, Nature. For this reason, the fallen reader, remaining subject to Nature, may hardly believe that the poet enjoys man's unfallen dominion over Nature. Yet proof that he does is shown in the images of perfection he creates: 'so true a lover as Theagenes, so constant a friend as Pylades, so valiant a man as Orlando, so right a prince as Xenophon's Cyrus, so excellent a man every way as Virgil's Aeneas'. Sidney implies that poetry derives from that element in man which remains unfallen, and he identifies that element with the poet's capacity to imagine states of perfection which existed only before the fall.

Sidney allows that perfection is known to fallen man by his 'erected wit', although his 'infected will' keeps him 'from reaching unto it'. His arguments will be understood by few because they are involved in religious controversy over man's fallen nature.[19] That man's will had become infected was generally accepted by Christians of all faiths. Protestant emphasis upon man's total depravity extended to his wit. The Calvinist position is expressed by William Tyndale: 'the will of man followeth the wit, and is subject unto the wit; and as the wit erreth, so does the will; and as the wit is in captivity, so is the will; neither is it possible that the will should be free, where the wit is in bondage'.[20] Yet Calvin himself allows that man's depravity is not absolute:

For even though something of understanding and judgment remains as a residue along with the will, yet we shall not call a mind whole and sound that is both weak and plunged into deep darkness. And depravity of the will is all too well known. Since reason, therefore, by which man distinguishes between good and evil, and by which he understands and judges, is a natural gift, it could not be completely wiped out; but it was partly weakened and partly corrupted, so that its misshapen ruins appear.[21]

This view that man is not totally fallen was seized upon by the Christian humanists who emphasized man's erected wit – what Sidney calls in the *Defence* man's 'own divine essence' and in a letter to Languet, 'that particle of the divine mind', and what Milton names as 'some remnants of the divine image [that] still exist in us, not wholly extinguished by. . .spiritual death'.[22] The poet's creative power displayed in his images of perfection manifests this 'divine image'.

More difficult to understand, and even more difficult to grant, is the poet's creative power over his readers, how he may 'bestow a Cyrus upon the world to make many Cyruses, if they will learn aright why and how that maker made him'. Evidently readers must do more than read Xenophon: from Sidney's poetic they must learn – and learn aright – both how and why the poet creates the image of perfection in Cyrus.

From that poetic, one may learn *why* the poet makes his images. Sidney accepts Horace's familiar concept of the end of poetry when he defines poesy as 'an art of imitation. . .with this end, to teach and delight' (79–80). These two ends become one when he goes on to claim that 'delightful teaching. . .must be the right describing note to know a poet by' (81–2). Yet he defends poetry on the ground that it teaches and delights in order to move. For him, 'moving is of a higher degree than teaching' (91), for the end of all knowledge is virtuous action. Since 'the poet, with that same hand of delight, doth draw the mind more effectually than any other art doth', he concludes that 'as virtue is the most excellent resting place for all worldly learning to make his end of, so poetry, being the most familiar to teach it, and most princely to move towards it, in the most excellent work is the most excellent workman' (94). While this rhetorical end of moving was allowed by earlier critics – Scaliger speaks of poetry '*docendi & mouendi, & delectandi*'[23] – none anticipates Sidney's emphasis. His defence of poetry rests upon its power through delight to move men to virtuous action.

Sidney's poetic is based on the Protestant emphasis on the doctrine of the Fall, and particularly on the Augustinian–Calvinist doctrine of the infected will. Since his will is infected, man must be moved to virtuous action. He may best be moved, Sidney believes, by the delight given by poetry. Horace's concept of the two ends of poetry implies that poetry teaches the reader by addressing his reason and delights him by appealing to his emotions. It combines the two ends when it delights in order to teach. For Sidney, however, poetry delights the reader in order to move his will. Since the will is radically infected, the reader must be ravished with delight. 'Delight' becomes a key word in what Sidney calls his 'defence of sweet poetry' (98). In the peroration he sums up his view of poetry when he speaks of it as 'full of virtue-breeding delightfulness' (120). Poetry teaches by delighting the readers with images of perfection, and by this means achieves the 'final end' of learning which is 'to lead and draw us to as high a perfection as our degenerate souls, made worse by their clayey lodgings, can be capable of' (82).

The second part of Sidney's argument, that the poet may 'make many Cyruses, if they will learn aright. . .how that maker made him', may be inferred from his own reading of poetry. His practical criticism is limited to the concluding pages of the *Defence* for he writes a defence of poesy, not of particular poets: as he says, 'I speak of the art, and not of the artificer' (89). Since that art is most fully realized in the genre of the heroic poem, his art of reading may be inferred from his comments on the heroic poets:

If the poet do his part aright, he will show you in Tantalus, Atreus, and such like, nothing that is not to be shunned; in Cyrus, Aeneas, Ulysses, each thing to be followed. (88)

The poet nameth Cyrus or Aeneas no other way than to show what men of their fames, fortunes, and estates should do. (103)

So is it in men (most of which are childish in the best things, till they be cradled in their graves): glad will they be to hear the tales of Hercules, Achilles, Cyrus, Aeneas; and, hearing them, must needs hear the right description of wisdom, valour, and justice. (92)

Who readeth Aeneas carrying old Anchises on his back, that wisheth not it were his fortune to perform so excellent an act? Whom doth not these words of Turnus move, the tale of Turnus having planted his image in the imagination, *Fugientem haec terra videbit? / Usque adeone mori miserum est?* (92)

Only let Aeneas be worn in the tablet of your memory, how he governeth himself in the ruin of his country; in the preserving his old father, and carrying away his religious ceremonies; in obeying God's commandment to leave Dido, though not only all passionate kindness, but even the human consideration of virtuous gratefulness, would have craved other of him; how in storms, how in sports, how in war, how in peace, how a fugitive, how victorious, how besieged, how besieging, how to strangers, how to allies, how to enemies, how to his own; lastly, how in his inward self, and how in his outward government – and I think, in a mind not prejudiced with a prejudicating humour, he will be found in excellency fruitful. (98)

Reading becomes a way of possessing poetry so actively that the reader is himself possessed. The poet's image is mnemonic and heuristic: it 'replenishes', 'inhabits', and 'enriches' the memory, and the knowledge it provides teaches man how to act. Yet Sidney refers to the knowledge that poetry provides as 'heart-ravishing' (76), for it inspires rather than instructs. The poet fashions his image not to teach directly but to 'strike, pierce, [and] possess the sight of the soul' (85).

Aeneas carrying Anchises on his back is adduced by Alciati as an emblem, with the motto '*Pietas filiorum*'. For Sidney, Virgil's image does not illustrate a moral tag but inspires a reader to similar virtuous action. It combines the philosopher's precept and the historian's example in a way that cannot be broken down into moral abstraction or historical event. What the poet imagines, he transplants directly into the reader's imagination. Hence Sidney speaks of the virtues, vices, and passions presented by the poet 'so in their own natural seats laid to the view, that we seem not to hear of them, but clearly to see through them' (86). If the reader heard of the virtues directly, poetry would supply knowledge of good and evil, as do the other arts and sciences. By seeing the virtues, and seeing through them, the reader reaches a higher state of illumination, which only poetry may provide. The distinction may be compared to that which Plato makes between knowledge which clarifies the world around us and that which illuminates a world of higher reality; and to Augustine's distinction between *scientia* and *sapientia*, that is, between the experiences that man's senses provide and what the mind provides by transcending experience through its contact with a higher reality.[24]

Sidney regards all learning in religious terms: its final end is 'to lead and draw us to as high a perfection as our degenerate souls, made worse by their clayey lodgings, can be capable of', and its scope is 'by knowledge to lift up the mind from the dungeon of the body to the enjoying his own divine essence' (82). As the highest form of learning, poetry lifts man from the brazen world of things as they are to a vision of the golden world of things as they should be. Accordingly, the illumination it provides suggests a religious vision. One may compare the wisdom which Agrippa urges his readers to find in Holy Scripture by rejecting the vanity of the arts and sciences:

If ye desire to attain to this divine and true wisdom, not of the tree of the knowledge of good and ill, but of the tree of life, the traditions of men set apart, and every search and discourse of the flesh and blood. . . .For the knowledge of all things is compact in you. . .Even as he [God] then hath created trees full of fruits, so also hath he created the souls as reasonable trees full of forms and knowledges; but through the sin of the first parent, all things were [concealed] and oblivion, the mother of ignorance, stepped in. Set you then now aside, which may, the veil of your understanding, which are wrapped in the darkness of ignorance. Cast out the drink of Lethe you which have made yourselves drunk with forgetfulness: await for the true light you which have suffered yourselves to be taken with unreasonable sleep; and forthwith when your face is discovered ye shall pass from the light to the light: for (as John saith) ye are anointed.[25]

In its revelation of the golden world, poetry provides a secular analogue to such religious vision. Accordingly, Sidney uses metaphors of light to describe how poetry affects the reader: it possesses the 'sight of the soul'; by its images, wisdom is 'illuminated or figured forth'; its pictures give 'insight' into the virtues and vices to make us 'see the form of goodness'; and he is prepared to entertain Plato's view that 'who could see virtue would be wonderfully ravished with the love of her beauty' (98).

For Plato, the teacher serves as a midwife to help give birth to man's innate virtues, or as a gardener to quicken the seeds of virtue within him. For Renaissance Platonists, man could fashion his virtues as he pleased. In *The heroic frenzies*, a work dedicated to Sidney, Giordano Bruno writes that nature has endowed him with an inward sense by which he 'can discern the most profound and incomparably superior beauty', that is, divine beauty.[26] But Sidney reserves such language for the divine poet: he refers to

David 'almost' (i.e. indeed) showing himself in the Psalms as 'a passionate lover of that unspeakable and everlasting beauty to be seen by the eyes of the mind, only cleared by faith'. He refers to 'the inward light each mind hath in itself' only after he has noted that reason must overmaster passion before the mind has 'a free desire to do well' (91). He prefaces Plato's view that man may be moved by the sight of virtue with an 'if': 'if the saying of Plato. . .be true' (98), for that mere 'saying' conflicts with religious doctrine on man's infected will.

Sidney's view of poetry remains stubbornly anti-mystical and severely practical. He avoids the extravagant claims made by some of his contemporaries, by Chapman, for example, who declares that poetry provides the means 'to the absolute redress, or much to be wished extenuation, of all the unmanly degeneracies now tyrannizing amongst us' by rooting out original sin.[27] He ignores the esoteric meanings claimed by the allegorists, such as Abraham Fraunce, who writes that in poetry the 'better born and of a more noble spirit, shall meet with hidden mysteries of natural, astrological, or divine and metaphysical philosophy, to entertain their heavenly speculation'.[28] Characteristic of his poetic is his claim that poetry is to be preferred to history on grounds of 'your own use and learning' (88). For him, poetry is rooted in man's life in this world, and the poet is concerned how best to move his infected will to lift him out of it.

For Sidney, poetry leads or draws the reader, always persuading him through delight. Its ethical and aesthetic functions are one and the same. It does not scold or harass the reader; even a lower poetical kind, such as tragedy, which 'maketh kings fear to be tyrants', does so by 'stirring the affects of admiration and commiseration' (96). It does not point to the guilt of man's fallen nature, but to the innocence of his unfallen nature, to that part of him which may be awakened by delight. Its way is 'sweet' as its means is delight, and its end is rapture and release.

Sidney says little about the way in which the poet makes his image. When he writes that the poet gives 'a perfect picture' of what man should do, he implies that the poet seeks to convey his vision of the virtues clearly and exactly. Since the poet may persuade his readers to 'steal to see the form of goodness (which seen they cannot but love)', it would seem that he tries simply to make them see the goodness which he has seen.[29]

When Sidney defines the work of the right poet, he compares him to the painter who shows 'the constant though lamenting look of Lucretia, when she punished in herself another's fault, wherein he painteth not Lucretia whom he never saw, but painteth the outward beauty of such a virtue'. Usually this comparison is made to claim that the poet does not set down the particular and individual but the general and universal. Shepherd compares Fracastorius's argument in *Naugerius*: other writers 'are like the painter who represents the features and other members of the body as they really are in the object; but the poet is like the painter who does not wish to represent this or that particular man as he is with many defects, but who, having contemplated the universal and supremely beautiful idea of his creator, makes things as they ought to be'.[30] Yet Sidney's point is not that the poet and painter present the appearance of an ideal, and ideally chaste, Roman matron but that her outward beauty reveals her inner state. More pertinent, then, is Lomazzo's argument in *Trattato dell' arte della pittura* (1584–5), that the poet and painter represent the *moti* or *passioni dell' animo*, showing outwardly what the soul suffers inwardly.[31] Further, Sidney points to Lucrece's conflicting passions: 'the constant though lamenting look. . .when she punished in herself another's fault'. That she should punish herself for Tarquin's fault led Augustine to challenge her legend: in Christian terms, she chose honour in the world before honour in the eyes of God.[32] Since her body was polluted, she chose to pollute her soul by suicide. Her story may be contrasted with Chaucer's tale of Virginia, the maiden who chose death at the hand of her father rather than be violated by the lustful judge. While Virginia stands as an emblem of virginity, there is no moral abstraction to which Lucrece, as described by Sidney, may be reduced. In the terms in which Greville read the *Arcadia*, she is shown rather as a 'pregnant image of life'.[33] Her contradictory action of punishing herself for another's fault expresses a complex inner moral state that reveals both innocence and guilt. That image cannot be reduced to precept or example but as a whole is planted in man's imagination for him to see and live by. When Sidney refers to 'the outward beauty of such a virtue', there is strangeness in the beauty, which arouses man's admiration and wonder at her act, and a complexity in her virtue, which leads him to understand her nature and his own.

Sidney does not extend the comparison between poet and painter because he recognizes clearly that to call a poem 'a speaking picture' is 'to speak metaphorically'. What the painter shows in Lucrece, the poet shows in a poem, such as Shakespeare's *Lucrece*. Yet his chief reason for not explaining further about the way in which the poet makes his image may well be that he had decided to show how such images are made by rewriting his *Old Arcadia*. 'The outward beauty of. . .virtue', such as the painter may show in Lucrece, is expressed only diffusely in that work. For example, after Philoclea has been seduced, she is first described in sleep as 'the natural image of exact beauty' and then her inner state is expressed by Pyrocles's claim that she 'had in truth never broken the bands of a true living virtue'. Yet that virtue is not expressed in her beauty, so she remains an admirable, yet pathetic, figure. In the *New Arcadia*, however, beauty and virtue become one as Sidney displays each virtue in its own outward beauty.

The *New Arcadia*:
'an absolute heroical poem'

The central facts about Sidney's later life and works may be summarized all too briefly. In the four years from spring 1578 to summer 1582, during which he was given no important public office, he wrote *The Lady of May*, the *Old Arcadia*, *Certain sonnets*, *Astrophel and Stella*, and the *Defence of poetry*, and probably translated the Psalms. During the next four years, until his death in October 1586, he wrote only a few original poems. He may have translated – the works are now lost – Du Bartas's *La Première Sepmaine* (a work of nearly 8000 lines), the first two books of Aristotle's *Rhetoric*, and part (or possibly all) of Duplessis-Mornay's *De la verité de la religion Chrestienne*.[1] Chiefly he was engaged in reworking the *Old Arcadia*. He never finished, and the incomplete version finally appeared in 1590 as *The Countess of Pembroke's Arcadia*, usually called the *New Arcadia* to distinguish it from the *Old*.

His final years were unusually busy. In January 1583 he was knighted. In September of that year he married Frances Walsingham, and, being deeply in debt, moved to her father's house in Surrey. The many books dedicated to him indicate his increasing reputation as a patron of the arts.[2] He established friendships with such famous contemporaries as Giordano Bruno, who noted that Sidney was his first friend in England. He continued to be actively interested in the New World as a place for settlement and a base from which to oppose Spanish power. In 1584 he became a member of the House of Commons and served on several special committees. From July 1583 he served in the Office of Ordnance under Warwick, becoming master in July 1585, with the responsibility of preparing the ports against an expected Spanish invasion. In July 1584 he was appointed to a mission, which was cancelled, to offer condolences to the French court on the death of Alençon and to persuade the French to oppose Spain. He was involved in various foreign affairs: to establish the Protestant faith in Scotland, to resist Spain in the Netherlands, and to defend his father's actions in Ireland. In 1585 he wrote a *Defence of Leicester* in reply to an anonymous tract, *Leicester's Commonwealth,* which attacked his uncle and the Dudley family. When he despaired of service in Europe and sought to accompany Drake on his expedition to the West Indies in September 1585, the Queen intervened and appointed him Lord Governor of Flushing. Ironically, he may no longer have wanted such a post. Greville claims that Sidney had decided that Spanish power could best be opposed in America rather than in the Netherlands.[3] If that is so, the fates were cruel to him. From November when he left for the Netherlands, he was totally caught up in preparations for war against the Spanish forces, in political intrigue, and in minor skirmishes and campaigns. His father died in May 1586, his mother in August. He was wounded in September, and – not yet 32 – died in October.

That final year fulfilled his ambition to serve actively the Protestant cause against Spain. In a letter to Walsingham, March 1586, he saw that cause directed by God:

I had before cast my count of danger, want, and disgrace, and before God, Sir, it is true that in my heart the love of the cause doth so far overbalance them all that with God's grace they shall never make me weary of my resolution. If her Majesty were the fountain I would fear, considering what I daily find, that we should wax dry; but she is but a means whom God useth, and I know not whether I am deceived but I am faithfully persuaded that if she should withdraw herself, other springs would rise to help this action. For methinks I see the great work indeed in hand, against the abusers of the world, wherein it is no greater fault to have confidence in man's power than it is too hastily to despair of God's work.[4]

Until that final year, however, Sidney had to find other ways to fulfil himself. As I have noted previously, he was like Pyrocles, 'formed by nature and framed by education to the true exercise of virtue'; and, like him, he was 'born to the greatest expectation'.[5] As time passed without the opportunity to express his virtues in some virtuous action, his fears must have increased that in the eyes of his father he would prove to be the false steward who buried his talents.

In the *Old Arcadia,* he tells the story of a son judged by his father to be worthy of death for what he has done, yet by his inner worth proving himself worthy of life. His revision of the work soon after he had completed it may indicate that he was not satisfied with an ending which simply set aside the father's judgment. He may have recognized that a son should be able to answer his father with something better than a trick ending. We cannot know this because at some point he became dissatisfied with piecemeal revision and decided to recast the whole work. Nor do we know why he decided to recast an old work rather than begin a new one. Perhaps in the course of writing the final books, he saw what was unrealized in it and wanted to clarify its 'idea or foreconceit'; or he may simply have lacked time. It seems most likely to me that writing the *Defence* in the interim showed him how the *Old Arcadia* could be recast as 'an absolute heroical poem' in terms of his own poetic.[6] While the earlier work was intended to fulfil the function of heroic poetry, the later work fulfils also the formal aspects of the genre, both in matter and manner, and may be regarded as 'an *absolute* heroical poem'. Sidney acts vicariously through his characters, manifesting his virtues in them, as Harvey recognizes when he says that 'the two brave knights, Musidorus and Pyrocles [are] combined in one excellent knight, Sir Philip Sidney'.[7] By writing the *New Arcadia*, Sidney proves himself finally to be the wise steward. Yet the work goes beyond the personal for its images of the virtues, vices, and passions display the work of the right poet. Its impersonality is indicated by his changed role within it: instead of appearing, as he does in each of the books of the *Old Arcadia*, as Philisides (*Phili*p *Sid*ney), he appears only once in the posture he had assumed near the end of his sonnet sequence, one looking up at the window to see his star; now he is named Philisides ($\phi\iota\lambda$, *sidus*) in his public role as the lover of the star. He need appear only briefly because his own life has been taken over by his characters and their story.

The one surviving manuscript of the incomplete work is dated 1584. Ringler assumes that Sidney began the revision in that year, but Robertson concludes, rightly I think, that 1584 is the date of transcription.[8] By that year time was running out for Sidney: it was too late for him to have begun that enormous labour of recasting the work, often sentence by sentence, for even in its incomplete state it is already over 50,000 words longer than the original.[9] The other evidence of date is Greville's letter to Walsingham in November 1586 written in response to Ponsonby's report that some publisher proposed to print the *Old Arcadia*: 'I have sent my lady your daughter [Sidney's widow] at her request, a correction of that old one done 4 or 5 years since which he left in trust with me whereof there is no more copies, and fitter to be printed than that first which is so common.'[10] From such evidence one may assume that the *Old Arcadia* in its final revised state may be dated 1581 or 1582, and that the 'correction' to which Greville refers is the newly-cast work which Sidney started in 1582 and completed by 1584.

The nature of the revised work may be shown by analysing the sequence of events which brings the princes into Arcadia. The *Old Arcadia* begins immediately with the main story: Basilius's decision to retreat into the pastoral life to escape threatened dangers is opposed by Philanax, and Pyrocles's decision to follow him to woo Philoclea is opposed by Musidorus. In the *New*, an elaborate introduction prepares for this story, as a list indicates (the starred items are revised from the *Old Arcadia*):

1. The laments of Strephon and Claius. Their encounter with Musidorus which leads to
2. The vision of Pyrocles at the shipwreck.
*3. The debate between Basilius and Philanax.
4. The story of Argalus and Parthenia.
*5. The princes debate the life of virtuous action.
6. Helen's story of her love for Amphialus.
*7. The princes debate the nature of love.

This introduction may be divided into four parts according to source or function: (i) the laments of the two shepherds imitate the opening laments of the shepherds in Montemayor's *Diana*; (ii) the vision of Pyrocles adrift at sea imitates the opening of Heliodorus's *Æthiopian history*; (iii) the story of Argalus and Parthenia illustrates Sidney's poetic; and (iv) the story of Amphialus serves as a foil to the story of the two princes.[11]

Montemayor and pastoral romance

The opening of Montemayor's *Diana* is superb even in Bartholomew Yong's workaday translation:

Down from the hills of *Leon* came forgotten *Syrenus*, whom love, fortune, and time did so entreat, that by the least grief, that he suffered in his sorrowful life, he looked for no less than to lose the same. The unfortunate shepherd did not now bewail the harm, which her absence did threaten him, and the fear of her forgetfulness did not greatly trouble his mind, because he saw all the prophecies of his suspicion so greatly to his prejudice accomplished, that now he thought he had no more misfortunes to menace him. But the shepherd coming to those green and pleasant meads, which the great river *Ezla* watereth with his crystalline streams, the great felicity and content came to his wandering thoughts, which sometimes he had enjoyed there, being then so absolute a lord of his own liberty, as now subject to one, who had wrongfully interred him in dark oblivion.[12]

Grief-stricken by memory of the year before when his love was faithful, the sad shepherd visits the place where his eyes 'first. . .beheld the beauty, grace, and rare virtues of the shepherdess Diana, she in whom skilful nature had consummated all perfections, which in every part of her dainty body she had equally bestowed'. He remembers particularly her grief at their parting. From these afflictions of memory, he is led to recall the pledges of faith given him by 'the fairest and most disloyal shepherdess that human eyes may behold'. When he is joined by a former co-rival in love, Sylvanus, their interspersed songs, renewed laments, and discussion of Diana's marriage to the aged and loutish Delius extend over some twenty pages, and might have gone on forever had they not been interrupted by Selvagia who tells her story of love's grief.

This opening episode defines the poignant, nostalgic mood of pastoral romance: within a pleasant pastoral setting, the grieving lover is overwhelmed by memory of earlier happiness. Memory of the past floods the present, bathing the lover in intense grief. Montemayor imitates the opening eclogue of Sannazaro's *Arcadia* in which Ergasto laments the loss of his beloved whom he had seen in a stream with her skirts raised to the knee, and whose vision of beauty he recalls now that she scorns him. The lover's grief, distanced and formalized in Sannazaro, is immediately present in Montemayor, spilling over from verse into prose and gathering into a moment of overwhelming agony.

In his opening scene Sidney imitates both:

It was in the time that the earth begins to put on her new apparel against the approach of her lover, and that the sun running a most even course becomes an indifferent arbiter between the night and the day when the hopeless shepherd Strephon was come to the sands, which lie against the island of Cithera; where viewing the place with a heavy kind of delight, and sometimes casting his eyes to the isleward, he called his friendly rival, the pastor Claius, unto him, and setting first down in his darkened countenance a doleful copy of what he would speak: 'Oh my Claius', said he, 'hither we are now come to pay the rent, for which we are so called unto by over-busy remembrance, remembrance, restless remembrance, which claims not only this duty of us, but for it will have us forget ourselves.'

During the year of Urania's absence, remembrance has forced Strephon and Claius to think of 'her ever-flourishing beauty', and now to visit the shore from which they may see the island where she dwells. Like Syrenus, Strephon remembers her grief at their parting and her 'heavenly beauty' at that time.

Sidney records the same poignant remembrance of things past which intensifies the lover's present agony. There is a sharp difference, however, in the object of remembrance. There is a mean, ordinary fickleness in Diana, while the heavenly nature of the goddess Urania appears in the simple shepherdess who inspires her lovers to lead virtuous lives and consider heavenly matters.[13] Accordingly, the one appears perfect 'in every part of her dainty body', while of the other it is said 'that as the greatest thing the world can show is her beauty, so the least thing that may be praised in her, is her beauty'. The one is displayed as a shapely shepherdess, the other as Venus in Botticelli's 'Birth of Venus': 'when she was embarked, did you not mark how the winds whistled, and the seas danced for joy, how the sails did swell with pride, and all because they had Urania?'. The more important difference is found in the effect of beauty. In Montemayor, as in Sannazaro, memory of the beloved withdraws the lover into self-regarding, self-pitying narcissism. In Sidney, the memory of Urania's beauty 'will have us forget ourselves' and withdraw from worldly matters in order not to 'let so much time pass without knowing perfectly her estate'. Strephon's lament for their loss is answered by Claius who urges him to remember their gains and 'love with joy in the midst of all woes'. He remembers not only her beauty but also her virtue which has inspired them. Through loving her they have moved (in ascending order) from knowledge more than ordinary, to heavenly knowledge, and finally to knowledge of themselves. Further, through them love has resolved (in ascending order) the greatest paradoxes: 'hath not she thrown reason upon our desires, and, as it were, given eyes unto Cupid? hath in any, but in her, love-fellowship maintained friendship between rivals, and beauty taught the beholders chastity?'. As Claius is the elder 'pastor' or guide, his address supplements and corrects Strephon's by showing how love leads to virtuous action. Their debate provides a prologue to the work: their love, which throws reason upon desires and maintains friendship between rivals, and this beauty, which teaches beholders chastity, display what love and beauty should be, in ironic contrast to the main story of the *Arcadia*.

In Montemayor, the lover's lament for lost happiness announces the theme of the entire work. Later episodes only repeat this theme in various ways. The key point which determines the structure of pastoral romance is the conclusion of the opening lament. What happens next? and why? In Sannazaro's second eclogue, two shepherds lament the cruelty of their mistresses. Of necessity, their story is analogous to the first because all love stories are similar. In Montemayor's second episode, Selvagia tells a story of the purity of love's passion as it leads to extreme confusion. Though love of another kind, such love takes its place in love's pageant. In both works the structure is repetitive and incremental: each new shepherd tells his tale and then joins the others in their journey into Arcadia or their pilgrimage to Lady Felicia's palace. It is the episodic structure of Henny Penny: 'they went along, and they went along, and they went along, and then they met Goosy Poosy', which Sidney mocks in Mopsa's story with its repeated 'And so's'.[14] In E. M. Forster's terms, this simple structure is a 'story', in contrast to the causality of a 'plot', which is the kind of structure Sidney seeks. His opening episode stands apart from the rest of the work: Strephon and Claius are the only true inhabitants of Arcadia but they have a very minor role in the work. No reader of pastoral romance would have anticipated what happens next.

Heliodorus and the effect of wonder

As Claius is about to praise their love, Strephon tells him to stop and look: they see 'a young man of. . .goodly shape, and well pleasing favour', drawn to the land 'by the favourable working of the sea'. A year earlier the sea had taken Urania away; now it brings Musidorus. His appearance leads very quickly to two startling visions when Musidorus, the shepherds, and a fisherman go out in a boat to find the shipwrecked Pyrocles. The first is 'a sight full of piteous strangeness':

...a ship, or rather the carcass of the ship, or rather some few bones of the carcass, hulling there, part broken, part burned, part drowned: death having used more than one dart to that destruction. About it floated great store of very rich things, and many chests which might promise no less. And amidst the precious things were a number of dead bodies...in sum, a defeat where the conquered kept both field and spoil: a shipwreck without storm or ill footing: and a waste of fire in the midst of water.

The second is another sight of a divine creature on the sea, a young man riding the ship's mast in the water:

...having nothing upon him but his shirt, which, being wrought with blue silk and gold, had a kind of resemblance to the sea...himself full of admirable beauty, set forth by the strangeness both of his seat and gesture: for, holding his head up full of unmoved majesty, he held a sword aloft with his fair arm, which often he waved about his crown as though he would threaten the world in that extremity.

The beholders are overcome with such amazement and astonishment that they worship the youth, who is Pyrocles, 'thinking it was some god begotten between Neptune and Venus, that had made all this terrible slaughter'. While Musidorus tries to persuade them that it is only a man they see, Pyrocles is taken prisoner by pirates.

Sidney imitates the opening episode of Heliodorus's *Æthiopian history* in which some thieves see two strange sights. The first is of a heavily laden ship at anchor deserted by her crew, and on the shore signs of a banquet at which all who had feasted lie dead or dying: 'God showed a wonderful sight in so short time, brewing blood with wine, joining battle with banqueting, mingling indifferently slaughters with drinkings, and killing with quaffings.' When they approach the ship, a second sight perplexes them: 'a maid endued with excellent beauty, which also might be supposed a goddess, sits upon a rock' with a knife in her hand. When she runs to aid a young man, the pirates retreat 'as well for wonder, as also for the fear they had', for she seems to them to be the goddess Diana or a priest of the gods who 'had made the great slaughter'.[15] They are persuaded that she is a maid when she kisses the man; but it is too late to seize her: she is taken away by another band of thieves.

Sidney's work combines the sweetness of Montemayor's pastoral romance with the strength of Heliodorus's heroic romance. In its sweetness Montemayor's world tends to softness: it becomes dream-like, overwhelmingly delicious, and oozes with self-satisfaction because everything is in the warm, capable hands of Felicia. In Alonso Perez's continuation, it degenerates into Enid Blyton for grown-ups. In contrast, Heliodorus's world tends to savagery: it can degenerate into the merely sensational and erotic. The points of similarity sharpen the differences between them. In Montemayor, three savages threaten to rape some nymphs, but they prove to be kindly savages: their tears of grief have caused streams to flood. Although Diana is unhappily married, adultery is unthinkable; in fact, all the varieties of love in the romance prove excruciatingly virtuous and move inexorably towards marriage. In Heliodorus, the entire plot turns upon episodes in which the heroine is threatened by rape and the hero is tempted by fornication. Sidney found in Montemayor a human world of fulfilled desire but wanted to go beyond the delight it provides the reader by adding the larger-than-human world of Heliodorus in which bizarre spectacle arouses amazement and heroic characters awaken wonder.

Argalus and Parthenia

The story of Argalus and Parthenia is Sidney's own in that he is not imitating any source: neither the characters nor their actions have any significant parallels or analogues in earlier literature. It impresses every reader first of all as a story in its own right, as an invented fiction rather than a true story or a *roman à clef*. Since it is Sidney's first story – and essentially the first, then, in English prose fiction (the prior claim for Gascoigne's *The adventures of Master F.J.*, 1573, only highlights the absence of imaginative literature in prose) – it deserves to be compared to the stories which he found in his chief sources.

In Sannazaro, the story exists to explain the lover's plight. Thus the despairing Ergasto tells how he saw a young girl in the water. To escape his gaze, she wades waist-high; when he faints through desire, she returns to aid him; but when he revives, she scorns him. The story itself doesn't matter; if it did, it would get in the way of what does matter: the vision of unattainable beauty which provokes the lover's despair. In Montemayor, the story does matter. For example, Selvagia tells how she fell in love with Ismenia believing her to be a man. Ismenia tells her lover, Alanius, who is her double, how she duped Selvagia; he sees her, falls in love, and abandons Ismenia. When Ismenia pretends to love Montanus, the jealous Alanius abandons Selvagia and woos her again, causing Montanus to leave Ismenia for Selvagia. At this juncture of love's comedy, Selvagia complains that Alanius has forsaken her, Ismenia complains that Montanus has forsaken her, Alanius complains that Ismenia loves Montanus, and Montanus complains that Selvagia doesn't love him. This complicated story is meant to delight the reader even as it delights the suffering Selvagia: 'it was the strangest thing in the world to hear how *Alanius* sighing said, Ah my *Ismenia*; and how *Ismenia* said, Ah my *Montanus*; and how *Montanus* said, Ah my *Selvagia*; and how *Selvagia* said, Ah my *Alanius*'.[16] While the story delights us by illustrating the delightful absurdities of lovers, it exists to illustrate a theme. One tenet of the work's sophisticated philosophy of love is love's irrationality: Selvagia's love for Ismenia, aroused by a glimpse of her eyes alone, shows love's pure intensity and how its infection spreads.

In Heliodorus, the story exists for its powerful, exciting appeal. Cnemon's story, for example, is rightly called 'an excellent tale' by the translator, Underdowne.[17] When Demeneta lusts after her stepson, Cnemon, but is rejected by him, he is tricked by her maid Thisbe into entering his father's bedroom with drawn sword, believing her there with her lover. Instead he confronts his father, and is exiled for threatening his life. Later, Thisbe tricks Demeneta into believing that she will bring Cnemon to her bed but in his place brings her own husband. The guilty Demeneta kills herself. The story is fiction in the simple sense that something happens. Nothing ever happens in Montemayor: its non-events could appear only on the lady's page of a small local newspaper. In Heliodorus, the story is all tabloid headlines: 'Mother claims that son spurned her on the belly', 'Son enters father's bedroom with drawn sword', 'Father beats son with rods', with follow-up stories on the lust-crazed mother who cries out: 'these things set me on fire; these things make me mad!'. In pastoral romance, everything has already happened, while in Greek romance everything happens now. In Montemayor, the story delights and amuses the reader; in Heliodorus, the story's brutal psychological impact, its sensational details, and its eroticism strongly move him.

Sidney found in Heliodorus, alone among his sources, stories in which characters act heroically within a plot that holds the reader for its own sake. The characters are 'larger than life' through their intensity of passion. Demeneta exists at an emotional pitch through which she becomes, in Renaissance terms, the very pattern or model of a lewd woman.[18] Unlike the 'soft' characters of pastoral romance, Heliodorus's characters are admirable in their superb extravagance and sustained excess. They are centres of energy with nothing mean or ordinary in them. Accordingly, they act in a grand style. Chariclea's first act is to display the knife with which she intends to kill herself should Theagenes be dead. That gesture so impressed Sidney that Musidorus's first act upon being saved from the sea is to throw himself back into the sea because he believes his friend is dead. In both, the act is a free, generous, and heroic gesture which displays a willingness to embrace death for the sake of love. Accordingly, the world in which such characters act is not the closed, stuffy garden of pastoral romance but the city, the sea, and the wilderness, with the dangerous adventures they bring. Threatened with death, characters live intensely in the present moment. Most important to Sidney, they are tested by these adventures and triumph over them in a way that arouses the reader's amazement, wonder, and awe.

Heliodorus satisfies Sidney's claim in the *Defence* that the poet 'cometh unto you with a tale which holdeth children from play, and old men from the chimney corner'. The work deserves his praise as 'an absolute heroical poem' for its 'sugared invention of that picture of love in Theagenes and Chariclea'. Yet erotic sensationalism becomes an end in itself and the work fails to satisfy Sidney's further claim that the poet delights the reader so that he will 'steal to see the form of goodness'.[19] Accordingly, when he fashioned his story of Argalus and Parthenia, he needed to outdo Heliodorus.

The story of Argalus and Parthenia, from their first meeting to their marriage, extends over four chapters. The first part is related to Musidorus by Kalander's steward. Parthenia is willing to marry Demagoras, her mother's choice, until she meets Argalus and wishes to marry him. Although he proves himself worthy through many heroic feats, the mother will not consent. Only after she dies through frustrated rage, may plans for the marriage proceed. Then Demagoras, seeking revenge, destroys Parthenia's beauty by a magic ointment. Although Argalus first loved her for her beauty, he wants to marry her even in her ugliness. Since she loves him, however, she leaves him, for she will not have him marry one as ugly as herself. Seeking revenge against Demagoras, he is captured by the Helots; and seeking to rescue him, Kalander's son, Clitophon, is captured. The second part of the story serves to reunite the two princes. Musidorus leads an attack against the Helots whose new leader turns out to be Pyrocles. When they recognize each other, a truce is arranged and Clitophon and Argalus are freed. Yet Argalus takes no pleasure in being free: his 'countenance well showed, while Parthenia was lost he counted not himself delivered' (48). The third and final act of the story initiates the main action of the *Arcadia*, for it serves to bring the princes into the Arcadian retreat. A woman who arrives at Kalander's house is thought to be Parthenia except that her complexion is more pure. She claims that the dying Parthenia had commanded Argalus to marry her by the authority of their love. When he refuses because he loves Parthenia for herself and not for her beauty or her likeness, she reveals that she is Parthenia now renewed in her beauty. At their marriage, Pyrocles wonders 'how happens it that beauty is only confined to Arcadia' (54) and later tells Musidorus that he decided to enter the Arcadian retreat 'when even Parthenia's fair face became a lecture to me of Philoclea's imagined beauty' (85).

Sidney guides the reader's response to this story by having the steward add at the end of the first part: 'the strangeness of it made me think it would not be unpleasant unto you'. Musidorus thanks him greatly 'being even passionately delighted with hearing so strange an accident of a knight so famous over the world as Argalus' (37–8). The reader, too, is meant to be 'passionately delighted' by the strange story of such a virtuous knight, one who is 'most rarely accomplished, excellently learned, but without all vainglory' (31). The praise of his 'valour of mind' nicely transfers

a classical virtue of the body to an inner Christian heroism, for
the chief point about him is that he 'manifested a most virtuous
mind in all his actions'. While he is an image of constancy, he is
not shown as an abstract virtue but rather as a constant man. It is
noteworthy that he is 'somewhat given to musing', a characteristic
personal to Sidney. Accordingly, although he is famous for 'over-
vehement constancy of yet spotless affection', he does not personify that virtue but appears rather as a man with that virtue in
excess.

Three events test Argalus's virtue, and their order is climactic.
The first establishes his nature in relation to his virtue. To prove
himself worthy of Parthenia, he undertakes many dangerous en-
terprises imposed by her mother: 'the more his virtue was tried,
the more pure it grew, while all the things she did to overthrow
him, did set him up upon the height of honour' (33). When Parthenia endures her mother's continued assaults designed to make
her yield, 'it was hard to judge, whether he in doing, or she in
suffering, showed greater constancy of affection'. In this first test,
his virtue is heroic but no more than that: it may be found in
Amadis or any similar knight who undertakes adventures to prove
himself worthy of his lady.

In the second test Argalus goes beyond this stage of virtue by
triumphing over himself. The wickedness of Demagoras in des-
troying Parthenia's beauty so that 'never leper looked more ugly
than she did' is the kind of violence which Sidney found in
Heliodorus as an end in itself.[20] Sidney hurries over the incident
to elaborate a paradox: although Argalus first loved Parthenia for
her great beauty, he loves her now in her ugliness; yet she loves
him so much that she rejects him. His constancy and her love
are meant to amaze the reader. Sidney calls the event 'a strange
encounter of love's affects, and effects: that he, by an affection
sprung from excessive beauty, should delight in horrible foulness;
and she, of a vehement desire to have him, should kindly build a
resolution never to have him' (35).[21] In medieval treatments of
the knight who is forced to accept the loathly hag – as in
Chaucer's *Wife of Bath's Tale* – he becomes comic as his courtesy
is strained, and she becomes ridiculous in being linked with him.
No knight so freely offers his love as does Argalus, and, of course,
no loathly lady so shows her love by refusing him, as does

Parthenia. The reader's amazement is not an end in itself but serves a witty paradox that illuminates the nature of virtue and love. His virtue is such that his love triumphs over his desire for beauty, and her love is such that she forsakes him.

In the third test, Argalus triumphs over earthly love itself. In the name of his love for Parthenia, he is tempted to marry the strange lady, an image of Parthenia yet even more beautiful. When he rejects her, he defines his constancy absolutely:

Excellent lady, know, that if my heart were mine to give, you before all other should have it; but Parthenia's it is, though dead: there I began, there I end all matter of affection. I hope I shall not long tarry after her, with whose beauty if I had only been in love, I should be so with you, who have the same beauty. But it was Parthenia's self I loved, and love; which no likeness can make one, no commandment dissolve, no foulness defile, nor no death finish. (50)

The miracle that Parthenia's beauty has been restored and increased, which is the typical stuff of romance, occupies less than a sentence. The true miracle is shown in Argalus's virtue: in his constancy he triumphs over even married love which is vowed 'until death us part', for his love endures after death.

When Argalus's virtue triumphs, Parthenia's love is fulfilled. Her love for him is such that in the first test she refuses to marry another, and in the second test she refuses to marry him. Is it sufficient, however, to allow him to marry another? In the *Old Arcadia*, Pyrocles fails that test: he is not sorry that Philoclea is to be imprisoned among vestal nuns because then no one else will be able to enjoy her. Parthenia allows Argalus to choose 'another' although she does not risk a substitute: she offers herself of whom she may truly say that 'nothing can please her soul more than to see you and me matched together'. This human gesture demonstrates the wit for which she is praised: 'a wit which delighted more to judge itself than to show itself' (32). Through her love she allows him the final victory: he gains her whether he passes or fails her test.

Argalus and Parthenia embody an absolute state of constancy and love apparently impossible for others to attain. 'As he gave this rare ensample, not to be hoped for of any other, but of another Argalus: so of the other side, she took as strange a course in affection' (35). Yet they do not personify abstract virtue, for both remain simply and fully human. To identify the ideal virtuous state with the fully human is one of Sidney's greatest triumphs in the *Arcadia*. His constant lovers represent a state which may be attained by all whose love survives the ravages of age and the separation of death. At one point in the *Arcadia*, Sidney distinguishes between virtue taken in one's self and virtue taken on: for him, virtue is the flowering of man's nature, rather than any imposition upon it. Argalus does not conform to a rule of constancy; instead, through love, he takes 'even a delight to be constant' (35).

The story of Argalus illustrates Sidney's poetic. As the right poet, Sidney feigns in his lovers 'notable images of virtue'. These images are 'so in their own natural seats laid to the view, that we seem not to hear of them, but clearly to see through them'. The lovers do not personify virtue but are shown as a constant knight and his loving lady. Through delight in their story, the reader is persuaded to 'steal to see the form of goodness'. Wonder at the actions of Argalus teaches him the nature of constancy. (It soon becomes clear that the reader, not Argalus, is being tested; for why should a state so natural to that knight seem so amazing?) The story teaches the reader to know his own nature, not the weakness of his fallen state but the strength of what Sidney calls 'his own divine essence'. As such, it is a story to be planted in the reader's imagination and worn upon his memory in order to move him to virtuous action.

Amphialus and Helen

Sidney's first story in the *Arcadia* treats constancy in love because that virtue is the basis of all the virtues. Argalus and Parthenia supply the pattern of constant affection which measures all the lovers. Their marriage is the ideal state which all should seek: 'he joying in her, she joying in herself, but in herself because she enjoyed him: both increasing their riches by giving to each other; each making one life double, because they made a double life; one, where desire never wanted satisfaction, nor satisfaction never bred satiety; he ruling, because she would obey; or rather, because she would obey, she therein ruling' (420). At the opposite pole to them are Amphialus and Helen who are constant in love but not to each other. Although Helen loves Amphialus, he hates her and later loves Philoclea. The heroic triumph of the first pair is balanced by the tragic ill-fortune of the second.

When Musidorus and Clitophon search for Pyrocles who has disappeared after the wedding of Argalus and Parthenia, they enter an Arcadian valley which shows the traditional features of the *locus amoenus*. As usual in the *Arcadia*, this setting announces the beginning of some major action. Here Clitophon finds Amphialus's armour but when Musidorus puts it on, he is attacked by Helen's twelve servants who take him for Amphialus. After he slaughters or maims them, he sees Helen gazing upon Amphialus's picture. He asks her to tell the story of her fortune 'lest hereafter when the image of so excellent a lady in so strange a plight come before mine eyes, I condemn myself of want of consideration in not having demanded thus much' (66). She tells how she favoured Philoxenus until he brought his close friend, Amphialus, to woo her for him. Amphialus rejects her love and leaves; but the jealous Philoxenus forces him to fight, and by an unlucky blow is killed. At this moment his friend's father, Timotheus, who is his own foster-father confronts him and dies through sorrow for his son's death but chiefly through Amphialus's unkindness. Thereupon Amphialus discards his armour and retires into the forest, an 'Orlando Furioso' overwhelmed by grief for what he has done.

Amphialus's subsequent history becomes central to the main plot of the *New Arcadia*. Philoxenus's spaniel, which has joined him in the forest, leads him to where the naked Philoclea is bathing. He falls in love and later is persuaded by his wicked mother, Cecropia, to imprison her in his castle. There besieged by Basilius's forces, he kills Argalus and later the disguised Parthenia who seeks death at his hands. In his despair, he allows his mother to try to persuade Philoclea to marry him, in effect abetting her use of torture. When he learns what she has done, unwittingly he causes her death and then stabs himself. Helen refers to the story of her love for Amphialus as 'my tragedy': it is also his tragedy for he destroys himself by his actions. In himself he remains entirely worthy: his mind is such as 'can be painted by nothing but by the true shape of virtue' (68) and he appears to Pyrocles as 'being indeed such a right manlike man, as Nature often erring, yet shows she would fain make' (222–3). For his virtues he is known as 'the courteous Amphialus'; yet all his actions outrage courtesy. Nothing turns out right for him: he seems wedded to misfortune. Despite the promise of his virtues (and for this reason his story appealed deeply to Sidney), his unlucky life seems fated to remain unfulfilled from that first moment when his foster-father died upon finding him the killer of his only son to the final moment when his resolve to take his own life causes his mother's death. The phrase used of that final moment, 'self-ruin' (494), sums up his life, for even his virtues seem to undo him. Love becomes the occasion of the disasters which befall him – Helen's love for him, his love for Philoclea, his mother's love for him, even Parthenia's love for Argalus, although if the work were completed Helen's love would restore him.

The story of Argalus and Parthenia and that of Amphialus and Helen provide the two poles for the main action of the *Arcadia*. The one shows what should be and the other what should not be. In Argalus, love and virtue are one, both when he upholds his love for Parthenia by virtuous action and later when he leaves her to serve Basilius. As a consequence, in Parthenia is seen 'the perfect picture of a womanly virtue and wifely faithfulness' (104). In Amphialus, love and virtue are divided, causing Helen to abandon her kingdom to pursue him. Though Argalus and Parthenia are killed by Amphialus, they live as an image of constancy in love. While they live in their oneness, he lives divided within himself – his name signifies 'between two seas' – and divided from Helen. Amphialus and Helen serve as an exemplum of the tragic possibilities of life despite the ideal virtue of the one and the constant love of the other.[22]

The debates

The three opening debates show that the work will carry a strong moral argument. Before ever the reader is allowed to enter Arcadia, he is fully armed to do so by debates on the public life in relation to the private life, and the private life in relation both to virtue and to love. The import of these debates may be indicated by brief quotation:

O no! he cannot be good that knows not why he is good, but stands so far good as his fortune may keep him unassayed: but coming once to that, his rude simplicity is either easily changed, or easily deceived; and so grows that to be the last excuse of his fault, which seemed to have been the first foundation of his faith. (26)

A mind well trained and long exercised in virtue. . .doth not easily change any course it once undertakes, but upon well-grounded and well-weighed causes. For being witness to itself of his own inward good, it finds nothing without it of so high a price, for which it should be altered. Even the very countenance and behaviour of such a man doth show forth images of the same constancy, by maintaining a right harmony betwixt it and the inward good, in yielding itself suitable to the virtuous resolution of the mind. (55)

Remember. . .that if we will be men, the reasonable part of our soul is to have absolute commandment; against which if any sensual weakness arise, we are to yield all our sound forces to the overthrowing of so unnatural a rebellion. (77)

Clearly the work will mingle instruction with delight in complex ways. The argument presented by Philanax in the first quotation is confirmed when the disasters overwhelm the kingdom after Basilius retires for fear of the oracle; but later it is refuted when the second oracle reveals that higher powers than reason direct men's affairs to a happy outcome. Musidorus, the speaker of the next two quotations, reverses himself when he falls in love, and his argument will be countered when virtue and love are finally reconciled. While his speeches befit him, they are not designed to reveal his character: in denouncing love, he leaves 'nothing unsaid, which my wit could make me know, or my most entire friendship to you required of me' (82). As a consequence, the reader must attend to what is said, not to who says it or why.

The tension throughout the work between instruction and delight is such that readers tend to stress one or the other. Greville emphasizes instruction, although he recognizes the work's 'pleasant and profitable diversity, both of flowers and fruits'.[23] Harvey emphasizes delight, although he allows instruction: for him Sidney's work is 'a gallant legendary, full of pleasurable accidents and profitable discourses', and he urges that it be read 'for three things especially very notable – for amorous courting (he was young in years), for sage counselling (he was ripe in judgement), and for valorous fighting (his sovereign profession was arms); and delightful pastime by way of pastoral exercises may pass for the fourth'.[24] For Milton, in contrast, the delight undermines the instruction: he refers to the *Arcadia* as 'a vain amatorious poem':

'in that kind full of worth and wit, but among religious thoughts and duties not worthy to be named; nor to be read at any time without good caution'.[25]

In the *Defence* Sidney anticipates the charge that the *Old Arcadia* may abuse man's wit by 'training it to wanton sinfulness and lustful love' when he defends love as the subject of the heroical poem. He argues that even if one should grant 'love of beauty to be a beastly fault (although it be very hard, since only man, and no beast, hath that gift to discern beauty)' and also grant 'that lovely name of Love to deserve all hateful reproaches', it does not follow that 'poetry abuses man's wit' but rather that 'man's wit abuseth poetry'. He defends poetry even though he recognizes that it is open to most abuse 'by the reason of his sweet charming force'.[26] In the *Old Arcadia*, especially in the erotic scenes, he seems deliberately to risk its condemnation as 'a vain amatorious poem'. While the revised work is more serious throughout, the three introductory debates and the moral arguments scattered throughout suggest that Sidney would agree with Milton that it should not be read 'at any time without good caution'. (He would have agreed with Milton that the work should never be named 'among religious thoughts and duties': he wrote only for man's 'own use and learning'.[27]) The delight it offers remains dangerous, and on his death-bed he asked that the *Arcadia* be burned, for he feared that 'even beauty itself, in all earthly complexions, was more apt to allure men to evil than to fashion any goodness in them'.[28] Earlier, however, he was prepared to allow that beauty could fashion goodness in man if it expresses virtue. Musidorus recants his attack on love and beauty when he sees the 'infinite beauty' of Pamela and falls in love: 'by love we are made, and to love we are made. Beasts only cannot discern beauty, and let them be in the role of beasts that do not honour it' (113). However, Sidney never presents images of beauty but only images of virtue in their 'outward beauty'.

BOOK I

For Book I, Sidney recast the abrupt opening of the *Old Arcadia* – chiefly by adding the stories of Argalus and Parthenia, Amphialus and Helen – in order to bring Pyrocles (and the reader) into

Basilius's Arcadian retreat. Then he appends the story of Phalantus and Artesia in order to include Musidorus. Phalantus challenges all knights in defence of Artesia's beauty by displaying the portraits of the eleven beauties whose knights he has defeated. He defends his possession of the portraits of Urania and Helen, and adds five more, including those of Gynecia and Philoclea. A black knight challenges him on behalf of Pamela but an ill-apparelled knight is allowed to fight for Philoclea. Phalantus is defeated; Artesia quarrels with him; and the two 'that came in masked with so great pomp, go out with so little constancy' (111). As the reader may readily guess, and soon learns, the black knight is Musidorus, who has fallen in love with Pamela, and the ill-apparelled knight is Pyrocles. This episode parodies the love and virtue shown in the other knights and their ladies, and also reflects on the present state of the two princes who engage in courtly combat to defend beauty apart from virtue.

Phalantus parodies the other knights, for he engages in knightly combat by choice rather than nature, and loves only because of fashion. Knightly courtesy in him becomes 'cunning cheerfulness' (97). Although Artesia engages him to prove that she is more beautiful than all others, she has less claim to that title (Basilius observes) than Helen, the princesses, and Parthenia. Moreover, she lacks virtue, for she 'called her disdain of him [Phalantus] chastity'.[29] As she was raised to believe that 'there is no wisdom but in including heaven and earth in oneself', she appears at the tournament as Phaethon, 'drawn by four winged horses with artificial flaming mouths and fiery wings, as if she had newly borrowed them of Phoebus' (101).

The muster of eleven beauties in chapter 16 is brilliantly designed and executed to discriminate kinds of beauty. The eleven are roughly paired in order of increasing beauty. Queen Andromana appears, as would Elizabeth to the young Sidney, a well-preserved older woman, having 'an exceeding red hair with small eyes', while Elis is beautiful only because she appears such to one who likes her; Artaxia is mannish while Erona is weak; and so on. Some portraits are wittily expanded: Baccha 'who though very fair, and of a fatness rather to allure than to mislike, yet her breasts over-familiarly laid open, with a mad countenance about her mouth, between simpering and smiling, her head bowed somewhat down, seemed to languish with over-much idleness, with an inviting look cast upward, dissuading with too much persuading, while hope might seem to overcome desire'. Others are brutally short: the Queen of Laconia 'was a queen, and therefore beautiful'. Beauty is finely discriminated in Helen: 'everything was full of a choice fineness, that if it wanted anything in majesty, it supplied it with increase of pleasure; and if at the first it strake not admiration, it ravished with delight. And no indifferent soul there was, which if it could resist from subjecting itself to make it his princess, that would not long to have such a playfellow.' In contrast, Parthenia's beauty expresses her virtue: her great-mindedness and humility are manifest in 'her great grey eye' and 'a large, and exceedingly fair forehead' (as Chaucer's Prioress) yet so carelessly attired, and far from all art that 'carelessness itself (in spite of itself) grew artificial'. As the story of Phalantus and Artesia educates the reader in the nature of love and virtue, the muster of beauties educates him in the nature of beauty.

For the rest of Book I, Sidney was content chiefly to revise the first book of the *Old Arcadia*. Since his revision often proceeds sentence by sentence, extended analysis would be required to show why some passages are omitted, others modified or shifted in context, others changed drastically, and new matter added.[30] The brief analysis that follows is guided by the response of early readers, which may be fairly represented by Molyneux's comment on the *Arcadia* as

...showing such excellency of spirit, gallant invention, variety of matter, and orderly disposition, and couched in frame of such apt words without superfluity, eloquent phrase, and fine conceit, with interchange of device, so delightful to the reader, and pleasant to the hearer, as nothing could be taken out to amend it, or added to it that would not impair it.[31]

What readers saw in the *Arcadia*, or wanted to see in such a work, often suggests what Sidney attempts.

From the kind of work Sidney chose to write, it is clear that he would have welcomed Sir William Temple's judgment that 'the true spirit or vein of ancient poetry in this kind [Romance] seems to shine most in Sir Philip Sidney'.[32] From the kind of story he told, it is clear also that he seeks Jonson's judgment: 'Sir Philip Sidney and Mr Hooker (in different matter) grew great masters of wit and language; and in [them] all vigour of invention and strength of judgement met',[33] and Thomas Howell's praise of the *Old Arcadia* as a 'most excellent book, full of rare invention'.[34] As a result, the *Arcadia* serves the reader in many ways: as a courtesy book, a moral treatise, a *Book named the Governour*, an anatomy of love, and (for its style) a rhetorical handbook.[35] Gabriel Harvey urged that it be read for its 'amorous courting', 'sage counselling', 'valorous fighting', and 'pastoral exercises'. Greville read it throughout as a moral and political treatise in which Sidney sought 'to turn the barren philosophy precepts into pregnant images of life; and in them, first on the monarch's part, lively to represent the growth, state, and declination of princes, change of government, and laws; vicissitudes of sedition, faction, succession, confederacies, plantations, with all other errors, or alterations, in public affairs'.[36] In some parts of the work, such as the tournament of Phalantus, Sidney may have added an historical allegory, as Sir Thomas Wilson suggests in the introductory matter to his translation of Montemayor's *Diana*: 'under the names and veils of shepherds and their lovers are covertly discoursed many noble actions and affections of the Spanish nation, as is of the English of the admirable and never enough praised book of Sir Philip Sidney's *Arcadia*'.[37] On more particular matters, such as the description of Arcadia, or Kalander's garden-house and garden, or the pastoral meadow at the end of Book I, Sidney invites Abraham Fraunce's praise of the natural logic shown by the 'poetical imaginations' of the best poets: 'read Homer, read Demosthenes, read Virgil, read Cicero, read Bartas, read Torquato Tasso, read that most worthy ornament of our English tongue, the Countess of Pembroke's *Arcadia*, and therein see the true effects of natural logic'.[38] In the various debates and moral arguments found throughout the work, he invites the general response given by John Hoskyns, that reading the *Arcadia* 'may make you eloquent and wise', and by Peter Heylyn, that it 'comprehendeth the universal art of speaking'. He invites also the specific response given by Hoskyns to the *sententiae* in the work and by Milton to the 'exquisite reasoning' on suicide found in Book IV of the 1593 *Arcadia*.[39]

In revising the *Old Arcadia*, Sidney seeks to produce a much more serious work. Everywhere he adds moral matter. The *Old Arcadia* simply mentions Basilius's skill in governing; in the *New*,

Kalander tells Musidorus: 'But to be plain with you, he excels in nothing so much as in the zealous love of his people, wherein he doth not only pass all his own foregoers but, as I think, all the princes living. Whereof the cause is, that though he exceed not in the virtues which get admiration, as depth of wisdom, height of courage, and largeness of magnificence, yet is he notable in those which stir affection, as truth of word, meekness, courtesy, mercifulness, and liberality' (19). This addition is all the more surprising because in the earlier work he appears hardly more than a doting, senile fool. All the other characters are described in moral terms, in particular, the two princesses, and especially Pamela. Her moral heightening becomes such that the *New Arcadia* omits the erotic moment in the *Old* when her fainting at the sight of the bear allows Musidorus 'to kiss and rekiss her a hundred times'. At this point she is not allowed to feel even a 'kind of inclination' towards him.[40]

The addition of such moral matter brings greater moral awareness to each point in the story of the two princes. For example, in the *Old Arcadia* Musidorus simply rejects the loving Pyrocles: 'give me leave rather in absence to bewail your mishap than to bide the continual pang of seeing your danger with mine eyes' (24). In the *New*, he says: 'give me leave to leave off this name of friendship as an idle title of a thing which cannot be, where virtue is abolished' (82), which asserts an important commonplace, deriving from Aristotle's *Ethics*, that friendship may exist only between the virtuous. In the original version, when Musidorus himself falls in love, the narrator intrudes to tell the fair ladies that 'for my part, I have not a feeling insight enough into the matter to be able lively to express it' (42). In the revised version, Musidorus says: 'I find indeed that all is but lip-wisdom which wants experience. I now (woe is me) do try what love can do. O Zelmane, who will resist it must either have no wit or put out his eyes. Can any man resist his creation? Certainly by love we are made, and to love we are made. Beasts only cannot discern beauty, and let them be in the role of beasts that do not honour it' (113). This revision shows clearly how he has abandoned his extreme idealism to accept the demands of human nature in an imperfect world. Now he shares Pyrocles's state, represented by the motto to the jewel he wears, which depicts Hercules with a distaff: 'Never more valiant', thus declaring both that he has shamefully abandoned the heroic life and that he has never been more valiant than now when he endures shame for the sake of love.[41] In the *Old Arcadia* when Musidorus laments the working of Fortune, he says:

Alas! What further evil hath fortune reserved for us, or what shall be the end of this our tragical pilgrimage? Shipwrecks, daily dangers, absence from our country, have at length brought forth this captiving of us within ourselves which hath transformed the one in sex, and the other in state, as much as the uttermost work of changeable fortune can be extended unto. (43)

This lament conveys little more than extravagant feeling, rather too self-pitying to be convincing. It summarizes past events in order to prepare for the future: the princes in prison at last rise above the assaults of fortune when they 'virtuously enable their minds against all extremities which they did think would fall upon them' (374). In the revised version, Musidorus says:

O heaven and earth...to what a pass are our minds brought, that from the right line of virtue are wried to these crooked shifts? But O Love, it is thou that doest it: thou changest name upon name; thou disguisest our bodies, and disfigurest our minds. But indeed thou hast reason, for though the ways be foul, the journey's end is most fair and honourable. (117)

Much more is said and of much more import. In the *Old Arcadia*, love knows no reason but only passion; now it transpires that love has reason to bring the princes through foul ways because the end is happiness in marriage. The revised lament affects our understanding of the whole work. Love promises to fulfil the lives of the princes rather than simply shame them.[42] That love's end is 'most fair and honourable' confirms what the heavens promised the princes at Pyrocles's birth, that 'love was threatened, and promised...as both the tempest and haven of their best years' (189).

This added moral matter supports Greville's comment on the 'finer moralities [which] offer themselves throughout that various and dainty work',[43] and Anne Bradstreet's praise of the 'learning, valour and morality, / Justice, friendship, and kind hospitality, / Yea and divinity within his book'.[44] Yet such matter does not add weight but rather a leavening, as Greville recognizes when he says that the 'moralities' serve 'for sounder judgements to exercise their spirits in' and defends the whole work as it 'shows the judicious reader how he may be nourished in the delicacy of his own judgement'.[45] The *New Arcadia* is never overtly didactic, as is the *Old* in Books IV and V, for moral matter is presented through characters in a story written to delight the reader. The reader responds only to images which free him to exercise his own judgment, in accord with the central argument in the *Defence* that he 'shall use the narration but [i.e. only] as an imaginative ground-plot of a profitable invention'.[46] Throughout the *New Arcadia* Sidney shows himself to be the right poet whose work is 'full of virtue-breeding delightfulness'.

It would be false to the whole work, however, to suggest that moral matter dominates our response: rather it provides a firm framework within which Sidney may delight the reader. One example, that may serve for many, is his description of Kalander's hunt:

The hounds were in couples staying their coming, but with a whining accent craving liberty; many of them in colour and marks so resembling that it showed they were of one kind. The huntsmen handsomely attired in their green liveries, as though they were children of summer, with staffs in their hands to beat the guiltless earth when the hounds were at a fault, and with horns about their necks to sound an alarm upon a silly fugitive. The hounds were straight uncoupled, and ere long the stag thought it better to trust the nimbleness of his feet than to the slender fortification of his lodging; but even his feet betrayed him, for, howsoever they went, they themselves uttered themselves to the scent of their enemies; who, one taking it of another, and sometimes believing the wind's advertisements, sometimes the view of their faithful counsellors, the huntsmen, with open mouths then denounced war, when the war was already begun. Their cry being composed of so well-sorted mouths that any man would perceive therein some kind of proportion, but the skilful woodmen did find a music. Then delight and variety of opinion drew the horsemen sundry ways; yet cheering their hounds with voice and horn kept still (as it were) together. The wood seemed to conspire with them against his own citizens, dispersing their noise through all his quarters; and even the nymph Echo left to bewail the loss of Narcissus and became a hunter. But the stag was in the end so hotly pursued that (leaving his flight) he was driven to make courage of despair; and so turning his head, made the hounds (with change of speech) to testify that he was at bay: as if from hot pursuit of their enemy, they were suddenly come to a parley. But Kalander (by his skill of coasting the country) was among the first that came in to the besieged deer; whom, when some of the younger sort would have killed with their swords, he would not suffer, but with a crossbow sent a death to the poor beast, who with tears showed the unkindness he took of man's cruelty. (60–1)

Even one opposed to hunting, as Sidney himself was reputed to be,[47] must delight in this description. The modern reader is rightly reminded of Theseus's hounds in *A Midsummer Night's Dream*,[48] or the pastoral scene with Jacques in *As You Like It*, or the account of the hare in *Venus and Adonis*. There is the same freeing of words from the demand that they be didactic or useful in order that they may delight the reader. Harvey responded to such art when he asked, 'is not the prose of Sir Philip Sidney in his sweet *Arcadia* the embroidery of finest art and daintiest wit?';[49] and so did Hoskyns when he noted that the work exemplified 'all the figures of rhetoric and the art of the best English';[50] and so did Joseph Hall when he called Sidney 'the prince of prose and sweet conceit'.[51]

BOOK II

In revising Book II of the *Old Arcadia*, Sidney was largely content to insert stories that trace the history of the two princes in Asia Minor – or involve them in some way – before they arrive in Arcadia. That history is summarized in extravagant terms by Musidorus as 'strange horrors. . .laboursome adventures [and] loathsome misadventures' (161) which reach a climax in their overthrow in Arcadia. The stories are divided among all the chief characters, except the Queen, and are spaced throughout the Book. In the *Old Arcadia* the narrator refers to the adventures of the princes only in passing, for 'it is a work for a higher style than mine'; in the *New*, Sidney is ready to display that style. The added stories serve mainly to reveal the active, heroic lives of the two princes before they assume their present shameful and paralysed state. Everywhere there is evidence of careful structuring. For example, the shipwreck, which brings the two princes to Arcadia, is finally explained in the concluding story of their adventures; and within the story they tell, it counters the shipwreck that brings them to Asia Minor. In Book I the action begins when Pyrocles falls in love with Philoclea's picture, 'resembling her he had once loved' (75): that statement is explained in the story of Zelmane which Pyrocles tells near the end of Book II. Or again, Pyrocles's first solo adventure, his 'monomachia' against Anaxius, which is interrupted by his succour of Dido, provides the climax to Book III.

In these stories, brilliant narrative art is displayed in a number of ways: in relating the teller to his tale, in connecting the past to the present in order to prepare for the future, in interweaving the stories, and chiefly in the moral complexity of the plot and the sustained fine writing, which is astonishing in the 1580s.[52] Sidney can tell a story well and memorably. He is particularly skilful in portraying characters. Hoskyns notes that he portrays characters with 'ever a steadfast decency and uniform difference of manners observed': '[his] course was (besides reading Aristotle and Theophrastus) to imagine the thing present in his own brain, that his pen might the better present it to you'.[53] An early seventeenth-century reader claims that choice passages gathered out of the *Arcadia* 'would make as good a book of Characters as is yet extant'.[54] Sidney's skill in an extended portrait is illustrated in the superb descriptions of the suspicious King of Phrygia in chapter 8 and the envious King of Pontus in chapter 9. Or in a brief portrait, the description in chapter 19 of the miser Chremes, 'the picture of miserable happiness and rich beggary': 'such a man as any enemy could not wish him worse than to be himself'. His entire character is expressed in the final moment when he is led to his death: neither the death of his daughter nor his own shameful end bother him as much as 'the loss of his goods and burning of his house, which often, with more laughter than tears of the hearers, he made pitiful exclamations upon'. Often Sidney's skill is shown when he defines a character in one sentence, as in his account of the proud Anaxius 'to whom all men would willingly have yielded the height of praise, but that his nature was such, as to bestow it upon himself before any could give it' (263).

The stories themselves reveal Sidney to be a master of prose. His skill in simple description is illustrated in the single sentence that describes Pamela when Philoclea finds her reading her lover's letter:

...she found her (though it were in the time that the wings of night doth blow sleep most willingly into mortal creatures) sitting in a chair, lying backward, with her head almost over the back of it, and looking upon a wax-candle which burned before her; in one hand holding a letter, in the other her handkerchief, which had lately drunk up the tears of her eyes, leaving instead of them, crimson circles like red flakes in the element when the weather is hottest. (175–6)

He is capable of sustained description, as in the account of the tempest at sea (192–3). For short description, one may cite his witty account of magnetism. When the two princes first put out to sea, they admire the instruments on board for their beauty and use, especially the compass:

And, O Lord, to see the admirable power and noble effects of love, whereby the seeming insensible loadstone, with a secret beauty (holding the spirit of iron in it) can draw that hard-hearted thing unto it, and (like a virtuous mistress) not only make it bow itself but, with it, make it aspire to so high a love as of the heavenly poles; and thereby to bring forth the noblest deeds that the children of the earth can boast of. (191–2)[55]

Here scientific explanation turns first to praise of love and then (startlingly) to praise of the English mariner. Sidney's control over words allows him to vary his description through an entire range from the simple and immediate to the elaborately ornate.

An example of his style at its simplest and most visual is his most famous story, that of the King of Paphlagonia in chapter 10. It begins as directly as any story may: 'It was in the kingdom of Galacia, the season being (as in the depth of winter) very cold, and then suddenly grown to so extreme and foul a storm that never any winter (I think) brought forth a fouler child.' When the princes shroud themselves from the tempest, they overhear a dispute between two men and go forward to see them. What they see is told as though it were a stage-direction: 'There they perceived an aged man, and a young, scarcely come to the age of a man, both poorly arrayed, extremely weather-beaten; the old man blind, the young man leading him; and yet through all those miseries, in both these seemed to appear a kind of nobleness, not suitable to that affliction.' The old man tells them how he had cast out his true son, who now befriends him, to favour his bastard son who has cast him out and blinded him. The pathos of his state is simply and memorably gathered in the concluding phrase of his account of his wanderings:

...if there were any who fell to pity of so great a fall, and had yet any sparks of unstained duty left in them towards me, yet durst they not show it, scarcely with giving me alms at their doors, which yet was the only sustenance of my distressed life, nobody daring to show so much charity as to lend me a hand to guide my dark steps. (209–10)

The conclusion in which he urges the princes to publish his true story to the world seems almost to invite Shakespeare's use of it in *King Lear.*

Such factual telling is not Sidney's norm, however, for generally he prefers to render speech in which the teller of a story conveys his response to what is said. An extreme, and therefore unfair, example is Pyrocles's account to Philoclea of the dying Zelmane's love for him:

> Such was therein my ill destiny, that this young lady Zelmane (like some unwisely liberal, that more delight to give presents than pay debts) she chose (alas for the pity) rather to bestow her love (so much undeserved, as not desired) upon me, than to recompense him [Palladius], whose love (besides many other things) might seem (even in the court of honour) justly to claim it of her. But so it was (alas that so it was) whereby it came to pass, that (as nothing doth more naturally follow his cause than care to preserve, and benefit doth follow unfeigned affection) she felt with me, what I felt of my captivity. . . . (282)

We are not told, we hear, or overhear, the sad tale of Zelmane (sad enough surely in itself) but more sad because the speaker conveys his sympathy, which we share, for the tale he tells.

More representative of the quality of Sidney's prose is Pyrocles's account to Philoclea of Helen in her court and her love for Amphialus:

> . . .she made her people by peace, warlike; her courtiers by sports, learned; her ladies by love, chaste. For by continual martial exercises without blood, she made them perfect in that bloody art. Her sports were such as carried riches of knowledge upon the stream of delight; and such the behaviour both of herself and her ladies as builded their chastity, not upon wayward-ness, but by choice of worthiness; so as it seemed that court to have been the marriage place of love and virtue, and that herself was a Diana apparelled in the garments of Venus. . .you may see by her example (in herself wise and of others beloved) that neither folly is the cause of vehe-ment love nor reproach the effect. For never (I think) was there any woman that with more unremovable determination gave herself to the counsel of love, after she had once set before her mind the worthiness of your cousin Amphialus; and yet is neither her wisdom doubted of, nor honour blemished. For (O God) what doth better become wisdom than to discern what is worthy the loving? what more agreeable to goodness than to love it so discerned? and what to greatness of heart than to be constant in it once loved? (283-4)

The paradoxes of life at her court are presented for the reader to meditate and then, surprisingly, shown not to be paradoxes at all but an ideal state in terms of which the reader may judge all others. The union in Helen of love and virtue, which in others (except the princesses) seem opposed, is shown to be natural in her. When Pyrocles defends love, he speaks as a lover to his beloved;

yet what he says gains authority from the story of Helen's love. The consequence is that his defence of love gains unique authority *because* he is a lover, and determines our understanding of the whole work.[56] While the passage is packed with moral doctrine, no reader feels that he is being instructed even though no reader, however well informed, can fail to be instructed.

The larger purpose of the stories of the princes is to serve the reader even as stories of princes served them during their early education: 'the delight of tales being converted to the knowledge of all the stories of worthy princes, both to move them to do nobly, and teach them how to do nobly; the beauty of virtue still being set before their eyes' (190). Since the stories are told by the princes themselves, the reader becomes intimately and powerfully involved. They teach him even as Musidorus taught Pyrocles: 'he taught me by word, and best by example, giving me in him so lively an image of virtue, as ignorance could not cast such mist over mine eyes as not to see and to love it' (264). Such statements, which occur so naturally within the work, show how the creative and critical responses are one in Sidney, and therefore in the reader: as he illustrates his poetic in the *New Arcadia*, the reader's delight in the work is converted into an understanding of his own nature.

The specific purpose of any story is to illustrate the nature of virtue. Parts of a story may illustrate aphorisms, which are found throughout:

...if that may be called love, which he rather did take into himself willingly than by which he was taken forcibly.
...a woman beautiful enough, if it be possible that the outside only can justly entitle a beauty.
...spies, the necessary evil servants to a king.
...the poor young prince, deceived with that young opinion, that if it be ever lawful to lie, it is for one's lover....

That such brief moral arguments may be found on only one page (243) of the *Arcadia*, indicates how seriously Sidney seeks to instruct the reader. Since they occur unobtrusively and inevitably in Pamela's powerful story of Plangus's misfortunes, Sidney's work as a whole deserves his description of Helen's sports: it is 'such as carried riches of knowledge upon the stream of delight'.

Usually a story gathers its aphorisms into some larger moral point. To cite one example. The worthy brothers, Tydeus and Telenor, are faithful servants to the vicious Plexirtus who rewards them only by treachery: he deceives them into fighting each other to the death. Pyrocles tells how at last they learn the truth, and lament that they had served faithfully so ungrateful a tyrant: 'accusing their folly in having believed he could faithfully love who did not love faithfulness; wishing us [the two princes] to take heed how we placed our good will upon any other ground than proof of virtue, since length of acquaintance, mutual secrecies, nor height of benefits could bind a savage heart; no man being good to other that is not good in himself' (294–5). Their story illustrates the specific moral point that one should not make friendship the father, rather than the child, of virtue (211). Almost the first fact we learn about them is that they choose to be good friends rather than good men. Although their story shows that their virtue serves vice, they are not judged: the foreboding they arouse in us remains entirely sympathetic. The climax of their story comes as a surprise: the two princes see 'one of the cruellest fights between two knights that ever hath adorned the martial story'. They watch, as we are meant to watch, 'a while. . .wondering, another while delighted with the rare bravery thereof'. When we learn with horror who they are, pity for them holds us. At the end, the pathos of their story merges with its moral in the same sentence:

But when they found by themselves, and us, no possibility [of cure], they desired to be joined; and so embracing and craving that pardon each of other, which they denied to themselves, they gave us a most sorrowful spectacle of their death; leaving few in the world behind them their matches in anything, if they had soon enough known the ground and limits of friendship. (295)

The moral instructs through the spectacle we see. Since that moral is fully justified, the story absorbs and contains it, remaining a story that seems only to delight the reader.

Together the stories serve to clarify the nature of virtue tested by the complexity of life. For example, the opening story demonstrates the nature of friendship by the actions of the two princes. When Pyrocles is condemned to death by the King of Pontus, Musidorus offers himself as substitute. Pyrocles is freed, much against his will, and returns disguised as the servant to Musidorus's executioner: 'he (even he, born to the greatest expectation, and of the greatest blood that any prince might be) submitted himself to be servant to the executioner that should put to death Musidorus: a far notabler proof of his friendship, considering the height of his mind, than any death could be' (199). Here friendship seems to be an absolute value. However, the story of Tydeus and Telenor questions friendship by showing its 'ground and limits'. These limits, which are defined in the brothers' service to Plexirtus, are themselves tested in the story that follows. Pyrocles abandons Musidorus in his greatest need in order to serve Plexirtus because he had vowed to the dying Zelmane that he would do so: 'by the strange working of unjust fortune, I was to leave the standing by Musidorus, whom better than myself I loved, to go save him whom for just causes I hated. But my promise given, and given to Zelmane, and to Zelmane dying, prevailed more with me than my friendship to Musidorus, though certainly I may affirm, nothing had so great rule in my thoughts as that' (299). In their sequence, the stories tend to replace simple, heroic action, which seems absolute and final, by action which, if not morally confusing, is morally ambiguous.[57] Increasingly they illustrate Musidorus's observation: 'see how virtue can be a minister to mischief' (160). Of his concluding and climactic action in which he kills the monster to save Plexirtus, Pyrocles reports that many greatly admired what he had done, but an old nobleman who loved him bewailed that 'my virtue had been employed to save a worse monster than I killed' (301).

In their sequence, the stories form a cyclical pattern. They begin with an account of how Evarchus, complete in all the virtues, reforms his corrupt kingdom. Presumably this opening prepares for a resolution in which he would reform the corrupt kingdom of Arcadia. His complete virtue measures all other characters, but chiefly the two princes. When Musidorus is born, it is prophesied that he will perform strange and incredible things, 'whether the heavens at that time listed to play with ignorant mankind, or that flattery be so presumptuous as even at times to borrow the face of divinity' (188). So, too, when Pyrocles is born, the heavens and earth promise 'the coming forth of an heroical virtue. The senate house of the planets was at no time to set, for the decreeing of perfection in a man' (189). Their natural virtue is fashioned by nurture, and first tested by their conduct in the shipwreck which brings them to Asia Minor. While the crew drown through fear, the princes save themselves by leaping on a rib of the ship, 'using the passions of fearing evil, and desiring to escape, only to serve the rule of virtue' (194). Then their two servants save them by leaving the rib when it begins to sink under their weight. Pyrocles is cast up on the shore of Phrygia and Musidorus on the shore of Pontus. The two kings of these countries embody respectively suspicion and envy, the two vices specifically named as absent in Evarchus.[58] Musidorus's 'divine' birth had led the King of Phrygia, acting like Herod, to seek to kill him. His determination to kill the captured Pyrocles leads now to 'a rare example of friendship' (197): Musidorus offers himself in place of Pyrocles. When freed, Pyrocles proves his friendship in turn when, in an attempt to release Musidorus, he is willing to aid the executioner. Although Musidorus overthrows the King, he refuses his throne, an action which 'set forth no less his magnificence than the other act did his magnanimity' (202).

Since the envious King of Pontus has killed their two servants, who had been rescued, the two princes seek revenge. They invade his kingdom and kill him. Now it is Pyrocles who refuses the throne; but the point of this second story is not in its parallel to the first but in its addendum. The princes kill two brothers, servants to the King of Pontus, who think 'nothing juster than revenge, nor more noble than the effects of anger'. Such anger is not 'a serviceable power of the mind to do public good' as it is in the two princes, but 'unbridled, and blind judge of itself, it made wickedness violent, and praised itself in excellency of mischief' (205). Such patterning of events in the *New Arcadia* is never schematic, as it would be in an allegory. Sidney does not spell out any response to anger, as he does in the *Defence* when he mocks the moral philosophers who are 'angry with any man in whom they see the foul fault of anger'. He only juxtaposes the two events, allowing the reader to connect them. In Greville's terms, he 'shows the judicious reader how he may be nourished in the delicacy of his own judgement'.[59]

In these first adventures, which follow the shipwreck, the princes are 'brought to heroical effects by fortune or necessity (like Ulysses and Aeneas)'. They want to overgo such classical heroes by deliberately seeking adventures – acting 'by one's own choice and working' (206) – in order to exercise and test their virtue. Later it is noted that they follow 'the course which virtue and fortune led them' (233). (Presumably, only at the end, as in the *Old Arcadia*, would they triumph over fortune.) Their virtue leads them because they have no choice, or rather, the choice they make is imposed by their own natures. Their virtue impels them to undergo virtuous action, in contrast to Phalantus, of whom it is said in scorn that 'it was rather choice than nature that led him to matters of arms' (97). Later when they enter Arcadia, they choose to submit to love: Pyrocles laments that his powers are 'with. . .inward treason spoiled' (76) and Musidorus sees himself as one 'who spoils himself of bliss' (113). Again, however, the choice is imposed by their own natures, for the reason that Musidorus gives: 'by love we are made, and to love we are made' (113). Accordingly, all their actions express their natures. Since virtue is natural to them, they need not be educated in it. They prove equal to any demand, however great, and appear to us as Sidney appeared to Sir Robert Naunton: 'born only to that which he went about'.[60]

In their next adventure, the princes undergo 'private chivalries' (213) by defending Leonatus and the King of Paphlagonia against Plexirtus. The larger significance of this adventure is specifically pointed to: the story is 'not so notable for any great effect they performed, yet worthy to be remembered for the unused [i.e. unusual] examples therein, as well of true natural goodness as of wretched ungratefulness' (206). The simple resolution of the earlier actions – replacing a bad king by a good one – is no longer possible: Plexirtus's 'wretched ungratefulness' deceives Leonatus because of his own 'true natural goodness', even as it deceives Tydeus, Telenor and the two princes. Treachery cannot be defeated, only exposed, because virtue is deceived by evil masked as good.[61] At the end of their Asian adventures, the princes leave in triumph but are shipwrecked by Plexirtus's treachery and then slandered by him. His treachery is rewarded by his marriage to Artaxia, and he 'sticked not to glory in the murder of Pyrocles and Musidorus, as having just cause thereto, in respect of the deaths of his sister Andromana, her son his nephew, and his own daughter Zelmane' (337).

In the next adventure, virtue itself leads to treachery. The princes undertake 'public chivalry' when they defend Erona against Tiridates and the three most famous men living, Plangus, Barzanes, and Evardes. In the Battle of the Six Princes, they display their virtue: Pyrocles kills Evardes, and Musidorus Barzanes. When her lover, Antiphilus, is captured by Plangus, Erona agrees to yield herself to Tiridates to save him. However, not telling the princes she has done so, she persuades them to rescue Antiphilus. They kill Tiridates in an action which his sister, Artaxia, rightly calls 'a most abominable treason' (236). From this battle, which taints virtue with treason, all future adventures of the princes follow. No resolution proves possible: Antiphilus's ungratefulness to the loving Erona leads to greater treason, for 'wickedness may well be compared to a bottomless pit into which it is far easier to keep oneself from falling than, being fallen, to give oneself any stay from falling infinitely' (262).

After the story of how the princes defend Erona, a new sequence of adventures begins: Pyrocles seeks to test his virtue without the support of Musidorus by agreeing to fight Anaxius who seeks revenge for the death of his uncle, Evardes. On his way, he intervenes to prevent Pamphilus from being castrated, blinded, and slain by nine ladies, led by Dido, whom he has seduced. He saves him but then must save Dido from Pamphilus's knights. Later while fighting Anaxius, he sees Dido abused by these knights, and is willing to suffer the shame of leaving the battle in order to rescue her. What should be simply an heroic quest becomes a shameful flight; but, as he confesses to Philoclea, 'the lady's misery over-balanced my reputation' (272). His second defence of Dido leads to the treachery of her father, Chremes: his plot to kill Pyrocles is foiled only by the arrival of Musidorus and the King of Iberia. Then follow stories of the lust of his queen, Andromana, for the princes; the love of her son, Palladius, for Plexirtus's daughter, Zelmane; and the culminating story, Zelmane's love for Pyrocles, which causes him to abandon Musidorus to rescue her father. This sequence is resolved in another Battle of Six 'Princes': in seeking revenge for Barzanes's death, Otaves and the two brothers of the two who served the evil King of Pontus challenge Pyrocles, Musidorus and the new King of Pontus. Pyrocles kills the monster to save Plexirtus; Musidorus, aided by Leonatus and the King of Pontus, captures Otaves. The Asian adventures of the two princes end with a final assembly of most of the princes of Asia to honour them, and the Arcadian adventures begin when Plexirtus, to win Artaxia as his wife, plots the mutiny designed to kill the princes at sea.

By this cycle of adventures, the history of the princes is brought to the present moment in which they woo the princesses in Arcadia. At the very end of Book II, Basilius tells the story of Erona in order to prepare for the action of the princes following their Arcadian romance: Erona is threatened with death unless the two princes come to her aid within the year, which is the limit of the working of the oracle.

BOOK III

Surprisingly, Book III is not a revision of the *Old Arcadia* but an addition to it. Not only does it not advance the plot but it makes revision of the later books difficult.[62] Since Pamela has declared that she would not marry without her parents' consent, 'for, without that, I know I should offend God' (405), she could hardly elope with Musidorus. All the chief characters gain such stature that they could not appropriately return to the love-game comedy that the original requires of them. Even more surprising, the Book spreads itself, unfolding leisurely and variously. For example, most of one chapter treats an encounter between Amphialus and Phalantus, which is in no way essential to the plot; yet Sidney expects the reader to share his interest and delight in the elaborate description. Phalantus rides a horse

milk-white but that upon his shoulder and withers, he was fretted with red stains, as when a few strawberries are scattered into a dish of cream. He had caused his mane and tail to be dyed in carnation; his reins were vine branches, which engendering one with the other, at the end, when it came to the bit, there, for the boss, brought forth a cluster of grapes, by the workman made so lively that it seemed, as the horse champed on his bit, he chopped for them, and that it did make his mouth water to see the grapes so near him. (415)[63]

When the two join battle, each detail invites attention, for 'it was a delectable sight in a dangerous effect; and a pleasant consideration that there was so perfect agreement in so mortal disagreement: like a music made of cunning discords' (416). With such leisurely expansion Sidney does not seem under any pressure to complete the earlier work. Yet through revision, the *Old Arcadia* is being foreshortened, as he may have realized. The triumph of love and virtue in Book III, in both the princes and princesses, now resolves the moral argument of the original, so that even in its unfinished state the *New Arcadia* is unified and essentially complete. Further, the revised work itself seems to be rounding out with the deaths of Argalus and Parthenia, Artesia and Cecropia, with the return of the mortally wounded Amphialus to Helen, and finally with the imminent death of Anaxius (and with it, the lifting of the siege).

It is notorious that there are many *Arcadias*, and this is especially true of Book III: by selective quotation one may make the work appear as one wishes.[64] It may be made to seem baldly didactic, as in Pamela's refutation of Cecropia's atheism:

It is as absurd in nature that from an unity many contraries should proceed still kept in an unity, as that from the number of contrarieties an unity should arise. I say still, if you banish both a singularity and plurality of judgement from among them, then (if so earthly a mind can lift itself up so high) do but conceive how a thing whereto you give the highest and most excellent kind of being (which is eternity) can be of the base and vilest degree of being, and next to a not-being; which is so to be as not to enjoy his own being? (409)

Or seem lushly pathetic, as in the description of the dying Parthenia:

For her exceeding fair eyes, having with continual weeping gotten a little redness about them; her roundly sweetly swelling lips a little trembling, as though they kissed their neighbour death; in her cheeks the whiteness striving by little and little to get upon the rosiness of them; her neck, a neck indeed of alabaster, displaying the wound, which with most dainty blood laboured to drown his own beauties; so as here was a river of purest red, there an island of perfect white, each giving lustre to the other.... (447)

At its most representative, however, Sidney's style seeks that ideal for which Musidorus strives in his letter: to show passion rather than art, but in such a way as to be 'forcibly moving' rather than 'foolishly passionate' (356). At its best, his style accommodates both elaborate conceit and direct realism, as in the description of a battlefield:

The earth itself (wont to be a burial of men) was now (as it were) buried with men: so was the face thereof hidden with dead bodies to whom Death had come masked in diverse manners. In one place lay disinherited heads, dispossessed of their natural seignories; in another, whole bodies to see to, but that their hearts wont to be bound all over so close were now with deadly violence opened; in others, fouler deaths had uglily displayed their trailing guts. (388)

The effect that Sidney seeks is a 'delightful terribleness' (42). As a tragedy renders violence 'sweet',[65] here 'deadly violence' becomes delightful through art, so that, for example, the earth 'buried with men' shows Nature herself to be unnatural. The 'face' of the earth hidden by dead bodies becomes other than mere metaphor when the work of 'masked' Death is seen in the unnatural exposure of the dead. In reading, the eye moves from head to heart to guts, as though seeing a picture. The passage is a picture in its realism, but being stylized, it becomes a 'speaking' picture: it addresses the mind and instructs the reader about the unnaturalness of war.

The central metaphor of Book III is the besieged castle. When Cecropia kidnaps Philoclea and Pamela, and Amphialus agrees to keep them in his castle because he loves Philoclea, two sieges follow: without, Basilius and his forces lay siege to the castle; within, Cecropia lays siege to the two princesses – to the castle of their bodies – in order to persuade one of them to marry her son. This metaphor gathers up the major concerns of the whole work: masculine virtue expressed in chivalric encounter and feminine virtue expressed in suffering, which are the twin themes of action and endurance, *agere et pati*. As a consequence, the argument of the Book contains the arguments of Homer's *Iliad* and *Odyssey*, as these are noted by Chapman: 'in one, the body's fervour and fashion of outward fortitude to all possible height of heroical action; in the other, the mind's inward, constant, and unconquered empire, unbroken, unaltered with any most insolent and tyrannous infliction'.[66]

The sieges alternate throughout the Book. Each is displayed in a variety of encounters, and each encounter is distinct in its display of virtue. For example, the battle between Musidorus and Amphialus is a heroical 'monomachia' fought to a finish, at which Musidorus is praised as 'the noble knight that had bettered the most esteemed knight in the world' (463). On the other hand, the battle between Amphialus and Argalus is interrupted at the point at which Amphialus offers a pardon which the other refuses to accept – 'a notable example of the wonderful effects of virtue, where the conqueror sought for friendship of the conquered, and the conquered would not pardon the conqueror; both indeed being of that mind to love each other for accepting, but not for giving, mercy, and neither affected to overlive a dishonour' (426). When Pamela rejects Cecropia's temptations to atheism by defending God's providence, 'she ended with so fair a majesty of unconquered virtue that captivity might seem to have authority over tyranny, so foully was the filthiness of impiety discovered by the shining of her unstained goodness' (411). In her encounter with Lycurgus, Philoclea rejects his wooing in a manner that was 'an excellent pastime (to those that would delight in the play of virtue) to see' (507). In all their variety, however, the two sieges move steadily to a resolution. The heroic battles reach a climax when Pyrocles single-handedly kills Zoilus and Lycurgus and then battles Anaxius, and the heroic resistance of the princesses reaches a climax when they resist physical torture.

The siege of Amphialus's castle is marked by a number of chivalric encounters, each of which is carefully discriminated. As one would expect, the greatest heroism is shown when Amphialus fights Musidorus in chapter 18. Sidney describes their wondrous heroism through paradox:

though reason and amazement go rarely together, yet the most reasonable eyes that saw it found reason to be amazed at the fury of their combat;

negatives:

never game of death better played; never fury set itself forth in greater bravery;

classical comparison:

the courteous Vulcan, when he wrought at his now more courteous wife's request, Aeneas an armour, made not his hammer beget a greater sound than the swords of those noble knights did; they needed no fire to their forge, for they made the fire to shine at the meeting of their swords and armours;

apparent miracles of nature:

if the astonished eyes of the beholders were not by the astonishment deceived, [the sun and wind] did both stand still to be beholders of this rare match. For neither could their amazed eyes discern motion in the sun, and no breath of wind stirred, as if either for fear it would come among such blows, or with delight had his eyes so busy as it had forgot to open his mouth;

and a flood of personifications:

spite, rage, disdain, shame, revenge came waiting upon hatred; of the other side came with love-longing desire, both invincible hope and fearless despair with rival-like jealousy, which (although brought up within doors in the school of Cupid) would show themselves no less forward than the other dusty band of Mars, to make themselves notable in the notableness of this combat;

until finally he reaches the point at which words fail:

as cruel a fight as eye did ever see, or thought could reasonably imagine; far beyond the reach of weak words to be able to express it;

although he manages to continue for another four pages.

Yet he uses none of these devices when he describes the fight between Amphialus and Phalantus; instead, there is exact, visual detail: 'he strake Phalantus just upon the gorget, so as he battered the lames thereof, and made his head almost touch the back of his horse' (416). Then, quite differently, Sidney seeks to arouse pathos when he describes the death of Parthenia after she is struck by Amphialus:

The very heavens seemed, with a cloudy countenance, to lour at the loss, and Fame itself (though by nature glad to tell rare accidents) yet could not choose but deliver it in lamentable accents, and in such sort went it quickly all over the camp: and, as if the air had been infected with sorrow, no heart was so hard but was subject to that contagion; the rareness of the accident matching together (the rarely matched together) pity with admiration. (448–9)

His skill is so assured that he can balance such pathos with a superbly comic account of the 'combat of cowards', Dametas and Clinias, 'mingling kings and clowns' with 'decency' and 'discretion' because 'the matter so carrieth it'.[67]

The siege of the castle centres upon Amphialus and traces the downward course of his tragic career. Love proves his undoing from the moment he sees Philoclea naked. At the beginning of Book III when she seeks to be released, he must refuse: 'alas, that tyrant love (which now possesseth the hold of all my life and reason) will no way suffer it. It is love, it is love, not I, which dis-

obey you' (369). Love forces him to encourage his mother to persuade Philoclea to yield to him; in effect, he drives her to assault
the princesses. Although he is noted as 'the courteous knight', he
undoes himself through increasingly discourteous actions. At the
end he catalogues the nine tragic actions in his life from the beginning when he killed his friend, Philoxenus, to the climax when
he causes the death of his mother after the tortured Philoclea
scorns him; and then he seeks to add a tenth by killing himself.
Being divided by passion, his virtue serves only to destroy him.

The limitations of masculine virtue are seen also in the two
princes. Neither is able to free the princesses despite his utmost
endeavour. Until the last battle against the three brothers, Pyrocles
remains a helpless Amazon, becoming comically effeminate when
he lies prostrate in grief believing Philoclea dead although she
spends most of the night with him. Until the end when he leads
forces for a final assault upon the castle, Musidorus is fought to a
standstill; he has good reason to castigate himself as 'worthy for
nothing but to keep sheep' (460). In effect, the disguised princes
become identified with their disguises. The explanation for their
failure would seem to be that love and virtue remain divided in
them, as they do in Amphialus. They are divided even in Argalus.
When he is summoned to leave Parthenia to fight Amphialus, he
goes as one 'in whom honour could not be rocked asleep by
affection' (420); yet later he is said to be 'carried away by the
tyranny of honour' (422). For honour means service to the foolish
whim of Basilius who thirsts for revenge against Amphialus in a
love-tournament. Argalus dies valiantly but vainly, and provokes
Parthenia to seek death at the hands of his killer.

More heroic than the knights in the siege of Amphialus's castle
are the two princesses under the assaults of Cecropia. They are,
in fact, 'above heroic' in their steadfast endurance. The explanation for their triumph over affliction is that in them love and
virtue are one. Yet in them together, for Sidney discriminates carefully between them in their harmonious relationship, associating
Philoclea primarily with love and beauty and Pamela with
virtue.[68]

The distinction between the sisters is established in Kalander's
account of Arcadia at the beginning of Book I, in a passage added
to the revised version:

The elder is named Pamela; by many men not deemed inferior to her sister; for my part, when I marked them both, methought there was (if at least such perfections may receive the word of more) more sweetness in Philoclea but more majesty in Pamela; methought love played in Philoclea's eyes and threatened in Pamela's; methought Philoclea's beauty only persuaded but so persuaded as all hearts must yield; Pamela's beauty used violence, and such violence as no heart could resist. And it seems that such proportion is between their minds: Philoclea so bashful as though her excellencies had stolen into her before she was aware, so humble that she will put all pride out of countenance; in sum, such proceeding as will stir hope but teach hope good manners. Pamela of high thoughts, who avoids not pride with not knowing her excellencies, but by making that one of her excellencies to be void of pride; her mother's wisdom, greatness, nobility, but (if I can guess aright) knit with a more constant temper. (20)

These distinctions are not developed in the first two books beyond associating Philoclea with beauty, for example, when she bathes in the river, and with love when she yields to Pyrocles; and Pamela with virtue in her virtuous disdain of Musidorus's suit. In Book III, however, their responses to Cecropia's assaults are elaborately compared in order to define their states.

When they are first seized by Cecropia, 'Philoclea (with a look where love shined through the mist of fear) besought her to be good unto them, having never deserved evil of her. But Pamela's high heart, disdaining humbleness to injury, "Aunt", said she, "what you have determined of us I pray you do it speedily; for my part I look for no service where I find violence" ' (363). The two key terms are 'humbleness' and 'majesty'. When Cecropia tempts them to yield to Amphialus, 'Philoclea with sweet and humble dealing did avoid their assaults, she [Pamela] with the majesty of virtue did beat them off' (384). When Cecropia points out to Philoclea that her son has released Philanax for her sake, she gets no answer 'but a silence sealed up in virtue, and so sweetly graced, as that in one instant it carried with it both resistance and humbleness' (402). When she uses atheistical arguments to persuade Pamela to yield, in virtuous anger Pamela replies to her at length and ends 'with so fair a majesty of unconquered virtue, that captivity might seem to have authority over tyranny'. Even Cecropia sees in her 'a light more than human, which gave a lustre to her perfections' (411). The resistance of the sisters to their aunt's temptations is summed up as 'majesty of virtue. . .in the one, . . ,silent humbleness in the other'

(411). These distinctions extend to each particular.[69] In posture and dress, for example, Philoclea is shown 'sitting low upon a cushion', her hair and apparel showing 'neither a careful art, nor an art of carelessness, but even left to a neglected chance' (376). In contrast, Pamela is seen in prayer (383), and some twenty pages later her apparel is described in contrast to her sister's: 'neither had she neglected the dainty dressing of herself, but as it had been her marriage-time to Affliction, she rather seemed to remember her own worthiness than the unworthiness of her husband. For well one might perceive she had not rejected the counsel of a glass, and that her hands had pleased themselves in paying the tribute of undeceiving skill to so high perfections of Nature' (403). Sidney stresses the contrast by adding that her appearance was 'so diverse from her sister, who rather suffered sorrow to distress itself in her beauty, than that she would bestow any entertainment of so unwelcome a guest'. Such careful balancing of the sisters extends to the closing episode of the Book, in which Philoclea responds to Lycurgus's suit with 'shamefastness and humbleness' and Pamela to Anaxius's suit with 'choler and disdain'.

The differences between the sisters may seem to suggest the usual conflict between beauty and virtue, variously expressed in the Renaissance as that between the earthly and heavenly Venus, profane and sacred love, or earthly and heavenly beauty. In place of conflict, however, the differences set up a *discordia concors* that is revealed in the harmony of their loving relationship. That harmony expresses the ideal relationship between beauty and virtue, as in Plato's identification of the beautiful with the good.

The climax of the assault upon the sisters leads to their 'identification' with beauty and virtue. Cecropia exhausts all means of persuasion to overcome Pamela's 'noble height' and Philoclea's 'sweet lowliness':

Pamela's determination was built upon so brave a rock that no shot of hers could reach unto it, and Philoclea (though humbly seated) was so environed with sweet rivers of clear virtue as could neither be battered nor undermined; her witty persuasions had wise answers; her eloquence recompensed with sweetness; her threatenings repelled with disdain in the one, and patience in the other; her gifts either not accepted, or accepted to obey but not to bind. (469–70)

When she resorts to terror, 'to all, Virtue and Love resisted, strengthened one by the other'. Finally, she whips them, first, Philoclea: 'she having a rod in her hand (like a fury that should carry wood to the burning of Diana's temple) fell to scourge that most beautiful body, love in vain holding the shield of beauty against her blind cruelty' (471). This image consolidates all earlier visions of Philoclea's beauty, from the moment Pyrocles first sees her picture in which 'all beauty seemed to speak' (18); to his first sight of her as 'the ornament of the earth, the model of heaven, the triumph of nature, the light of beauty, queen of love' (90); to the catalogue of her beauty in his poem (218–22); to his first moment alone with her when he is struck by 'a lightning of beauty' (257). In describing her whipping, Sidney seeks to move the reader, even as Cupid is moved:

The sun drew clouds up to his face from so pitiful a sight; and the very stone walls did yield drops of sweat for agony of such a mischief; each senseless thing had sense of pity; only they that had sense were senseless. Virtue rarely found her worldly weakness more than by the oppression of that day; and weeping Cupid told his weeping mother that he was sorry he was not deaf, as well as blind, that he might never know so lamentable a work. (471)

Such pathos is designed to fix the present moment as an image of Beauty in Philoclea (and an image of vice in Cecropia) which, in terms of the *Defence*, will 'strike, pierce, [and] possess the sight of the soul'.[70]

When Pamela is whipped, in place of a description of her suffering, there is the direct statement: 'if ever the beams of perfection shone through the clouds of affliction, if ever Virtue took a body to show his (else inconceivable) beauty, it was in Pamela' (472). More than a virtuous woman, she is an image of Virtue itself: she manifests, realizes, and literally embodies virtue. She expresses virtue in herself, rather than revealing or symbolizing it: instead of representing virtue as a moral abstraction, she re-presents it 'so in its own natural seat laid to the view, that we seem not to hear of it, but clearly to see through it'. She is what Christophoro Giarda calls 'a symbolic image', one that does not simply display virtue but contains it so far as it may be grasped by the human mind:

We owe it to them [the symbolic images] that the mind which has been banished from heaven into the dark cave of the body, its actions held in bondage by the senses, can behold the beauty and form of the Virtues...

divorced from all matter and yet adumbrated, if not perfectly expressed, in colours, and is thus roused to an even more fervent love and desire for them.[71]

Again in the language of the *Defence*, Sidney presents in Pamela a 'notable image of virtue', one that makes us 'see the form of goodness'. As such, she may be contrasted to the revelation which Pyrocles provides – and which Sidney takes over largely unchanged from the *Old Arcadia* – when he reveals himself to Philoclea as 'a living image, and a present story of what love can do when he is bent to ruin'. He is, as he says, 'a miserable miracle of affection', at most, therefore, an image of passion that warns the reader against giving all for love. As with the image of beauty in Philoclea, the image of virtue in Pamela is designed to move the reader profoundly – not, however, by an appeal to his emotions but by a vision sustained by Plato's faith that 'who could see virtue would be wonderfully ravished with the love of her beauty'. Or in the language of the *New Arcadia*, the reader is 'mind-stricken by the beauty of virtue' in Pamela, as the nobleman of Pontus was by Evarchus; and her effect upon him is that described by Amphialus: 'did ever man's eye look through love upon the majesty of virtue, shining through beauty, but that he became (as it well became him) a captive?' (451–2). At the same time, Pamela remains a woman sustained by her love for Musidorus, and the moment confirms Pyrocles's earlier claim: 'if we love virtue, in whom shall we love it but in a virtuous creature?' (80).[72]

Through the two sieges, Book III analyses human conduct comprehensively, both in doing and suffering. The siege of Amphialus's castle is comprehensive in its display of masculine endeavour: from the purely heroical in the battle between Amphialus and Musidorus, to the comically heroical in the battle between Pyrocles and the three brothers, to the chivalric in the battle between Amphialus and Phalantus, to the anti-chivalric, which ranges from the pathetic encounter between Amphialus and Parthenia to the comic Combat of Cowards. The siege of the princesses is comprehensive as it shows the variety of suffering in the differing responses to Cecropia's assaults, and as the princesses fulfil an ideal of human conduct at the same time that they become fully human.

Book III provides the climax to the *New Arcadia*: it fulfils Sidney's intent to revise the *Old Arcadia* into 'an absolute heroical poem'. As a right poet, he satisfies his own poetic by feigning notable images of virtues, vices, and passions. The 'virtue-breeding delightfulness' of the work brings the reader such knowledge of himself that he becomes capable of virtuous action. In moving him to such action, the whole work achieves the final end of knowledge, which is 'to lead and draw us to as high a perfection as our degenerate souls, made worse by their clayey lodgings, can be capable of'. If its chapters are read as Sidney urges poets to read earlier works – 'devour them whole, and make them wholly theirs' – so that in reading one may 'exercise to know' rather than 'exercise as having known', the reader may so possess the work that he himself is possessed. It will inhabit his memory and judgment for his 'own use and learning' in his private and public lives. So Gabriel Harvey read the work, saying of it: 'he that will love, let him learn to love of him that will teach him to live'.[73] No one may enter truly into the work without leaving it a better person.

On the proper reading of the *New Arcadia*, the final word – as it was in point of time the first – must be given to Greville. Early in his life of Sidney, he notes the changes of fortune of the characters in the *Arcadia*, and says:

In which traverses (I know) his purpose was to limn out such exact pictures of every posture in the mind, that any man being forced, in the strains of this life, to pass through any straits, or latitudes, of good or ill fortune, might (as in a glass) see how to set a good countenance upon all the discountenances of adversity, and a stay upon the exorbitant smilings of chance.[74]

He adds, 'I know this was the first project of these works'; he knows because Sidney told him. At the conclusion to the *Life*, he makes the same point more powerfully: Sidney's end in the *Arcadia* 'was not vanishing pleasure alone, but moral images and examples (as directing threads) to guide every man through the confused labyrinth of his own desires, and life'.[75] Even when one allows that his judgment of Sidney and his works is special pleading – their friendship is recorded from Sidney's comment in a school book, 'foulke griuell is a good boye' to his own epitaph, 'Friend to Sir Philip Sidney' – and admits that he writes nearly a quarter of a century after Sidney's death to honour and idealize him, what he says remains essentially sound, even authoritative.

THE 1593 'ARCADIA'

In 1593 the *Arcadia* was again published, 'now since the first edition augmented and ended'. The text is, in fact, a conflation, or rather a juxtaposition, of the 1590 *Arcadia* and the final three books of the *Old Arcadia*, which have not been revised but only altered and amended. At the break between the two works, a note allows that it is not known how the siege of Amphialus's castle would end, but 'what afterward chanced, out of the author's own writings and conceits hath been supplied'. In a preface H.S. (known to be Hugh Sanford) writes that the 'disfigured face' with which the work had appeared moved the Countess of Pembroke 'to take in hand the wiping away those spots wherewith the beauties thereof were unworthily blemished'. He explains that her work, 'begun in correcting the faults, ended in supplying the defects'. One infers that by 'faults' he means the division of the 1590 *Arcadia* into chapters, the chapter summaries, and chiefly the selection and arrangement of the eclogues, and by 'defects', its unfinished state. Sanford allows that the amended version is 'the conclusion, not the perfection of *Arcadia*' but claims that this is 'no further than the author's own writings, or known determinations, could direct'. Since the new edition has been edited by the Countess 'most by her doing, all by her directing', he concludes by noting that as the *Arcadia* was first done 'for her' now it is done 'by her'. Unfortunately, what is said as flattery may be taken to imply (wrongly, I believe) that the Countess, abetted by Sanford, went beyond Sidney's 'known determinations'.

The only other evidence of Sidney's 'determinations' is Greville's letter to Sir Francis Walsingham in November 1586: he refers to a correction of the *Old Arcadia* which he believes 'fitter to be printed than that first, which is so common; notwithstanding, even that to be amended by a direction set down under his own hand, how and why'.[76] The 'correction', edited by him, became the 1590 *Arcadia*; for him, 'fitter to be printed than that first' because of its higher seriousness. Sidney left him the manuscript of the revised *Arcadia* because it is his book, even as the

Old Arcadia, which he wrote for the Countess, is her book. Greville seems to have been no more concerned with its incomplete state than was Spenser whose *Faerie Queene* was published in the same year – and by the same publisher – similarly incomplete. (Readers of both works are left with parallel questions: how will Pamela and Philoclea / Britomart and Florimell join their lovers?.) Greville would not amend any of Sidney's unpublished works, 'for I think it falls within the reach of no man living', even though he was aware of Sidney's direction 'how and why' the concluding books of the *Old Arcadia* should be amended.

The general nature of Sidney's direction becomes clear when the final books of the *Old Arcadia* are compared to the 1593 text.[77] There is one major revision and one major alteration. In the *Old Arcadia*, Pyrocles goes to Philoclea's room to seduce her, and he does so. In the 1593 version, he goes to persuade her to elope; and although they fall asleep on her bed, their embrace extends no lower than their necks. In the *Old Arcadia*, Musidorus determines to rape the sleeping Pamela but is interrupted by rebels; in the 1593 version, he is interrupted when he is engaged only in placing his face near hers to suck up her breath. These two changes require many minor revisions. For example, in the *Old Arcadia* when Pyrocles arranges to go to Philoclea, he plans to use the time 'to the full performance of her [i.e. his] violent affection': in the 1593 version, he plans to use the time 'to the best purpose'; the two lovers fall asleep in the *Old Arcadia* from 'the too high degree of their joys': in the 1593 version, from 'the unresistible force of their sorrows'; and Philoclea's 'uttermost point of contentment' becomes the 'uttermost point of woefulness'. The suggestion in the *Old Arcadia* that they fall asleep because their souls were 'lifted up with extremity of love after mutual satisfaction' is deleted. The 1593 version omits all references to Musidorus's attempted rape of Pamela, such as the statement that she was 'in a shrewd likelihood to have had great part of her trust in Musidorus deceived, and found herself robbed of that she had laid in store as her dearest jewel', and that, upon being interrupted, he was enraged 'betwixt a repentant shame of his promise-breaking attempt and the tyrannical fire of lust, which, having already caught hold of so sweet and fit a fuel, was past the calling back of reason's counsel'.

Such revisions and omissions could be made by any close reader of the text who was instructed by a direction to delete the seduction and rape, especially since he was shown 'how' to do it by Sidney's own careful revision of the erotic climax at the end of the *Old Arcadia*, Book III.[78] The reason 'why', is simply that the *New Arcadia* makes such conduct unthinkable. The direction may have suggested also that the *Old Arcadia* be accommodated to the *New* in its names, places, conventions, and added episodes, but that would hardly be necessary.

Yet this direction has not survived. Nor is it known when Sidney made it. Robertson suggests that the changes were intended for the *New Arcadia* as it stood before the new Book III was written, because Sidney's revised account of Evarchus's journey to Arcadia in Book v of the 1593 version takes no account of events in that Book.[79] An equally persuasive reason to me is that Book III makes the continuation of the story in the *Old Arcadia* inadequate, however much revised. The two sisters could not be subject to absurd masculine aggression after what they have endured from Cecropia.[80] As a consequence, the 1593 *Arcadia* remains two separate works, or rather, one work which is essentially complete as it stands, even though unfinished, and a fragment of a different work.

When Sanford defended the new edition, he digressed to attack worthless readers who 'can never worthily esteem of so worthy a writing', and in particular those poor souls who cannot delight in the flowers in Arcadia: 'they are roses, not flowers, must do them good'. John Florio, who may have helped Greville edit the 1590 *Arcadia*, seems to have interpreted these words – his name signifies 'flowers' – as a personal attack; if he did, he would have been offended by the allusion to Apuleius's *Metamorphoses* – Lucius, transformed into an ass, must search for roses to restore him to human shape. In the preface to *A World of Words* (1598) he mocks an H.S. for his name,[81] and in dedicating his translation of Book II of Montaigne's *Essays* (1603) to the Countess of Rutland (Sidney's daughter) and to Lady Penelope Rich, he replies to Sanford's attack on the 'disfigured face' of the 1590 *Arcadia*: 'I know, nor this [i.e. Montaigne's *Essays*], nor any I have seen, or can conceive, in this or other language, can in aught be compared to that perfect-unperfect *Arcadia*.' His argument against the composite 1593 text is unanswerable: since Sidney 'lived not to mend or end it', 'this end we see of it, though at first above all [he speaks in praise of the trial-scene in the *Old Arcadia*], now is not answerable to the precedents'. The result of patching the 1590 text was 'more marring that was well, than mending what was amiss'. Unfortunately, for the reader's proper appreciation and understanding of both the *Old Arcadia* and the *New*, the unnatural 1593 hybrid became the standard text until the present century.

CONCLUSION

Sidney's greatness as a writer rests finally on the 1590 *Arcadia*. It is his major work, unique in its kind and the prose equivalent to Spenser's *Faerie Queene*, as both poets 'honour right virtue and brave valour'.[82] In exemplifying the nature and working of the right poet, it becomes 'a kind of touchstone' for the English literary Renaissance, as C. S. Lewis notes:

What a man thinks of it, far more than what he thinks of Shakespeare or Spenser or Donne, tests the depth of his sympathy with the sixteenth century. For it is, as Carrara says of the earlier Italian *Arcadia*, a work of distillation. It gathers up what a whole generation wanted to say. The very gallimaufry that it is – medieval, Protestant, pastoral, Stoical, Platonic – made it the more characteristic and, as long as that society lasted, more satisfactory.[83]

Its relation to Sidney, and to the reader, may be indicated even by its unfinished state.

There is no evidence to explain why Sidney left the work incomplete, with even the final sentence incomplete, allowing Pyrocles and Anaxius to fight forever, as though in a painting. It is tempting to imagine him scribbling furiously until the final moment when he was forced to exchange his pen for a sword and sail for the Netherlands. However, the unfinished sentence may well be the fault of the scribe, or of the foul papers from which he copied. (The latter possibility would explain why, after Greville's letter in 1586 urging that the revised *Arcadia* was 'fitter to be printed than the first', there was a delay of two years before it was registered and two more before it was published.) Possibly, as noted above, it may have been difficult for Sidney to revise the later books after adding Book III. Or the obvious explanation may

be the correct one – Sidney's death. At the end of the 1590 text,
the editor of the 1613 edition adds: 'thus far the worthy author
had revised or enlarged that first written Arcadia of his. . .having
a purpose likewise to have new ordered, augmented, and concluded the rest, had he not been prevented by untimely death'.[84]

If none of these explanations is correct, it may be that the
truncated ending is deliberate. Greville records of Sidney that 'his
end was not writing, even while he wrote. . .but both his wit and
understanding bent upon his heart, to make himself and others,
not in words or opinion, but in life and action, good and great'.[85]
If it is true, as I have argued, that Sidney sought to fulfil in the
work the virtues which he despaired of being able to fulfil in virtuous action for his country – in it fashioning images of virtue
even as his life had been fashioned from birth – the *Arcadia*
rightly remains incomplete. It is unfinished because his life was
unfinished, and he expected always to be summoned to virtuous
action; but chiefly because it is to be finished by the reader. After
nearly three books had been written, and particularly after the
visions of Beauty and Virtue in Philoclea and Pamela, there was
no need to continue, as there was no need for Spenser to complete
the *Faerie Queene* after its six books, and particularly after the
vision of the source of the virtues in the four Graces. Both poets
had written enough, no matter how much more could be written,
'to fashion a gentleman or noble person in virtuous and gentle
discipline'. Accordingly, at the end of the *Life*, Greville may
praise 'that unperfected shape' of Sidney's work because of its
'excellent intended pattern'.

Whatever the explanation of its unfinished state, the 1590
Arcadia stands as Sidney's central and climactic work in that it
feigns notable images of virtues, vices, and the passions. Of his
other writings, perhaps *The Lady of May* is too slight to deserve
a significant place in the canon. As his first work, however, it
showed him how a modest entertainment could treat seriously the
nature and quality of human life. In the *Old Arcadia* and in
Astrophel and Stella, he presents images of passion in conflict with
virtue. Writing these works, he came to understand that the business of the poet is to present images also of the virtues and vices.
Images of virtue show all that life should be; images of vice all
that life should not be; and images of passion show the variety of

man's conduct in his present life in relation to these antithetical visions. By presenting all three kinds of image, the 1590 *Arcadia* becomes Sidney's most comprehensive work.

Yet that work is central and climactic chiefly because it is designed to move the reader to virtuous action. In possessing its images so that he is possessed by them, the reader is involved wholly, immediately, and profoundly. Other poets in his tradition seek this same end through different methods, as Spenser in the *Faerie Queene* sensuously assaults his reader by his descriptions and Milton in *Paradise Lost* entangles him by his argument.[86] For Sidney, reading is rapture, yet also release, for its further end is to make 'life and action good and great'. This further end adds to the gaiety and wonder of his poem a profound seriousness.

Such a view of the poet's relation to the reader is fragile, because it requires profound faith in the power of the word, in eloquence allied to wisdom, and in delight as natural to man. That delight upon which poetry depends may be abused, as Sidney recognized on his death-bed when he asked that the *Arcadia* be burned. Earlier, however, his faith was sustained by youthful optimism: he was about 23 when he started to write the *Old Arcadia*, about 26 when he was engaged in writing the *Defence*, and under 30 when he completed the *New Arcadia*. It was also sustained because he lived and wrote in the sixteenth century before the power over nature, which he claims for poetry, was claimed by an increasingly strident Puritanism and the growth of modern science.

In turn, his faith sustains the literary Renaissance in England in the late sixteenth and early seventeenth centuries. In large part through Sidney's influence, English Renaissance literature is secular, as it serves immediately to move men to virtuous action in the world, and Christian, as its final end is 'to lead and draw us to as high a perfection as our degenerate souls, made worse by their clayey lodgings, can be capable of'. That influence extends even to Milton, the last and greatest exponent of Sidney's faith, in his claim that literature is 'doctrinal and exemplary to a nation' and serves 'beside the office of a pulpit, to imbreed and cherish in a great people the seeds of virtue, and public civility'.[87]

Appendix

The genealogy of the chief characters in the *New Arcadia*

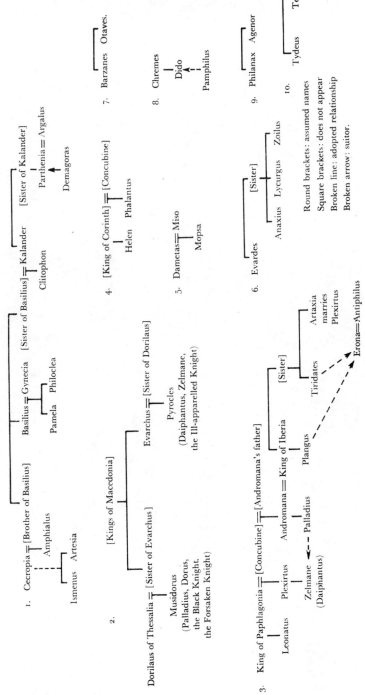

Abbreviations

ଊଊଊଊଊଊଊଊଊଊଊଊଊଊଊଊଊଊଊଊଊଊଊଊଊଊଊଊଊଊଊଊଊ

ABBREVIATIONS FOR SIDNEY'S WORKS

AS   *Astrophel and Stella*
CS   *Certain sonnets*
LM *The Lady of May*
NA *New Arcadia*
OA *Old Arcadia*

REFERENCES FOR EDITIONS OF SIDNEY'S WORKS

Feuillerat *The complete works of Sir Philip Sidney,* ed Albert Feuillerat. Cambridge 1912–26. Volumes cited: I. *NA*; II. 1593 *Arcadia*; III. Correspondence

Levy *The correspondence of Sir Philip Sidney and Hubert Languet, 1573–1576*, tr. and ed Charles Samuel Levy, unpub. doctoral diss. Cornell 1962

Pears *The correspondence of Sir Philip Sidney and Hubert Languet,* tr. Steuart A. Pears. 1845

Prose *Miscellaneous prose of Sir Philip Sidney,* ed Katherine Duncan-Jones and Jan von Dorsten. Oxford 1973. Prose cited: *Defence of the Earl of Leicester; A defence of poetry; Discourse on Irish affairs; LM; A letter written...to Queen Elizabeth;* George Gifford, *The manner of Sir Philip Sidney's death*

Ringler *The poems of Sir Philip Sidney,* ed William A. Ringler, jr. Oxford 1962

Robertson Sir Philip Sidney, *The Countess of Pembroke's Arcadia* (The *Old Arcadia*), ed Jean Robertson. Oxford 1973

Shepherd Sir Philip Sidney, *An apology for poetry,* ed Geoffrey Shepherd. 1965

ABBREVIATIONS FOR JOURNALS

CBEL *Cambridge Bibliography of English Literature*
CL   *Comparative Literature*
ELH   *Journal of English Literary History*
ELN   *English Language Notes*

ELR	*English Literary Renaissance*
ES	*English Studies*
HLQ	*Huntington Library Quarterly*
JEGP	*Journal of English and Germanic Philology*
JWCI	*Journal of the Warburg and Courtauld Institutes*
MLQ	*Modern Language Quarterly*
MLR	*Modern Language Review*
MP	*Modern Philology*
PLL	*Papers on Language and Literature*
PQ	*Philological Quarterly*
RES	*Review of English Studies*
RQ	*Renaissance Quarterly*
SEL	*Studies in English Literature*
SP	*Studies in Philology*
TSLL	*Texas Studies in Literature and Language*

Notes

CHAPTER 1

1 James M. Osborn, *Young Philip Sidney, 1572–1577* (New Haven 1972) 54.
2 Malcolm William Wallace, *The life of Sir Philip Sidney* (Cambridge 1915) 69.
3 *Defence of the Earl of Leicester*, in *Miscellaneous prose of Sir Philip Sidney*, ed Katherine Duncan-Jones and Jan van Dorsten (Oxford 1973) 134.
4 Osborn 246.
5 George Whetstone, *Sir Philip Sidney: his honourable life, his valiant death and true virtues* (1587) $B_3{}^r$.
6 *The copy of a letter [Leicester's commonwealth]* (1584) 196.
7 *Prose* 139.
8 The motto is Ulysses's reproof to Ajax who claims that he deserves Achilles's arms because of the deeds of his ancestors (Ovid, *Metamorphoses* xiii 141). Like Spenser's Red Cross Knight, Sidney wears borrowed armour for which he must prove himself worthy. On his keen interest in *imprese*, see Katherine Duncan-Jones, 'Sidney's personal *imprese*', *JWCI* 33 (1970) 321–4.
9 *The complete works of Sir Philip Sidney*, ed Albert Feuillerat (Cambridge 1912–26) iii 139.
10 See Lawrence Stone, *The crisis of the aristocracy 1558–1641* (Oxford 1965) 385. He notes (403) that 'by the 1580s the key to advancement lay at the Court'.
11 Sir Fulke Greville, *Life of Sir Philip Sidney* etc. (1652), ed Nowell Smith (Oxford 1907) 146, 148. The work was written between 1610 and 1614; see Joan Rees, *Fulke Greville, Lord Brooke* (1971) 25.
12 William Camden, *Remains concerning Britain* (1605) 174.
13 Feuillerat iii 140.
14 Greville 67–8.
15 Noted Edmund Molyneux, in Holinshed, *Chronicles* (1587) 1550.
16 Wallace 71.
17 Wallace 169.
18 Roger Howell, *Sir Philip Sidney, the Shepherd Knight* (1968) 5. Virgil B. Heltzel and Hoyt H. Hudson, ed and tr. *Nobilis* [1589] by Thomas Moffet (San Marino 1940) xxiii, note that 'all of the early writers upon Sidney laid as much stress upon his death as upon his life', for they felt

that his death 'was as great and as full of significance as his life – that, indeed, the end crowned the work'.

19 Greville 41.

20 Sir Walter Raleigh, 'Epitaph upon the right honourable Sir Philip Sidney', in Spenser, *Minor poems*, ed Ernest de Sélincourt (Oxford 1910) 366. Unfortunately, the elegies on Sidney must be heavily discounted because they compete in fulsome praise. Sidney's reputation and influence have been traced by W. H. Bond, unpub. diss. (Harvard 1941) and his emerging legend by R. S. Esplin, unpub. diss. (Utah 1970). See also Jan van Dorsten, *Poets, patrons, and professors: Sir Philip Sidney, Daniel Rogers, and the Leiden humanists* (1962) 152–66 and Appendix I.

21 Desiderius Erasmus, *The education of a Christian prince*, tr. Lester K. Born (New York 1936) 154. On the humanist emphasis upon public service, see John M. Major, *Sir Thomas Elyot and Renaissance humanism* (Lincoln, Neb. 1964). Wallace 373 notes that the Burgomaster and Council of Flushing esteemed Sidney an ideal governor.

22 John Stow, *The annals of England* (1592) 1245.

23 *Sir Philip Sidney* B$_2$^{v}.

24 Greville 129–30.

25 Greville 138, 16. In *The Ruins of Time* 594–5 Spenser records that Sidney, 'most sweetly sung the prophecy / Of his own death in doleful elegy'.

26 Greville 135. George Gifford, 'The manner of Sir Philip Sidney's death', in *Prose* 169.

27 Greville 137. On Sidney's interest in 'the opinion of the ancient heathen', see D. P. Walker, *The ancient theology* (1972) 132–63.

28 Chapter 15 is entitled 'That the immortality of the soul hath been taught by the philosophers of old time'.

29 Arthur Collins, *Letters and memorials of state* (1746) 1 246. Greville 6 records that he heard Sir Henry call his son *lumen familiae suae*.

30 Epistle to *The tragedy of Philotas* (1605) 77–87. Cf. Gabriel Harvey, *Pierce's supererogation* (1593), *Elizabethan critical essays*, ed G. Gregory Smith (Oxford 1904) ii 260: 'England, since it was England, never bred more honourable minds, more adventurous hearts, more valorous hands, or more excellent wits, than of late.' See Harry Levin, *The myth of the golden age in the Renaissance* (New York 1969).

31 Shelley, *Adonais* (1821) XLV 5–7.

32 Wallace 401, 400. Richard A. Lanham, 'Sidney: the ornament of his age', *Southern Review* (Adelaide) 2 (1967) 319–40, seeks to debunk the legend but all he is able to suggest is that the idealistic Sidney was not cunning enough in political matters.

33 *Prose* 143.

34 *Apology for Smectymnus, Complete prose works*, ed D. M. Wolfe *et al.* (New Haven 1953–. The Yale edn) 1 890. Cf. Jonson, Preface to *Volpone, Works*, ed C. H. Herford, P. and E. M. Simpson (Oxford 1925–52) v 17: 'the impossibility of any man's being the good poet, without first being a good man'.

35 Scipio Gentili, Dedication to *The assembly of Plato* (1584); cited

Thomas Zouch, *Memoirs of the life and writings of Sir Philip Sidney* (York 1808–9) 308. The few contemporary references are noted by William A. Ringler, jr, ed, *The poems of Sir Philip Sidney* (Oxford 1962) lxi–lxii, and by John Buxton, *Sir Philip Sidney and the English Renaissance* (1954) chap. 5. Especially noteworthy is Geoffrey Whitney's praise of Sidney's 'vein in verse' as Surrey's successor: 'More sweet than honey, was the style, that from his pen did flow, / Wherewith, in youth he us'd to banish idle fits; / That now, his works of endless fame delight the worthy wits. / No halting verse he writes, but matcheth former times, / No Cherillus he can abide, nor poet's patched rhymes' (*A choice of emblems*, Leiden 1586, 196–7). Whitney adds that Sidney refused his praise, saying that it belonged to Dyer. See Dorsten, *Poets* 137–8. Dorsten 62–7 adds a poem by Daniel Rogers, dated 14 January 1579, in praise of Sidney as a poet: 'when your [poetic] passion seizes our arts, then how abundant are the streams in which your wit flows forth'. See also Dorsten, 'Gruterus and Sidney's *Arcadia*', *RES* 16 (1965) 174–7.

36 His first work, *The Lady of May*, remained untitled until 1725. His *Defence of poetry* was published in 1595 in two independent editions, one entitled *The defence of poesy* and the other *An apology for poetry*. The *Arcadia* has appeared in three separate texts: an original version (called the *Old Arcadia*) in 1926, a revised but incomplete version (called the *New Arcadia*) in 1590, and a composite version (the *New Arcadia* completed by the *Old*) in 1593. To compound confusion, *Astrophel and Stella*, which appeared twice in 1591 in pirated editions, has been re-entitled *Astrophil and Stella* in Ringler's edition. I prefer the spelling 'Astrophel' for the sake of assonance, as I note in *ELH* 36 (1969) 60: for the sake of the Greek root and the play upon Philip, 'Astrophil' by itself may be allowed, as Ringler 458 argues, following Mona Wilson in her edition of the poem (London 1931, xvi–xvii); but the only spelling when coupled with Stella can be 'Astrophel'. No one can *say* 'Astrophil and Stella'.

37 Thomas Nashe, 'Preface to *Astrophel and Stella*', *Works*, ed R. B. McKerrow (1904–10) iii 329; Ringler 542.

38 Ringler lviii.

39 *Prose* 186.

40 Virginia Woolf, *The second common reader* (New York 1932) 48. Buxton 135 writes: 'the *Arcadia* was probably the first literary work of any kind to be translated from English into either French or Italian. Truly Sidney had set English on the way to become one of the chief literatures of Europe.'

41 Ringler xxxvi.

42 Sir Philip Sidney, *An apology for poetry*, ed Geoffrey Shepherd (1965) 9.

43 Ringler li.

44 Richard B. Young, *English Petrarke: a study of Sidney's 'Astrophel and Stella'* (New Haven 1958); C. S. Lewis, *English literature in the sixteenth century* (Oxford 1954) 339; Shepherd 11.

45 Shepherd 11. Robert Kimbrough, *Sir Philip Sidney* (New York 1971)

Preface, claims that 'the life of Sidney and the nature of his art must be studied together'.

46 Greville 77–8.

47 *Defence* 89.

48 *Discoveries, Works* VIII 595.

49 As source of the prison scene, Walter R. Davis, *A map of Arcadia: Sidney's romance in its tradition* (New Haven 1965) 63, cites Duplessis-Mornay's *Trueness of the Christian religion* (1587) 246, part of which Sidney translated: 'And therefore we ought surely to say that this mind or reason ought not to be ever in prison...as man is prepared in his mother's womb to be brought forth into the world, so is he also after a sort prepared in this body and in this world to live in another world.'

50 *Defence* 79.

51 H. J. C. Grierson, *Cross currents in English literature of the seventeenth century* (1929). For the general background to the two views of man's nature, see Theodore Spencer, *Shakespeare and the nature of man* (Cambridge, Mass. 1942) and Thomas Greene, 'The flexibility of the self in Renaissance literature', *The disciplines of criticism*, ed Peter Demetz *et al.* (New Haven 1968) 241–64. G. F. Waller, '"This matching of contraries": Bruno, Calvin and the Sidney circle', *Neophilologus* 56 (1972) 331–43, discusses the intellectual tension in Sidney between the Magical tradition of Bruno and the Calvinist tradition.

52 Douglas Bush, *English literature in the earlier seventeenth century 1600–1660* (Oxford 1962) 37. To illustrate Bush's point briefly: when Sidney refers in the *Defence* to the mind 'not enclosed within the narrow warrant of her [Nature's] gifts, but freely ranging', he suggests his affinity with Pico, who urges: 'let us fly beyond the chambers of the world to the chamber nearest the most lofty divinity' (*On the dignity of man*, tr. C. G. Wallis, New York 1965, 7). Yet he is careful to add that man's mind ranges 'only within the zodiac of his own wit'. Similarly, when he writes that learning may 'lift up the mind from the dungeon of the body to the enjoying his own divine essence', he would seem to endorse Bruno's sonnet on the soul: 'I spread proud pinions to the wind, and contemn the world, and further my way toward heaven' (*The heroic frenzies*, tr. P. E. Memmo, jr, Chapel Hill 1966, 118). Yet he has already noted that man's soul is 'degenerate' and may be drawn only 'to as high a perfection' as it 'can be capable of', which may not prove very high.

53 *Of education, Complete prose works* II 366–7.

54 *Tetrachordon, Complete prose works* II 587.

55 Greville 35.

CHAPTER 2

1 The 'fundamental unity and inner consistency', which Neil L. Rudenstine, *Sidney's poetic development* (Cambridge, Mass. 1967) viii, traces in Sidney's poetry, one would expect to find in a major poet whose career is crammed into four to six years (1578–84). Rudenstine

fully supports his claim for 'the technical aspects of Sidney's growth as a poet'.

2 *OA* 334–5.

3 See Katherine Duncan-Jones, 'Sidney and Samothea', *RES* 25 (1974) 174–7.

4 The purpose of the trip was 'for his attaining the knowledge of foreign languages' (see John Buxton and Bent Juel-Jensen, 'Sir Philip Sidney's first passport rediscovered', *Library* 5th ser. 25, 1970, 42–6); in so doing, he attained European stature as a future leader of the Protestant League. His tour has been exhaustively treated by Buxton 33–80 and by Osborn. Buxton 34 writes: 'How did the boy of seventeen who set out for France in the spring of 1572 achieve, in three years' residence on the Continent, a reputation from Italy to the Low Countries, from France to Poland, that no other Englishman would rival till the days when Marlborough went there to war, and that only Byron among the English poets has ever equalled? The story is astonishing, almost incredible; and yet the evidence remains.'

5 *The correspondence of Sir Philip Sidney and Hubert Languet*, tr. Steuart A. Pears (1845) 2.

6 *OA* 365.

7 Holinshed, *Chronicles* 1554.

8 Osborn 138.

9 Greville 42. Osborn 525–8 reproduces the Queen's instructions to Sidney. Jan van Dorsten, 'Sidney and Languet', *HLQ* 29 (1966) 221, notes that Sidney sought also 'an all-embracing Confession of Faith, to be drawn up by the Protestant churches of England, Poland, Germany, and other countries'. On the political aspirations of the Leicester-faction, of which Sidney was spokesman, see R. C. Strong and Jan van Dorsten, *Leicester's triumph* (1964).

10 Osborn 477.

11 Collins I 100.

12 Greville 27. Osborn 529–31 argues that 'Certain notes concerning the present state of the Prince of Orange in May 1577' (see 481–90) was written by Sidney as a summary of their conversations to be presented to the Queen.

13 Collins I 193. Pietro Bizari, *Senatus populique genuensis rerum* (1579), cited Osborn 495, writes that the embassy proved Sidney to be 'so clearly the exemplar of the heroic spirit and the prudent, well-educated young man, that almost anyone could anticipate where his precocious and unique talent might direct him'.

14 Collins I 193.

15 See Marion Jones, 'The court and the dramatists', *Elizabethan theatre* (Stratford-upon-Avon studies 9, 1966) 180.

16 Ringler 362.

17 Sir Philip Sidney, *The Countess of Pembroke's Arcadia* (The *Old Arcadia*), ed Jean Robertson (Oxford 1973) xviii. Duncan-Jones, *Prose* 13, concludes that 'the evidence on neither side seems strong enough for one to make a firm decision between the two years'.

18 C. H. Herford in Jonson, *Works* II 256; Ringler 361. Stephen Orgel,

The Jonsonian masque (Cambridge, Mass. 1965) 44–57, discusses Sidney's handling of the masque. In it, he finds that 'the validity of the conventional antithesis of pastoral – contemplation versus action – is to be thought through again from the beginning, debated, and judged'. Duncan-Jones, *Prose* 15, notes its literary achievement: 'on a small scale it is an authentic drama with characters, rather than an assemblage of allegorical lay-figures or rustic grotesques'.

19 Ringler 363 notes that the concluding song 'was ingeniously devised to be appropriate to whichever suitor was adjudged victor by the Queen'. Kimbrough 64–6 speculates that the Queen was expected to choose the forester, Therion, who is 'clearly a Leicester-figure', rather than the shepherd, Espilus; but Duncan-Jones, *Prose* 14, concludes soundly that 'it is unlikely that Sidney would be so foolish as to devise an entertainment in which the Queen could make a blunder'. Ringler 362 speculates that there may be some hidden topical allusion: Therion may represent Leicester and his followers who advocated a warlike policy on the continent, and Espilus those who favour peace. In the absence of evidence, one may speculate equally that Therion represents the Dudley's who had served the Queen well but violently, and Espilus the Sidney family who had served her faithfully but drably. However, both allusions ignore the poverty–wealth antithesis which is central to the difference between the suitors.

20 David Kalstone, *Sidney's poetry: contexts and interpretations* (Cambridge, Mass. 1965) 43, notes that 'both works share a playful attitude not only toward the abuses of rhetoric, but also toward the extravagances of pastoral'. On the verbal spectacle in *Love's Labour's Lost*, see my *The early Shakespeare* (San Marino 1967) 128–42.

21 George Puttenham, *The art of English poesy*, ed Gladys Doidge Willcock and Alice Walker (Cambridge 1936) 299.

22 Guarini, *Il pastor fido*, IV Chorus.

23 *The Faerie Queene* IV viii 30.

24 It is fitting that among the last poems that Sidney wrote is a 'Dispraise of a courtly life'. In it, he prefers 'shepherd's treasure' to 'this false, fine, courtly pleasure', for life is 'Better filled with contenting, / Void of wishing and repenting'.

25 Charles Wilson, *Queen Elizabeth and the revolt of the Netherlands* (1970) 43, sees the years from 1576–9 as 'a political and military watershed in European history. What was at stake was not merely the future of a sizable territory and the most advanced economy of the contemporary world: it was the future of Europe itself for the next three centuries.' See Osborn 497. Howell provides the best recent account of the political affairs in which Sidney was involved during these years.

26 Wallace 199.

27 Pears 146.

28 *Prose* 11.

29 The date offered tentatively by Duncan-Jones, *Prose* 34. She notes correctly that 'there is in fact no contemporary evidence that the Queen in any sense banished Sidney'. At most one may infer that the

Letter would not further his fortunes and, with other factors, led him in a sense to banish the court.

30 Sir Thomas More, *Utopia*, ed J. Churton Collins (Oxford 1904) 40–1. For Castiglione, it was essential for the courtier to retain the favour of his prince. G. K. Hunter, *John Lyly: the humanist as courtier* (1962) chap. 1, traces the frustration of the humanists in their effort to be politically effective as courtiers to Elizabeth.

31 Pears 170. The closest Greville ever comes to criticizing his idol is to ask of Sidney's opposition to the proposed marriage, 'whether it were not an error, and a dangerous one, for Sir Philip, being neither magistrate nor counsellor, to oppose himself against his sovereign's pleasure in things indifferent?' (60–1). As one would expect, he concludes that Sidney was right to do so.

32 Pears 185.

33 Holinshed, *Chronicles* 1552.

34 Wallace 401. Cf. Osborn 500: 'he lacked the agility, adaptability, and capacity to accept what was possible in place of what was desirable, qualities necessary for continuing success in court politics. Duplicity, the standard practice at court, was not one of Sidney's skills.'

35 Anthony Esler, *The aspiring mind of the Elizabethan younger generation* (Durham, N. C. 1966) 67–8, 59.

36 Greville 35.

37 *The correspondence of Sir Philip Sidney and Hubert Languet, 1573–1576*, tr. and ed Charles Samuel Levy, unpub. doctoral diss. (Cornell University 1962) 193. Cf. Languet's letter of 3 December 1575: 'Do not think that God bestowed so fine a mind upon you for you to let it decay through disuse; but believe instead that he demands more of you than of others to whom he has been less generous' (Levy 301).

38 Pears 75–6.

39 Pears 144.

40 Wallace 69.

41 Greville 6.

42 Moffet 71, 83. Languet, who knew Sidney best, warns him that 'by nature and inclination you are formed for gentleness' (Pears 177).

43 See Dorsten, *Poets* 66. James E. Phillips, 'Daniel Rogers: a neo-Latin link between the Pléiade and Sidney's "Areopagus" ', *Neo-Latin poetry of the sixteenth and seventeenth centuries* (Los Angeles 1965) 7, argues that the movement of the Areopagus, which included Sidney, Dyer, and Spenser, 'was at least highly conscious of itself as a group concerned with new literary, philosophical, and religious ideas far more significant than mere versifying'.

44 Levy 49. In another letter in the same month, Languet urges Sidney to 'shake off that occasionally excessive melancholy of yours' (Levy 61).

45 Levy 69–70. Cf. *AS* 23.

46 Pears 127.

47 Pears 143.

48 Pears 150. Osborn 501–2 notes that Sidney was awarded a post in the Admiralty that was never confirmed.

49 Pears 182–6.
50 Feuillerat III 129.
51 As summarized by Wallace 226.
52 Pears 167.
53 Jonson, 'To Sir Henry Savile', *Works* VIII 61. Cf. Belphoebe's defence of the active life, which includes the life of the scholar–writer, against the life of courtly ease: 'Abroad in arms, at home in studious kind / Who seeks with painful toil, shall honour soonest find' (*The Faerie Queene* II iii 40). Rudenstine 292 cites a pertinent letter by Languet to Sidney in 1579: 'you wrote to me that you had long struggled to attain a state wherein it would be possible for you to be lazy (*ut tibi liceat esse pigrum*), and that those who called laziness in you a vice were being unfair'. Sidney may have expressed Aristotle's claim, *Ethics* 1177b, that the end of life is leisure, conceived not as idleness but as a state to which man aspires to the extent that a divine principle dwells in him. See Josef Pieper, *Leisure the basis of culture*, tr. Alexander Dru (1952) on the medieval distinction between leisure and laziness. In the previous year, Sidney had spoken of 'that particle of the divine mind [*divinae mentis particula*]' (Pears 143) possessed by man.
54 Pears 143. He makes the same point in the *Defence* 91: 'as Aristotle saith, it is not γνῶσις but πρᾶξις, must be the fruit'.
55 Osborn 537.
56 *Defence* 83.
57 Holinshed, *Chronicles* 1554. Apparently, Molyneux does not distinguish between the *Old Arcadia* and the *New*.
58 Feuillerat III 132. Robertson xvi suggests the reading 'books'. She concludes that 'the evidence points to the composition of the bulk of the story when he [Sidney] was at Wilton and Ivy Church from March to August 1580'.
59 *The history of the Houses of Douglas and Angus* (Edinburgh 1644) 362.
60 Thomas Howell, *Devises* (1581), ed Walter Raleigh (Oxford 1906) 44–5.
61 Cited Ringler 530.
62 Spenser, 'Letter to Harvey', 5 October 1579, *Poetical works*, ed J. C. Smith & E. de Sélincourt (Oxford 1912) 635. The archaisms in one of the third eclogues of the *OA* lead Ringler 413 to conclude that it 'may be a deliberate experiment in the Spenserian manner'.
63 Rudenstine 16–19 has established the close connection between the Languet letters and the *Old Arcadia*, and cites a number of the parallels noted below.
64 Pears 155.
65 Pears 2. Pyrocles admits twice that love for Philoclea leads him to reject his father. He tells her that she has made him 'neglect his country, forget his father, and lastly forsake himself' (120); and when he contemplates the consummation of their love, 'all the great estate of his father seemed unto him but a trifling pomp, whose good stands in other men's conceit' (228).

66 Rudenstine 293.

67 *OA* 254–9. Philisides's enigmatic fable on the subject of monarchical government may convey the general moral that 'a powerful aristocracy is the best safeguard of the common people against tyranny' (Ringler 413) but Jan van Dorsten, *Terug naar de toekomst* (Leiden 1971) 7, 16, argues convincingly that the fable applies genearlly to Sidney's role in the political events of 1579 and specifically (in a typically mannerist manner) to the theme of responsibility treated in the *Old Arcadia*.

68 Kalstone 59.

69 Mark Rose, 'Sidney's womanish man', *RES* 15 (1964) 353–63, argues that the Amazon disguise is the mark of spiritual effeminacy, which follows his yielding to passionate love. Musidorus argues the same – 'this effeminate love of a woman doth so womanize a man that, if you yield to it, it will...make you a famous Amazon' (*OA* 20) – until love teaches him otherwise.

70 See Richard A. Lanham, *The Old Arcadia* (New Haven 1965) chap. iv. Rudenstine 33 claims that Sidney's attitude to his lovers 'remains generally sympathetic, indulgent, worldly-wise'.

71 Robertson uses the spelling 'Euarchus', which I find persuasive for its etymology, εὔαρχος, good ruler; on balance, however, I am persuaded by the claims for 'Evarchus' given by Franklin B. Williams, jr in *RQ* 27 (1974) 240–2. Yet see her rejoinder, *RQ* 28 (1975) 298–9.

72 The princes share the conviction provised in Evarchus: 'the secret assurance of his own worthiness (which, although it be never so well clothed in modesty, yet always lives in the worthiest minds)' (362). Ironically, this conviction leads him to accept the role of judge over his son and nephew. Cf. Sidney's comment, as narrator, in praise of Pyrocles's trust in his own courage: 'for, indeed, the confidence in oneself is the chief nurse of true magnanimity' (289).

73 *AS* 21.

74 *NA* 185.

75 That Sidney would not regard romances simply as 'light reading' is indicated by his defence of *Amadis of Gaul* (*Defence* 92). Lacking any evidence of his personal reading habits, one clutches at straws, for example, Languet's exhortation to him in December 1575 that he need not yield to idle pleasure if he remembers the many excellent writers he has read from whom he has learned so many things...which concern the right ordering of one's life' (Levy 300). Since the writers whom Sidney read under Languet's direction would have been philosophers and historians, perhaps he found that they helped him little, and that in the company of his sister he began to learn, what later he expresses in the *Defence*, that poetry may best teach man the 'right ordering' of his life, for 'the poet ... doth draw the mind more effectually than any other art doth' (94). One may compare John Stuart Mill's mental crisis when his beliefs collapsed and he turned to poetry, specifically to Wordsworth, as 'a medicine for my state of mind'.

76 Thus Petrarch refers to his *Rime* as 'little trifles'; Anthony Munday

refers to *Amadis of Gaul* as 'but a toy' (tr. of *The second book* 1595);
Richard Johnson refers to his *Seven champions* (1596) as 'this simple
toy'; and Heminge and Condell refer to Shakespeare's plays as 'these
trifles'. Molyneux, in Holinshed 1554, refers to the *Arcadia* as 'a
mere fancy, toy, and fiction'. In his letter to his brother, Robert,
Sidney refers to the *Arcadia* as 'my toyful book' (Feuillerat III 132);
in the *Defence* 120–1, he refers to 'this ink-wasting toy of mine'; and
in *Astrophel and Stella* 18, he laments that 'My youth doth waste, my
knowledge brings forth toys.'

77 Greville 153–4. Kenneth Myrick, *Sir Philip Sidney as a literary craftsman* (Cambridge, Mass. 1935), attributes Sidney's disparagement of
his works to the courtier's *sprezzatura*, 'the urbane nonchalance which
seems to treat lightly what must be treated seriously if one is to win
distinction' (40). (It is 'nonchalance' in its etymological and modern
sense: not being warm, i.e. 'keeping one's cool'.) The underlying
seriousness of the poet's studied indifference to his works emerges in
Chapman's comment that he has spent time writing a poem on 'so
trifling a subject' as Musaeus's *Hero and Leander*: 'it goes much
against my hand to sign that for a trifling subject, on which more
worthiness of soul hath been showed, and weight of divine wit, than
can vouchsafe residence in the leaden gravity of any money-monger
in whose profession all serious subjects are concluded' (*Poems*, ed
P. B. Bartlett, New York 1941, 132). Margaret E. Dana, 'Heroic and
pastoral: Sidney's *Arcadia* as masquerade', *CL* 25 (1973) 320, applies
the *sprezzatura* displayed by the disguised princes to Sidney himself:
'the pastoral disguise offers a way in which, even as a young man, he
could begin to explore, with all the courtly grace and nonchalance
so characteristic of him, the possibilities of heroic narrative. There is
a kind of *sprezzatura* in the very conception of the *Arcadia*. It is the
performance of a writer who was content to claim less that he might
achieve more.'

78 *Defence* 112.

79 My argument in the following pages was first presented in 'Sidney's
Arcadia as prose fiction: its relation to its sources', *ELR* 2 (1972) 29–
47.

80 John Hoskyns, *Direction for speech and style* [written 1599], ed Hoyt
H. Hudson (Princeton 1935) 41.

81 'To the reader', *The English Arcadia* (1607); 'To the understanding
reader', *The second part* (1613).

82 Unpub. MS honours thesis (Harvard 1894). See also R. W. Zandvoort,
Sidney's 'Arcadia': a comparison between the two versions (Amsterdam
1929) 189–95, and John J. O'Connor, *'Amadis de Gaule' and its
influence on Elizabethan literature* (New Brunswick 1970) 183–201.
O'Connor 186 concludes that 'in basing his central narrative upon
Amadis, Sidney did not so much follow as blend and transform'.
Robert W. Parker, 'Terentian structure and Sidney's Original *Arcadia*',
ELR 2 (1972) 74, notes that 'the economy with which Sidney inte-
grates the diverse elements he finds in the *Amadis* (and elsewhere)
into a tightly knit pattern of cause and effect suggests the great dif-

ference between an episodic, romantic story, and a dramatic, comedic plot'. Davis, chaps. 1 and 2, relates the two *Arcadias* to the extended tradition of pastoral romance. Since he uses this tradition to interpret Sidney's work as a religious allegory, I differ strongly; see my '*Et in Arcadia ego*', *MLQ* 27 (1966) 332–50. I agree with Lanham 385 that 'in studying the *Old Arcadia*, genres rather than particular works, and source areas rather than sources, are most important'. Apuleius's *Golden Ass* may be ignored: while it provided Sidney with some matter (see Ringler xxiv*n* and Robertson xxiii), it did not serve him as an 'imitative pattern'.

83 Osborn 540.
84 *Defence* 78.
85 Erwin Panofsky, *Meaning in the visual arts* (New York 1955) 299. On Sidney's transformation of Arcadia, see Kalstone 9–39.
86 Lewis 333.
87 Jacopo Sannazaro, *Arcadia and Piscatorial eclogues*, tr. Ralph Nash (Detroit 1966) 32.
88 Sannazaro 72.
89 Sannazaro 105.
90 *Defence* 78. Sidney seems to allude to 1 John 2:15: 'love not the world, neither the things that are in the world'.
91 *OA* 183. Walter R. Davis, 'Actaeon in Arcadia', *SEL* 2 (1962) 95–110, shows how the cave provides the symbolic centre of the work.
92 Elizabeth Dipple, 'Harmony and pastoral in the *Old Arcadia*', *ELH* 35 (1968) 313, claims that Sidney 'takes the myth of a harmonic paradise common to Greek and Christian thought and places it within the norms of action typical of real, post-lapsarian men. The result is a moral exemplum illustrating the ultimate inadequacy of the romance heroes.'
93 *Amadis of Gaul*, tr. Robert Southey (1872) II xiv. Most likely, Sidney read *Amadis* in the expanded French translation, which reached some twenty-one books by 1581, and for the summary here I used the 1573 edition in the Houghton Library, Harvard. However, Southey's abridged translation of the first four Spanish books provides an adequate sense of the genre of chivalric romance.
94 *The Faerie Queene* III i 49.
95 *Amadis* I iii.
96 Heliodorus, *An Æthiopian history*, tr. Thomas Underdowne (1587), ed George Saintsbury (Abbey Classics, n.d.) 5.
97 Roger Ascham, *The Schoolmaster* (1570), *English works*, ed William Aldis Wright (Cambridge 1904) 231.
98 *Defence* 92.
99 *Defence* 81, 79.
100 *Poetices libri septem* (3rd edn 1586) III xcv.
101 Heliodorus 257, 258.
102 Heliodorus 265.
103 Ibid.; *OA* 412.
104 *Defence* 98.
105 Heliodorus 282.

106 Ringler 379. Kenneth Thorpe Rowe, *Romantic love and parental authority in Sidney's 'Arcadia'*, Univ. Michigan *Contributions in Modern Philology* 4 (1947) 16, argues that we are on the side of the lovers *and* parental authority: 'the result is that the reason is divided while the sympathies remain intact, and the *Arcadia* ends on an effect of ethical confusion'. Rudenstine 44 claims that the trial scene exposes 'the limitations of moral rigor and old age as well as those of ardent youth'. Walter R. Davis, *Idea and act in Elizabethan fiction* (Princeton 1969) 66, calls the ending ambivalent.

107 Robertson xxxvii.

108 Ringler xxxvi–xxxviii classifies the *Old Arcadia* as a prose pastoral tragicomedy with a serious double plot combined with a comic underplot, using the Renaissance Terentian five-act structure with its movement of protasis, epitasis, and a catastrophe with an unexpected anagnorisis and peripeteia. His view is expanded by Parker, 'Terentian structure'. A more complex structure – and one which I find mind-boggling – is claimed by Jon S. Lawry, *Sidney's two 'Arcadias': pattern and proceeding* (Ithaca 1972) 23: 'in bald terms, it [the *Old Arcadia*] must be read: *three* vertical or triadic elements, moving in *three* appropriate horizontal or sequential "practices", each of which is multiplied into *two* aspects (the political and the ethical), within *five* conventional partitions of time or movement'. The kind of structure found in the work usually depends on one's understanding of its genre, and the kind of genre depends on the relative stress given the twin themes of love and war, or ethics and politics. If the reader regards the work as a romance, he tends to sympathize with the lovers; if he takes it as a 'serious' work, such as an allegory or heroic poem, he tends to condemn them. Among contemporary readers, Greville stresses the political matter; accordingly, he comments on the plot: 'who sees not that these dark webs of effeminate princes be dangerous forerunners of innovation, even in a quiet and equally tempered people' (13). Among modern readers, his approach has been continued by Edwin A. Greenlaw, 'Sidney's *Arcadia* as an example of Elizabethan allegory', *Kittredge anniversary papers* (Boston 1913), who writes of Basilius's retreat: 'it is no idyllic existence in the forest of Arden, but a criminal evading of responsibility that will bring ruin to any state' (337). Philanax judges much the same, and critics who agree – notably Lanham and Marenco – endorse his later judgment against the princes. While Davis 175 declares that each prince emerges at the end as 'the supreme Christian hero', Lanham 275 concludes that 'the whole purport of [Sidney's] romance is to show how ridiculous his characters are'. Franco Marenco, *Arcadia puritana* (Bari 1968), analyses the experiences of the princes as a fall, a progressive degeneration into sin. In 'Double plot in Sidney's *Old Arcadia*', *MLR* 64 (1969) 250, he calls the work 'a gloomy, almost desperate book, mocking and not glorifying the worldly hero'. Similarly, P. Jeffrey Ford, 'Philosophy, history, and Sidney's *Old Arcadia*', *CL* 26 (1974) 41, notes 'the emergence of a clear and unequivocal condemnation of the behavior of the principal characters'. Stephen

J. Greenblatt, 'Sidney's *Arcadia* and the mixed mode', *SP* 70 (1973) 269–78, argues that Sidney wrote in a mixed mode, playing one genre against another, by exposing the tragic possibilities in the comic and romantic, in order to mock human actions, human judgments, and human values. His view of Sidney as 'a connoisseur of doubt' strikes me as suspiciously modern. I do not take sides in the controversy whether the *Old Arcadia* is centrally concerned with love or politics, for clearly it is centrally concerned with both. I agree with Clifford Davidson, 'Nature and judgment in the *Old Arcadia*', *PLL* 6 (1970) 361: 'Sidney assumes that his readers will easily sympathize with the plight of those who are inclining toward earthly love, while at the same time they will accept as inevitable the judgment which threatens the lovers.' That the work as a romance could be regarded also as an heroic poem in sixteenth-century terms is noted by John Buxton, *Elizabethan taste* (1963) 255, and by Alan D. Isler, 'Heroic poetry and Sidney's two *Arcadias*', *PMLA* 83 (1968) 368–79. Robertson xxxv–xxxvii agrees that the *Old Arcadia* 'was intended to fulfil the function of heroic poetry' but notes its mingling of genres and its affinities with the mixed kind of tragicomedy.

109 Marenco, 'Double plot' 251–4, finds an 'allegorical conflation' of the princes and the beasts: in their lust, 'they are a pair of beasts'. What he calls lust, Sidney describes as 'all sorts [i.e. kinds] of passions lively painted out in the young lovers' faces' (46–7). Further, his reading must ignore the fact that the princes heroically slay the beasts to save the lives of the princesses.

110 1 Sam. 17:34–5. Arthur F. Marotti, 'Animal symbolism in *The Faerie Queene*', *SEL* 5 (1965) 79, notes that David's killing of the beasts is glossed as a defeat of the destructive passions. He interprets the princes' victory over the beasts, together with the parallel episode in *The Faerie Queene* VI x, Calidore's victory over the tiger, as 'an internal triumph over the concupiscible passions': 'thus the presentation of the trophies from the slain beasts is symbolic proof of the good intentions of the individual lover'. These beasts had been allegorized in literary tradition: in Sannazaro's *Arcadia* 88, Eugenio cries out in response to his friend despairing in love: 'A bear in the midst of my soul, a lion roars.' The bear is connected with love's violence in Giordano Bruno's *Expulsion of the triumphant beast* (1584), tr. Arthur D. Imerti (New Brunswick 1964) 113: Jove says that when he raped Callisto, 'the ugliness of my foul debauchery was presented before me in the form of a bear'. The lion is, of course, the Nemean lion, as Gynecia says: 'she saw the very face of young Hercules killing the Nemean lion' (*OA* 53). Its killing was the first labour of Hercules, as it is of the transformed Pyrocles, to prove himself.

111 That this address is retained in the revised *Arcadia*, which elsewhere excludes the narrator's role, indicates the central importance of the 'love-famed' Philoclea in the story.

112 Marenco, 'Double plot' 255, identifies the princes with the rebels: 'eversion in Arcadia is but the external manifestation of the inner chaos the princes are experiencing'. Again, however, he ignores the

fact that the princes defeat their foes, a service which Evarchus allows to be 'truly honourable and worthy of great reward' (*OA* 405).

113 While Evarchus is famous for his equity (*OA* 351, 354), as a judge in Arcadia he may exercise only justice. Mercy is the exclusive prerogative of Basilius. Mark Rose, *Heroic love: studies in Sidney and Spenser* (Cambridge, Mass. 1968) 72, interprets Basilius's abrogation of the law as 'the triumph of equity over law, the accommodation of justice to the actual circumstances of the world'. Cf. Elizabeth Dipple, ' "Unjust justice" in the *Old Arcadia*', *SEL* 10 (1970) 83–101.

114 Eccles. 7:18 (Geneva).

115 *Defence* 89.

116 Rudenstine 46.

117 Greville 223.

118 Lewis 342.

119 Robertson xxix.

CHAPTER 3

1 *Defence* 73.

2 Gabriel Harvey, *Marginalia*, ed G. C. Moore Smith (Stratford-upon-Avon 1913) 226.

3 While the *Defence* may have been written as late as 1580–2, as I argue on p. 108, Sidney's views on the contemporary state of English poetry may have been reached earlier.

4 *Defence* 111.

5 'A pastoral eclogue', in Spenser, *Minor poems* 354.

6 Buxton 91 understands that Sidney is renowned for his study of the Muses as a patron, but Dorsten, *Poets* 51, interprets the reference (and I agree) to Sidney as a poet.

7 Ringler lix–lx.

8 *Poetical works* 635.

9 *Poetical works* 611. Derek Attridge, *Well-weighed syllables: Elizabethan verse in classical metres* (Cambridge 1974) 187, concludes that Sidney's quantitative verse shows 'a mind consciously and carefully experimenting with the poetic potential of the English language'.

10 Ringler 392.

11 *Defence* 120.

12 *Defence* 112.

13 Ringler 385–6.

14 John Thompson, *The founding of English metre* (1961) 143.

15 Rudenstine 97.

16 Kalstone 67.

17 Ringler xxxviii–xxxix.

18 Davis 113. Cf. Lanham 210–20. Elizabeth Dipple, 'The "fore conceit" of Sidney's eclogues', *Literary monographs*, vol 1, ed Eric Rothstein and Thomas K. Dunseath (Madison 1967), argues that the eclogues by themselves form a whole work, with each poem contributing to the end Sidney had planned. She sees the 'idea' of the eclogues to be a vision

of the lost golden age: 'the poems teach the beauties of divine harmony even as they warn of and define human limitation' (47).

19 Davis 107.

20 Cf. Anthony Scoloker, Epistle to *Daiphantus, or The passions of love* (1604) on the proper epistle: 'it should be like the never-too-well read *Arcadia*, where the prose and verse, matter and words, are like his mistress's eyes, one still excelling another and without co-rival; or to come home to the vulgar's element, like friendly Shakespeare's tragedies, where the comedian rides when the tragedian stands on tiptoe: faith, it should please all, like Prince Hamlet'.

21 John 12:36.

22 *Defence* 79.

23 Moffet 74.

24 Katherine Duncan-Jones, ed, *Sir Philip Sidney: selected poems* (Oxford 1973) xvi. Rudenstine 284–6 supports the date 1580–1.

25 Ringler 501.

26 *The divine poems*, ed Helen Gardner (Oxford 1952) 33–5.

27 James 5:13.

28 *Defence* 119.

29 Hallett Smith, 'English metrical psalms in the sixteenth century and their literary significance', *HLQ* 9 (1946) 269.

30 *The poetry of meditation: a study in English religious literature of the seventeenth century* (New Haven 1962) 278.

31 *The whole book of psalms* (1582).

32 The Geneva bible (1560).

33 Ringler 514. Coburn Freer, 'The style of Sidney's Psalms', *Language and Style* 2 (1969) 64, notes that Sidney 'is not merely a skilful versifier, but a poet who thinks *through* or by means of his forms'. In his edition of *The Psalms of Sir Philip Sidney and The Countess of Pembroke* (Garden City, N.Y. 1963) xiii, J. C. A. Rathmell notes that the Sidneian psalms have 'an energy, intensity, and emotional piquancy which are conspicuously absent from the popular version'.

34 A facsimile is reproduced in P. J. Croft, *Autograph poetry in the English language* (1973) 1 14.

35 See Ringler 424–5.

36 *AS* 63.

37 See Ringler 423–4.

38 A poem by Dyer, which Sidney includes, raises the total to 33. It tells the fable of a satyr who, 'fond of delight', kisses fire; like him, the lover, seeing his beloved, is inwardly burned. In *CS* 25, the lover compares himself 'to the silly sylvan, / Burn'd by the light he best liked, / When with a fire he first met'. A central theme of *Astrophel and Stella* is the contrasting effects of light and fire: although the light of the lady's beauty illuminates the lover, it becomes an inward fire which burns him. The image of burning has a wide reference from syphilis to hell-fire.

39 Rudenstine 151 argues that 'Sidney's development between 1580 and 1582...can be described largely as an effort to achieve energia within the decorum of the private, courtly-love lyric'. Forcibleness is displayed

in the whole sonnet and particularly in the complexity of the concluding line. Leonard Barkan, *Nature's work of art: the human body as
image of the world* (New Haven 1975) 182–3, notes the two readings:
1. since the lover finds his lady in his heart, she inspires him to write
of her; 2. since he finds himself by looking in his heart, 'the muse is
urging him to write his own self, and this self is identified with the
body'. In support of the second reading, Barkan adds: 'the idea is
quite appropriate to the imagery which develops in the whole sonnet
sequence, for the human body is seen as nature's real work of art'. By
either reading, the traditional allegorization of the heart prepares for
the concluding sonnet in which Astrophel's body, now the closed
furnace, becomes the traditional emblem of the lover frustrated by
passion.

40 Sidney reveals his strictly pragmatic view of the poet's purpose in
writing love sonnets in the *Defence* 107, where he argues that Plato
cannot have banished poets from an ideal commonwealth which allows
community of women on account of effeminate wantonness 'since little
should poetical sonnets be hurtful when a man might have what
woman he listed'. He concludes the work with a curse against the
poetry-haters: 'while you live, you live in love, and never get favour for
lacking skill of a sonnet'.

41 There is an extended controversy on whether the sonnets should be
read as fact or fiction, biography or convention, that usually takes the
form of gathering the facts or denying their relevance. The facts are
given by Ringler 435–47. Hoyt H. Hudson, 'Penelope Devereux as
Sidney's Stella', *Huntington Library Bull* 7 (1935) 89–129, concludes
that 'informed people, from 1591 onwards, thought or knew that
Penelope Devereux was Sidney's Stella'. Jack Stillinger, 'The biographical problem of *Astrophel and Stella*', *JEGP* 59 (1960) 617–39,
concludes to the contrary that the evidence is not sufficient to prove
any love affair between Sidney and Penelope. However, any simple
'either-or' position is too simple and reductive for the complex relationship that exists between Sidney's life and his poetry. While more
recent critics tend to allow both biography and fiction as important
elements in the sonnets, the division remains. For example, Buxton,
Elizabethan taste 271, sees a continual shift between fact and fiction.
J. G. Nichols, *The poetry of Sir Philip Sidney* (Liverpool 1974) 82,
treats the sonnets as 'a dramatic fiction'. Richard A. Lanham, '*Astrophil and Stella*: pure and impure persuasion', *ELR* 2 (1972) 100–15,
finds the poem biographical throughout because Sidney uses it as a
vehicle of direct courtship: 'I am not saying that the sequence cannot
survive extraction from its biographical matrix. It can and has. But
why extract it when it obviously gains from being left as the anomalous
artifact, half art and half life, which it was?' (108). I agree with his
question but not with his conclusion that the poem remains 'half art
and half life': the 'life' is transmuted into 'art'.

42 Feuillerat III 132.

43 *Defence* 111. Buxton, *Elizabethan taste* 278, claims that Sidney's
thoughts were not about any woman but 'how to make English poetry

comparable to the Italian and French poetry that he had lately discovered during his Continental tour'. Perhaps his thoughts were of both, as matter and form.

44 Lewis 327–8.

45 Ringler 440, 447.

46 *Fables of identity: studies in poetic mythology* (New York 1963) 91–2. Cf. 45: 'it is not the experience of love but practice in writing love sonnets that releases the floods of poetic emotion'.

47 Cf. J. W. Lever, *The Elizabethan love sonnet* (1956) 74: 'the principal theme of *Astrophel and Stella* appears...as a study of the inner conflicts that romance precipitates in the personality of a contemporary man'.

48 Ringler xliv.

49 Lewis 329; Robert L. Montgomery, jr, *Symmetry and sense: the poetry of Sir Philip Sidney* (Austin 1961) 118. Cf. J. W. Lever ed, *Sonnets of the English Renaissance* (1974) 11: 'No other sonnet sequence in English so vividly projects the ardours and frustrations of sexual love in its impact on a brilliant, many-sided young man.'

50 Greville 16.

51 *'Orlando Furioso' in English heroical verse* (1591) 126, 30. In the *Golden treasury*, Palgrave claims that Sidney's poem 'offers the most intense and powerful picture of the passion of love in the whole range of our poetry'. Cf. Dylan Thomas, *Quite early one morning* (1954) 120: 'in these sonnets we see, held still in time for us, a whole progress of passion, physical and spiritual, coursing through rage and despair, self-pity, hope renewed, exultancy, moon-loved dreams, black fear, and blinding bright certainty of final loss'.

52 Young emphasizes Sidney's use of Petrarchan convention, seeing it as the subject of his sonnet sequence. Kalstone shows his departure from it, noting that 'the voice of Astrophel is almost the opposite of Petrarch's: recognizing conflicts where Petrarch enforces harmonies; tentative and critical where Petrarch is sure about the relation of beauty and philosophic meditation' (150).

53 J. P. Castley, S.J., *'Astrophel and Stella* – "high Sidnaean love" or courtly compliment?'*, Critical Review* (Melbourne) 5 (1962) 54–65, concludes that the sonnets must be considered 'not in terms of high seriousness and passion, but of lightness, touching feeling, and sophisticated good humour. Not in terms of Sidney's nobility of soul, but of his poise, courtliness, amiability and sense of fun.' Sidney's stubborn English bent is inherited from Wyatt, of whom Patricia Thomson, *Sir Thomas Wyatt and his background* (1964) 146, writes: 'In his "English" love poems he is, with the English poets, bent on satisfying his "love as to a creature". He was not [Chaucer's] Palamon's "affection of holiness". He is not searching for a transcendental reality or a spiritual satisfaction.'

54 Myrick 192.

55 *LXXX Sermons* (1640) 549; cited Helen Gardner, *The business of criticism* (1959) 70. Cf. *AS* 71.

56 Leland Ryken, 'The drama of choice in Sidney's *Astrophel and Stella*',

JEGP 68 (1969) 649, cites sonnet 2 to illustrate the element of active moral choice which contributes to the dramatic quality of the sequence.

57 *Pierce's supererogation* (1593), Smith II 259. Cf. Harington 126: 'Petrarch in his infinite sonnets in the midst of all his lamentation, still had this comfort, that his love was placed on a worthy lady; and our English Petrarch, Sir Philip Sidney, or (as Sir Walter Raleigh in his Epitaph calleth him) the Scipio and the Petrarch of our time, often comforteth himself in his sonnets of Stella, though despairing to attain his desire, and (though that tyrant honour still refused) yet the nobility, the beauty, the worth, the graciousness, and those her other perfections, as made him both count her, and call her inestimably rich, makes him in the midst of those his moans, rejoice even in his own greatest losses.'

58 Cf. Jean Robertson, 'Sir Philip Sidney and his poetry', *Elizabethan poetry* (Stratford-upon-Avon studies 2, 1960) 117: 'secure in the knowledge of her unassailability, he [the Petrarchan poet] was free to assail her with all his might'.

59 *Works* III 329.

60 Ringler xlvi.

61 I consider the various attempts to discover a three-part structure and then present my own, which is summarized below, in 'Sidney's *Astrophel and Stella* as a sonnet sequence', *ELH* 36 (1969) 59–87. The more recent attempts, which do not persuade me but contribute to our understanding of the complexity of the sonnets in their sequence, are by Leonora Leet Brodwin, 'The structure of Sidney's *Astrophel and Stella*', *MP* 67 (1969) 25–40; B. P. Harfst, '*Astrophil and Stella*: precept and example', *PLL* 5 (1969) 397–414; and Andrew D. Weiner, 'Structure and "fore-conceit" in *Astrophil and Stella*', *TSLL* 16 (1974) 1–25.

62 *Marginalia* 228.

63 Argent, a fesse, gules in chief three torteaux (three red disks with a broad band over a silver field), alluding to Stella's cheeks and face. See Young 21.

64 Perhaps for this reason Sir John Davies imitates this sonnet to describe the 'Meditations of a gull', *Epigrams, Works*, ed Alexander B. Grosart (1876) II 43–4.

65 The indirection is evident in the lament, 'I…could not see my bliss.' Sidney may pun on the name Devereux, from *heureux*, happiness, as does Spenser in the *Prothalamion* 153–4: 'And endless happiness of thine own name [addressing Robert Devereux] / That promiseth the same.' For a contrary reading, which denies the biographical inferences in this sonnet, see Ephim G. Fogel, 'The mythical sorrows of Astrophil', *Studies in language and literature in honour of Margaret Schlauch* (Warsaw 1966) 146–52.

66 *The elegies, and The songs and sonnets*, ed Helen Gardner (Oxford 1965) 52. Puttenham 47 notes that the love poet makes 'the very grief itself (in part) cure of the disease'. On this function of poetry, see Rosemond Tuve, *Elizabethan and metaphysical imagery* (Chicago 1947) 171. Alexander Sackton, 'Donne and the privacy of verse', *SEL* 7

(1967) 67–82, argues that Donne's poem is built on the idea that the poet's art destroys its curative value when it is made an object for others to sing and hear. Much the same may be said of Astrophel's sonnets once they have become public.

67 *OA* 112.

68 The double assault of the lady upon the lover's eye and ear – the combined powers of nature and art – is a common motif in Renaissance poetry. See, e.g. Marvell, 'The fair singer': 'while she with her eyes my heart does bind, / She with her voice might captivate my mind'. Since the fall of Eve (and man) was caused by the voice of the serpent, the hearing was regarded as the sense by which the soul may be captured or captivated. On the power accorded to music in the Renaissance, see John Hollander, *The untuning of the sky: ideas of music in English poetry 1500–1700* (New York 1970), esp. 252.

69 *Orchestra* (1596) 130, lines 2–3.

70 Sidney would seem to pun on 'quake', in the sense of 'quack' (*OED* quake v.²). On his name, Fr. Cygne, see, e.g. the 1624 French engraving of Sidney reproduced by Buxton. In his elegy on Sidney in *The ruins of time*, 589–601, Spenser doubles the pun: Sidney is 'a snowy swan' who after death becomes a 'heavenly sign' (Cygne but also Cycnus whom Apollo metamorphosed into a swan and placed among the stars). The connection was fitting because the swan was the popular symbol for the poet (see, e.g. Whitney, *Emblems* 126).

71 As Lalus in *OA* 159, 'since he had gotten his desire, he would sing no more'.

72 See the analyses of this sonnet by Lever 58–62 and Kalstone 117–22. The latter notes that the sonnet is 'a rare example of what appears to be a direct response to a poem by Petrarch' and concludes (172) that the sequence 'reaches a climax in sonnets 69–72'.

73 Castiglione, *The book of the courtier*, tr. Sir Thomas Hoby (1561), Everyman edn 313–14.

74 James Finn Cotter, 'The "baiser" group in Sidney's *Astrophil and Stella*', *TSLL* 12 (1970) 381–403, treats these poems as Sidney's analysis of the *baiser* genre: 'he not only wrote *in* the genre but also *about* it'.

75 Ringler xlv–xlvi. Ann Romayne Howe, '*Astrophel and Stella*: "why and how"', *SP* 61 (1964) 164–7, re-orders certain songs in order to improve the narrative relation between them and the sonnets, e.g. placing song i after sonnet 28, song iii before sonnet 36, song iv before sonnet 63, and associating songs vi and vii with sonnets 57 and 58. The order of the songs and sonnets in the authoritative 1598 text is accepted by James Finn Cotter, 'The songs in *Astrophil and Stella*', *SP* 67 (1970) 178–200, in showing the function of the songs, and by Alastair Fowler, *Triumphal forms: structural patterns in Elizabethan poetry* (Cambridge 1970) 177–80, in tracing elaborate numerological patterns and symmetrical arrangements of the songs in relation to the sonnets, and their stanza and line totals.

76 On the title-page of *Arcadian rhetoric* (1588), Abraham Fraunce refers to Sidney's *Songs and sonnets*.

77 Robert Herrick, 'Hell fire', *Poetical works*, ed L. C. Martin (Oxford 1956) 387. The cause of Astrophel's exile is 'tyrant honour' (song viii 95), the absence of which, in Tasso's *Aminta*, marks the golden age. That age was called golden 'only for that name, /...that empty sound / Called honour, which became / The tyrant of the mind, /...Was not yet vainly found' (tr. Daniel, *Works*, ed A. B. Grosart [1885–96] 1 260).

78 The Clifford MS reading, in place of 'give us sight to see', is supported by Sidney's translation of Psalm 36:9: 'And in thy light shall we see light'.

79 Petrarch, *Secretum*, tr. W. H. Draper (1911) 109–10.

80 Donne, 'The ecstasy' 65–8.

81 David Kalstone, in *English poetry and prose, 1540–1674*, ed Christopher Ricks (1970) 53, finds the resolution in Astrophel's 'emerging clarification of and commitment to his own fallen nature as an earthly lover'.

CHAPTER 4

1 *Poetical works* 635.

2 Arthur F. Kinney, 'Parody and its implications in Sidney's *Defence of poesie*', *SEL* 12 (1972) 1–19, argues that Sidney parodies the *School of Abuse* through parallel and burlesque 'because he was in many ways in agreement with Gosson's position and so could not directly oppose it'. William A. Elwood, 'A critical old-spelling edition of Sir Philip Sidney's *Defence of poesie*', unpub. diss. (Chicago 1966) argues that Sidney replies to Gosson's *Plays confuted* (1582), and dates the *Defence* in 1582–3.

3 'Argument' to *The shepherd's calendar*, October eclogue.

4 Dorsten, *Prose* 59–63, argues that the *Defence* was written during the winter of 1579–80.

5 As I argue in 'Sidney's idea of the "right poet"', *CL* 9 (1957) 51–9.

6 Dorsten, *Prose* 60, notes that Sidney spent his time discussing poetry 'while his political friends could at least be busy preparing the treatises that served to denounce the living tyrants of their time'.

7 *Select translations from Scaliger's 'Poetics'*, by F. M. Padelford (New York 1905) 1. For the Latin text, I use the third edition, 1586.

8 Shepherd 199.

9 tr. James Sanford (1569) 142. For Sidney's extended and witty use of Agrippa as a framework within which he attacks the other arts and sciences and defends the art of poetry, see my 'Sidney and Agrippa', *RES* 7 (1956) 151–7.

10 Dorsten, *Prose* 64, notes that Sidney's style creates 'an authentic tone of almost *extempore* oral delivery'. Catherine Barnes, 'The hidden persuader: the complex speaking voice of Sidney's *Defence of poetry*', *PMLA* 86 (1971) 422–7, finds the voice so complex – 'smiling at the excesses of his argumentation and chuckling at its effect on the listener' – that she must add: 'this is not to say that Sidney scorned poetry'. O. B. Hardison, jr, 'The two voices of Sidney's *Apology for poetry*', *ELR* 2 (1972) 83–99, hears two distinct and discordant voices in the two parts: an affirmative and inclusive tone in the first and a

negative and exclusive tone in the second. I find no such distinction. When Sidney complains in the second part that English verse has become 'a confused mass of words, with a tingling sound of rhyme, barely accompanied with reason', Hardison asks: 'where, one wonders, are the "unspeakable beauties" seen only by the mind cleared by faith?' However, in the second part Sidney denounces mere rhymers, not poets; and the phrase quoted from the first part does not apply to the right poet, whom he defends, but only to the divine poet, specifically to David in the Psalms.

11 Lewis 346.

12 Shepherd 11.

13 In demonstrating Sidney's originality in 'Sidney's idea of the "right poet"', I conclude that, as a right poet himself, he 'delivers the Idea of what poetry should be; and the end of his treatise is through delightful teaching to defend poetry from the *Mysomousoi*, with the further end of moving the age to make the highest kind of poetry'. Cf. Elizabeth Story Donno's more recent and cogent argument, 'Old mouse-eaten records: history in Sidney's *Apology*', *SP* 72 (1975) 298: 'Skilfully manipulating matter and words (*res et verba*) and thus illustrating the *right* use of Art and Imitation, in contrast to current practice, he made the *Apology* itself a demonstration of his proposition that a "fiction" indeed has the power to move, to instruct, and, above all, to delight.'

14 *Poetices* I ii.

15 Ibid.

16 On the contrast between Plato's concept of divine inspiration and Sidney's 'Christian' concept, see Morriss Henry Partee, 'Anti-Platonism in Sidney's *Defence*', *English Miscellany* 22 (1971) 7–29.

17 *Prose* 64. Davis, *Idea and act* 31, calls it 'the most daring passage of the *Defence*'.

18 Shepherd 27 finds that 'Sidney's religious temper exercises a control upon his theory of poetry'. Frank B. Evans, 'The concept of the Fall in Sidney's *Apologie*', *Renaissance Papers* 1969 9–14, shows that the Fall is the logical starting-point of Sidney's argument.

19 Evans 12 notes that 'in crediting fallen man with "erected wit"'... Sidney has taken a theological position unusual for his time'.

20 *Doctrinal treatises*, ed H. Walker (Cambridge 1848) 182; cited Evans 13. For the common Elizabethan understanding of man's nature, Evans cites Sir John Davies: 'I know the heavenly nature of my mind, / But 'tis corrupted both in wit and will' (*Works* I 24).

21 *Institutes* II ii 12, tr. F. L. Battles, Library of Christian Classics 20 (1961) I 270.

22 *Defence* 82; Pears 143; *De doctrina Christiana* i 12, *Works*, ed F. A. Patterson *et al.* (New York 1931–8. The Columbia edn) xv 209.

23 *Poetices* III xcvii. Robert M. Strozier, 'Poetic conception in Sir Philip Sidney's *An apology for poetry*', *Yearbook of English Studies* 2 (1971) 49–60, considers Sidney's argument that the reader is moved to virtuous action more effectively by the poet than by the historian or philosopher, and concludes that 'while Sidney is not a philosopher of art – as is

Scaliger – he is certainly original, coherent, and systematically theoretical'. Andrew D. Weiner, 'Moving and teaching: Sidney's *Defence of poesie* as a Protestant poetic', *Journal of Medieval and Renaissance Studies* 2 (1972) 259–78, claims that Sidney emphasizes moving over teaching because his aesthetics is based on Calvin's theology.

24 See Eugene F. Rice, jr, *The Renaissance idea of wisdom* (Cambridge, Mass. 1958) chap. 1.

25 *Vanity* 186. For 'concealed', Sanford reads 'revealed'; but the Latin text has *velata*.

26 Bruno 184.

27 'A defence of Homer', Smith II 302.

28 *Amintas dale, the third part of The Countess of Pembroke's Ivychurch* (1592) 4.

29 Jan van Dorsten, 'The arts of memory and poetry', *ES* 48 (1967) 419–25, suggests that Sidney's 'speaking pictures' resemble 'mnemonic *imagines*', being didactic visualizations which the reader remembers. Forrest G. Robinson, *The shape of things known: Sidney's 'Apology' in its philosophical tradition* (Cambridge, Mass. 1972), argues that Sidney's poetic derives from the common assumption that thought is a form of internal vision; hence Sidney describes poetry as 'a verbal rendering of ideas visible in the poet's mind as he composes and visible in the reader's mind as he reads' (vii–viii). Davis, *Idea and act* 28–54, considers how the poet's image in Sidney's theory is intended to lead the reader's mind from the concrete to the idea in order to test ideas of value by means of experience.

30 tr. Ruth Kelso (Urbana 1924) 60; cited Shepherd 162.

31 Shepherd 64–6 stresses the importance of Lomazzo and Zuccaro as spokesmen for a mannerist theory of art, which he finds central to Sidney's theory of poetry.

32 On the legend of Lucrece, rendered complex by her sin of suicide, see my *Early Shakespeare* 170–81.

33 Greville 15.

CHAPTER 5

1 See Wallace 325–7.

2 Ringler lxi notes that the 38 dedications addressed to him are 'a greater number than were addressed to any other contemporary of similar position'. See the list in F. B. Williams, jr, *Index of dedications* (Oxford 1962) and a supplement by Ringler, New *CBEL* I 1050. Buxton, chap. 5, provides a full account of Sidney's influence on the literary and intellectual life of the time. His central thesis is that Sidney and his sister played an essential part in bringing about the poetic achievement of the English Renaissance.

3 Greville 76–7, 110–20. Roger Howell, jr, 'The Sidney circle and the Protestant cause in Elizabethan foreign policy', *Renaissance and modern studies* 19 (1975) 31–46, concludes that Sidney 'had shifted his views to a more naval New World policy'.

4 Feuillerat III 166. The reader may well be reminded of Milton's words, 'methinks I see in my mind a noble and puissant nation' (*Areopagitica*), for both poets share an apocalyptic vision of Protestant England ushering in the kingdom of God.

5 *OA* 18; *NA* 199 (a passage added to the *Old Arcadia;* but cf. *OA* 19).

6 For modern readers of the *New Arcadia*, the seminal critical essay has been Greenlaw's 'Sidney's *Arcadia* as an example of Elizabethan allegory', *Kittredge anniversary papers* 327–37, in which he supports the view of Sidney's contemporaries, such as Fraunce, Harington, and Harvey, that the work is a serious heroic poem, and argues that 'the revision changed the earlier version from a pastoral romance, with the simplicity of a direct tale, into a complicated heroic "poem"'. In line with Greenlaw, E. M. W. Tillyard, *The English epic and its background* (1954), writes on the *New Arcadia* as 'an epicising fragment' (319). The pioneering study of the revisions, to which all later critics are indebted, is Zandvoort's *Sidney's 'Arcadia': a comparison between the two versions*. However, I do not accept his central thesis that the difference between the *Old Arcadia* and the *New* shows that 'Sidney had made great progress in psychological insight and artistic skill' (74). To me, they are different works which required from him different insight and skill. Unfortunately, most comparisons defend one version by attacking the other. It is generally allowed that the critical basis for Sidney's revision is his *Defence*. Myrick 299 writes: 'The *Arcadia* and the *Defence of Poesie* belong together; for the one exemplifies what the other states as theory'. Cf. Robinson 150: 'Sidney revised and expanded his romance in order to bring it into alignment with the main principles of his critical treatise.'

7 *Pierce's supererogation*, Smith II 263. The connection of the heroes to Sidney is presented visually on the title-page of the 1593 edition: the porcupine of the Sidney crest appears in the top central medallion as the Arcadian boar, flanked on the left by the bear of the Dudley arms and on the right by the lion of the Sidney arms (reproduced on the 1590 title-page). Supporting the crest, and alluding to their slaying the beasts, are the two princes: Musidorus as a shepherd on the left and Pyrocles as an Amazon on the right. The allusion is enforced, as Robertson xlviii–xlix notes, by having the bear unchained and the lion uncrowned. See Roderick L. Eagle, 'The *Arcadia* (1593) title-page border', *The Library*, 5th ser. iv (1949) 68–71. One suspects that the Sidney circle would see connections between the writer and his work not evident to outsiders: knowing, for example, that Pyrocles's colours, blue and gold (*NA* 10), are Sidney's.

8 Ringler l; Robertson lvii. Mary R. Mahl, *ELN* 10 (1972) 90–1, records her discovery that the same hand prepared the Norwich MS of the *Defence* and the Cambridge MS of the *New Arcadia*, which suggests that both manuscripts may have been prepared during Sidney's stay at Wilton in 1584.

9 The revision extends to each particular, for example, the use of *imprese* (see Katherine Duncan-Jones, 'Sidney's pictorial imagination', Oxford B.Litt. thesis 1964), geographical settings (see Ringler 376–7), and the

strict economy in the number of characters and their relationships (see Appendix).

10 Ringler 530.

11 Part of my argument in the following pages was first presented in 'Sidney's *Arcadia* as prose fiction: its relation to its sources', *ELR* 2 (1972) 47–60.

12 *A critical edition of Yong's translation of George of Montemayor's 'Diana' and Gil Polo's 'Enamoured Diana'*, by Judith M. Kennedy (Oxford 1968). In her Introduction xxxiii–xxxix, Kennedy analyses Sidney's indebtedness to Montemayor and his continuators.

13 Katherine Duncan-Jones, 'Sidney's Urania', *RES* 17 (1966) 129, argues that 'the point about Urania, above all, is that she has gone away. Heavenly Beauty, Venus Urania, has left for the island of Cythera...and only her earthly counterpart, Venus Pandemos, remains in Arcadia.' Alastair Fowler, *Conceitful thought: the interpretation of English Renaissance poems* (Edinburgh 1975) 57, adds: 'Urania's departure... may rather mythologize the loss of harmony, of *iustitia originalis*, at the Fall, and simultaneously serve as an invocation'.

14 *NA* 241.

15 Heliodorus 8–10.

16 Montemayor 42.

17 Argument to Book I. Cnemon's story extends through pp. 15–26.

18 Cf. Underdowne's address 'To the gentle reader': 'what a king is Hydaspes? What a pattern of a good prince? ...Contrariwise, what a lewd woman was Arsace? What a pattern of evil behaviour?'

19 *Defence* 92, 81, 93.

20 He found such violence also in life, as Myrick 235 notes, and at a very impressionable age: his mother contracted smallpox when he was eight. Over twenty years later his father had not recovered from her disfigurement. In a letter to Walsingham, he writes: 'when I went to Newhaven, I left her a full fair lady, in mine eye at least the fairest, and when I returned I found her as foul a lady as the smallpox could make her' (Wallace 22). According to Moffet 71, Sidney's own beauty was laid waste by smallpox. Osborn 517–22 cites Sidney's horoscope which confirms his early illnesses.

21 Sidney's characteristic technique in the *New Arcadia* is to resolve an episode with a paradox, which is often presented as a visual image. For example, the debate between the two princes in Book I ends when both are overcome: 'they rested, with their eyes placed one upon another, in such sort as might well paint out the true passion of unkindness to be never aright, but betwixt them that most dearly love' (83).

22 It is in relation to these two pairs of lovers that Sidney tells the story of the two princes and the two princesses. See, e.g. 31, 32, 100, 302.

23 Greville 14.

24 *Pierce's supererogation*, Smith II 263.

25 *Eikonoklastes, Complete prose works* III 362.

26 *Defence* 104.

27 *Defence* 88.

28 Greville 16. When Greville adds that Sidney 'bequeathed no other

legacy but the fire to this unpolished embryo', he implies that the reason for burning is simply the work's incomplete state. Without the concluding trial scene, the moral pattern remains unrealized. Not too much should be made of Sidney's dying wish, not because it is traditional – he would know Virgil's dying wish that the *Aeneid* be burned – but because, being near death, he is 'fixing. . .a lover's thoughts upon those eternal beauties' (Greville 137). With David, he becomes at last 'a passionate lover of that unspeakable and everlasting beauty to be seen by the eyes of the mind, only cleared by faith' (*Defence* 77).

29 Compare the scorn of courtly ladies in *AS* 31: 'Do they call virtue there ungratefulness?', and contrast the ladies at Helen's court who 'built their chastity, not upon waywardness, but by choice of worthiness' (283). In *OA* 107, Musidorus persuades Pamela to elope because of 'virtuous gratefulness for his affection'.

30 One kind of revision, which I must ignore because it is a separate study in itself, follows from what Sidney had written in the interim. One example from each of the three works may illustrate the matter. Since he had completed the *Old Arcadia*, he adds to the opening account of Dametas that he 'will stumble sometimes upon some songs that might become a better brain' (28) because he had given him a witty response to Charita's 'My true love hath my heart' in Book III. That the shepherds had their fancies 'opened' to high conceits (*OA* 4) is changed to 'lifted' (*NA* 19) to agree with the claim made in the *Defence* 78 that the poet is 'lifted up with the vigour of his own invention'. The 'perfect blackness' of Philoclea's eyes (*OA* 37) is extended into an elaborate conceit (*NA* 90) because Sidney had mastered the art of praising Stella's black eyes in *AS* 7.

31 Holinshed 1554.

32 'Of poetry', *Critical essays of the seventeenth century*, ed J. E. Spingarn (Oxford 1909) III 91.

33 *Discoveries*, *Works* VIII 591.

34 *Devises* 44-5.

35 Greville saw the *New Arcadia* serving as a book for the governor; hence he says of it, 'this representing of virtues, vices, humours, counsels, and actions of men in feigned and unscandalous images, is an enabling of free-born spirits to the greatest affairs of states' (2-3). Abraham Fraunce read the *Old Arcadia* (in the St John's College MS) as a rhetorical handbook, as his title-page indicates: *The Arcadian rhetoric: or the precepts of rhetoric made plain by examples,. . .English. . .out of. . .Sir Philip Sidney's 'Arcadia'* (1588).

36 Greville 15. Sidney's generally orthodox political thought is described by Ernest William Talbert, *The problem of order: Elizabethan political commonplaces* (Chapel Hill 1962) 89-117. He concludes that 'a treatment of political commonplaces emerges which is more complicated, more realistic, more conducive to ironies than that represented by any Elizabethan world-picture of a musically simple order and degree'. One radical theory, which Sidney seems to endorse, the Huguenot theory of rebellion against an unlawful tyrant or evil ruler, is noted by Martin Bergbusch, 'Rebellion in the *New Arcadia*', *PQ* 53 (1974) 29-41.

37 The manuscript of Wilson's translation, dated 1596, was presented to Greville. It was first published in *Revue Hispanique* 50 (1920) 367–418. The personal allegory in the *New Arcadia* is examined by Ephim G. Fogel, 'The personal references in the fiction and poetry of Sir Philip Sidney', unpub. doctoral diss. (Ohio State Univ. 1958).

38 *The lawyer's logic* (1588)B$_3$^{v}.

39 Hoskyns 42; Peter Heylyn, *Microcosmos* (1621) 208: 'a book which besides its excellent language, rare contrivances, and delectable stories, hath in it all the strains of poesy, comprehendeth the universal art of speaking, and to them which can discern, and will observe, notable rules for demeanour, both private and public'; Milton, *Commonplace book*, *Complete prose works* 1 371. In the *Commonplace book* 463, Milton also notes the 'excellent description' of nobles seeking to ruin royal sovereignty (referring to *NA* 185–6).

40 *OA* 52; deleted in the *New*.

41 Sidney explains in the *Defence* 115–16 that the picture of Hercules with the distaff 'breedeth both delight and laughter: for the representing of so strange a power in love procureth delight, and the scornfulness of the action stirreth laughter'. In his study of heroic love in Sidney and Spenser, Rose 139 concludes that the two poets do not pit war against love: 'instead they cast over love itself the atmosphere of the heroic, transforming the torments of the soul aspiring to marriage into a struggle worthy of the epic hero'.

42 Cf. Rose 38: 'in making his original pastoral romance into a heroic poem, one of the things Sidney did was to restore the balance between reason and passion: the *New Arcadia* permits the serious claims of love to be put forward for consideration'.

43 Greville 14.

44 'Elegy upon Sir Philip Sidney' (1638), *Works*, ed J. H. Ellis (Gloucester, Mass. 1962) 347.

45 Greville 14, 11.

46 *Defence* 103. The same active response is indicated by Greville's speculation that if Sidney had lived to complete his work, 'what a large field an active, able spirit should have had to walk in' (15).

47 As Spenser records in 'A pastoral elegy' (1595) 79–80: 'in hunting, such felicity / Or rather infelicity he found', and Harington, in *Metamorphosis of Ajax* (1596), ed Elizabeth Story Donno (1962) 108: 'the noble Sir Philip Sidney was wont to say, that next [to] hunting he liked hawking worst'.

48 Michel Poirier, 'Sidney's influence upon *A Midsummer Night's Dream*', *SP* 44 (1947) 483–9.

49 *Pierce's supererogation*, Smith 11 282.

50 *Directions*, title-page.

51 'To Camden', *Poems*, ed Arnold Davenport (Liverpool 1969) 105.

52 Drayton, 'Epistle to Reynolds', Spingarn 1 136, praises Sidney because he 'thoroughly pac'd our language, as to show / The plenteous English hand in hand might go / With Greek and Latin'. Mona Wilson, *Sir Philip Sidney* (1931) 150, cites Samuel Johnson's Preface to his Dictionary in which he claims that Sidney's work and Spenser's provided

the dialect of fiction and poetry beyond which he needed to make few excursions, and comments: 'the *Arcadia* is the earliest example of a book written throughout in standard English speech. Hardly any word that Sidney uses has become obsolete'. Cf. Buxton, *Elizabethan taste* 266.

53 Hoskyns 42.

54 Cited John Buxton, 'Sidney and Theophrastus', *ELR* 2 (1972) 81, from an early seventeenth-century MS in his possession.

55 Cf. *NA* 166–7: 'as a perfect magnet, though put in an ivory box, will through the box send forth his embraced virtue to a beloved needle'. The 'scientific' basis is expressed by Du Bartas, *Divine weeks*, in *Works* (1613) 256: the 'hidden love' which exists between steel and loadstone 'is but a spark or shadow of that love / Which at the first in everything did move, / When as th' earth's Muses with harmonious sound / To heav'ns sweet music humbly did resound'.

56 Kalstone, 'Sir Philip Sidney' 49, comments: 'Sidney's emphasis is never on simple participation in the stream of events, or even simple delight in or fear of the images before one, but rather on control and mastery. His heroes become *readers* of their experience.'

57 Cf. Nancy Rothwax Lindheim, 'Sidney's *Arcadia*, Book II: retrospective narrative', *SP* 64 (1967) 169: 'the two sets of tales [of the two princes] move, in a sense, from the simple to the complex, from situations in which issues are clear and responses unequivocal to situations where both sides are often partially wrong and values must be ranked one above the other before response is possible'.

58 Noted by Lindheim 170.

59 Greville 11.

60 *Fragmenta regalia* (1641) 22.

61 'For neither man nor angel can discern / Hypocrisy, the only evil that walks / Invisible, except to God alone' (Milton, *Paradise lost* iii 682–4).

62 See Robertson lx. Joan Rees, 'Fulke Greville and the revisions of *Arcadia*', *RES* 17 (1966) 56, observes that 'Book III moves the *New Arcadia* so far away from the *Old* that it is difficult to see how Sidney was going to get it back on to anything like the old lines'. Cf. Lanham 400–1.

63 Sidney expects his reader to enjoy the witty variation in the description – some forty pages later – of the Black Knight's horse. The reins are snakes, 'which finely wrapping themselves one within the other, their heads came together to the cheeks and bosses of the bit, where they might seem to bite at the horse, and the horse (as he champed the bit) to bite at them; and that the white foam was engendered by the poisonous fury of the combat' (455). The delight which Thomas Nashe took in such description is evident in his description of the trappings of Surrey's horse, which are shaped like an ostrich: 'he reached out his long neck to the reins of the bridle, thinking they had been iron, and still seemed to gape after the golden bit, and ever, as the courser did raise or curvet, to have swallowed it half in' (*Works*, ed R. B. McKerrow [1904–10]) II 272. See Werner von Koppenfels, 'Two notes on *imprese* in Elizabethan literature', *RQ* 24 (1971) 21–2. Sidney's

keen interest in tilts is noted by Frances A. Yates, 'Elizabethan chivalry: the romance of the Accession Day tilts', *JWCI* 20 (1957) 4-9.

64 See Lewis 336-7. Tillyard 300-5 seeks to answer T. S. Eliot's judgment that 'the *Arcadia* is a monument of dulness' by demonstrating that Sidney 'commands a style of considerable range, a range that admits the possibility of the work attaining to the rank of epic'.

65 *Defence* 96. In *Defence* 92, Sidney cites Aristotle, *Poetics* 1448^b, to support his claim that 'cruel battles...are made in poetical imitation delightful'. It is noteworthy, then, that Aristotle in that section refers to the poet's imitation through which we may delight to gaze on dead bodies, which is just the effect that Sidney seeks in his description. In commenting on the passage, Robinson 156 concludes enigmatically that its language 'is pictorial not only in the sense that it describes a visualizable battle but also because the words limn out the conceptually visible structure of thought itself'. See n. 72 below.

66 'To the Earl of Somerset', *Poems* 406.

67 *Defence* 114. Robert Nicholas Reeves III, *The ridiculous to the delightful: comic characters in Sidney's 'New Arcadia'* (Cambridge, Mass. 1974) 26, in the course of demonstrating that Sidney merges the ridiculous and the delightful in his work observes that the Combat of Cowards comments on the heroic jousting.

68 Zandvoort 74 notes that 'one of the most remarkable features of the *New Arcadia* is the deliberate and subtle retouching of the figures of the two sisters'. John F. Danby, *Elizabethan and Jacobean poets* (1952) 59, finds in Pamela 'a conscious and deliberately maintained virtue' and in Philoclea 'a perfection of nature'. The distinction that I find between the sisters is implicit in the opening description of Urania: as the encompassing feminine figure, she is praised both for 'her everflourishing beauty' and for her 'unspeakable virtues'. Alan D. Isler, 'The allegory of the hero and Sidney's two *Arcadias*', *SP* 65 (1968) 171-91, claims that Pyrocles and Musidorus also are carefully discriminated, the one representing courage and the other wisdom.

69 Lewis 338 observes that 'the contrast between the two cynosures, worked out in every detail,...helps to save them from abstraction'.

70 *Defence* 85. The final vision of Philoclea's beauty balances the opening vision of Urania's 'heavenly beauty'. When Pyrocles sees her, believing her to be dead, he addresses her as an angel, 'by that excellent beauty, so beloved of me'. When he believes instead that she is the soul of Philoclea, he begs that he may join her in heaven, 'there eternally to behold, and eternally to love your beauties' (487).

71 *Icones symbolicae* (Milan 1626); cited E. H. Gombrich, *Symbolic images: studies in the art of the Renaissance* (1972) 124. Compare Sidney's claim for the effect of the poet's images of virtue, that 'we seem not to hear of them, but clearly to see through them' with Giarda's claim that the symbolic images 'leap to the eyes of their beholders and through the eyes they penetrate into the mind, declaring their nature before they are scrutinized' (Gombrich 145).

72 Robinson 145 claims that the reader is meant to discover that Pamela 'is not a person at all. Her personality is a thin tissue of particularities

that scarcely obscure the cold, bare bones of the Idea that is her raison d'être'. In Sidney's terms, he prefers the abstraction of the philosopher's precept to the vision given by the poet's image; accordingly, he urges that we read by closing our eyes: 'by closing our eyes to the literal, concrete image. . .and by accepting an abstract, figurative alternative, we are able to see what the poet–painter means' (150).

73 *Pierce's supererogation*, Smith II 263.

74 Greville 16.

75 Ibid. 223.

76 Ringler 530. 'even that' would seem to refer to the *Old Arcadia*, as Rees, 'Fulke Greville and the revisions of *Arcadia*' 54–7 argues; but it may refer to the *New Arcadia*, as Ringler 376 assumes. Either way, Greville refers to the rest of Book III and Books IV and V.

77 The textual apparatus in the Robertson edition of the *Old Arcadia* records all the changes made in the 1593 *Arcadia*. See also William Leigh Godshalk, 'Sidney's revision of the *Arcadia*, Books III–V', *PQ* 43 (1964) 171–84. Zandvoort's comparison of the texts is undercut by his assumption that the changes result from the Countess of Pembroke's bowdlerizing.

78 The changes that the scribe could have made but failed to make are minor, such as allowing Basilius to remain a Duke. More interesting are those which ought to have been made but were beyond his power. To offer an example briefly, I italicize the phrases added to the *Old Arcadia*. In the 1593 *Arcadia* 103–12, Pyrocles plans to take his own life when he perceives that '*his being*' (in place of 'all his action') with Philoclea has been discovered, and '*by the folly or malice, or rather malicious folly of Dametas, her honour therein touched in the highest degree*' because they had been found '*as Dametas reported of them*' in act of marriage without solemnity of marriage'. She counters that, being left 'dishonoured as *supposed* unchaste', she would '*though untruly*' confess to her father. Unfortunately, the scribe must allow what she would confess: 'that with her consent this act had been committed'; for it would need major revision to omit any reference to the 'act' between them. He could only hope that her reference to 'our virtuous action' (in the revised St John's College, Cambridge MS but not in the earlier Clifford MS) would disguise its real nature. For such changes possibly the scribe was Sidney himself, engaged in revising the remaining books preparatory to radically recasting them if time allowed. But not for those which result from misreadings. For example, when Pyrocles disguised as Gynecia and in her bed pretends to be asleep so that Basilius may leave for the cave, the *Old Arcadia* 227–8 reads: 'Pyrocles. . .having. . .so naturally measured the manner of his breathing that Basilius made no doubt of his sound sleeping, having lain a pretty while with a quiet unquietness *to satisfy his greedy desire*'. That is, Pyrocles lies quietly to satisfy Basilius's 'greedy [i.e. eager] desire' that he be asleep. Presumably it was a scribe, not Sidney, who took the italicized phrase to refer to Pyrocles's desire for Philoclea, and awkwardly substituted 'to perform his intended enterprise'.

79 *OA* lxi.

80 Nancy R. Lindheim, 'Vision, revision, and the 1593 text of the *Arcadia*', *ELR* 2 (1972) 136–47, concludes that the major revision of the plot by the addition of Book III and the change in the basic conception of the main characters 'make us wonder whether the reason for Sidney's failure to complete the *New Arcadia* was not that his original plan was no longer workable'. Cf. Elizabeth Dipple, 'The captivity episode and the *New Arcadia*', *JEGP* 70 (1971) 424.

81 The title-page, with a pig halting before sweet marjoram around which is the motto '*Non tibi spiro*', caused offence by implying that the work was not meant for the vulgar; see Eagle 68–71. (Cf. the title-page of Olney's edition of the *Defence* [1595]: *odi profanum vulgus, et arceo.*) As a consequence, the offended Florio berates H.S. as Humfry Swineshead, Hodge Sowgelder, and 'twice as much and a half as half an ass'.

82 Harvey, *Four letters* (1592), Smith II 234.

83 Lewis 339. Cf. Buxton, *Elizabethan taste* 268: 'the *Arcadia*, being the most successful work of fiction of the English Renaissance, reveals the taste of the age more vividly than any other'.

84 Greville 14 suggests the same when he speculates on the conclusion of the *Arcadia* 'if this excellent image-maker had lived to finish, and bring to perfection, this extraordinary frame of his own commonwealth'. At the opposite extreme, Kimbrough 142 believes that Sidney 'quit writing in disgust'.

85 Greville 18.

86 On Spenser, see Paul J. Alpers, *The poetry of 'The Faerie Queene'* (Princeton 1967); on Milton, Stanley Eugene Fish, *Surprised by sin: the reader in 'Paradise Lost'* (1967).

87 *Reason of Church-government, Complete prose works* I 815, 816.

Bibliography

List of editions cited more than once.
Unless otherwise stated, the place of publication is London.

Agrippa, Cornelius. *Of the vanity and uncertainty of arts and sciences*, tr. James Sanford. 1569
Bruno, Giordano. *The heroic frenzies* (1584), tr. Paul Eugene Memmo, jr. Chapel Hill 1966
Buxton, John. *Elizabethan taste*. 1963
   Sir Philip Sidney and the English Renaissance. 1954, 1964
Castiglione, Count Baldassare. *The book of the courtier*, tr. Sir Thomas Hoby (1561). Everyman edition
Chapman, George. *Poems*, ed Phyllis Brooks Bartlett. New York 1941
Collins, Arthur. *Letters and memorials of state*. 1746.
Davies, Sir John. *Works*, ed Alexander B. Grosart. 1876
Davis, Walter R. *Idea and act in Elizabethan fiction*. Princeton 1969
   A map of Arcadia: Sidney's romance in its tradition. New Haven 1965
Donne, John. *'The elegies', and 'The songs and sonnets'*, ed Helen Gardner. Oxford 1965
Dorsten, Jan van. *Poets, patrons, and professors: Sir Philip Sidney, Daniel Rogers, and the Leiden humanists*. Leiden 1962
Eagle, Roderick L. 'The *Arcadia* (1593) title-page border', *The Library*, 5th ser. iv (1949) 68–71
Evans, Frank B. 'The concept of the Fall in Sidney's *Apologie*', *Renaissance Papers* (1969) 9–14
Fraunce, Abraham. *The Arcadian rhetoric* (1588), ed Ethel Seaton. Oxford 1950
Greenlaw, Edwin A. 'Sidney's *Arcadia* as an example of Elizabethan allegory', *Kittredge anniversary papers*. Boston 1913
Greville, Sir Fulke. *Life of Sir Philip Sidney* etc. (1652), ed Nowell Smith. Oxford 1907
Hamilton, A. C. *The early Shakespeare*. San Marino 1967
   'Sidney's *Arcadia* as prose fiction: its relation to its sources', *ELR* 2 (1972) 29–60
   'Sidney's *Astrophel and Stella* as a sonnet sequence', *ELH* 36 (1969) 59–87
   'Sidney's idea of the "right poet"', *CL* 9 (1957) 51–9
Harington, Sir John tr. *'Orlando Furioso' in English heroical verse*. 1591

Harvey, Gabriel. *Marginalia,* ed G. C. Moore Smith. Stratford-upon-Avon 1913

Pierce's supererogation (1593), in Smith

Heliodorus. *An Æthiopian history,* tr. Thomas Underdowne (1587), ed George Saintsbury. Abbey Classics n.d.

Holinshed, Raphael. *The chronicles of England, Scotland and Ireland.* 1587

Hoskyns, John. *Directions for speech and style,* ed Hoyt H. Hudson. Princeton 1935

Howell, Roger. *Sir Philip Sidney, the Shepherd Knight.* 1968

Howell, Thomas. *Devises* (1581), ed Walter Raleigh. Oxford 1906

Jonson, Benjamin. *Works,* ed C. H. Herford, P. and E. M. Simpson. Oxford 1925–52

Kalstone, David. *Sidney's poetry: contexts and interpretations.* Cambridge, Mass. 1965

'Sir Philip Sidney', *English poetry and prose, 1540–1674,* ed Christopher Ricks. 1970

Kimbrough, Robert. *Sir Philip Sidney.* New York 1971

Lanham, Richard A. *The Old Arcadia.* New Haven 1965

Lawry, Jon S. *Sidney's two 'Arcadias': pattern and proceeding.* Ithaca 1972

Lever, J. W. *The Elizabethan love sonnet.* 1956

Lewis, C. S. *English literature in the sixteenth century.* Oxford 1954

Marenco, Franco. 'Double plot in Sidney's *Old Arcadia*', *MLR* 64 (1969) 248–63

Milton, John. *Complete prose works,* ed D. M. Wolfe *et al.* New Haven 1953–. The Yale edn

Works, ed F. A. Patterson *et al.* New York 1931–8. The Columbia edn

Moffet, Thomas. *Nobilis,* ed Virgil B. Heltzel and Hoyt H. Hudson. San Marino 1940

Molyneux, Edmund. In Holinshed

Montemayor. *A critical edition of Yong's translation of George of Montemayor's 'Diana' and Gil Polo's 'Enamoured Diana',* by Judith M. Kennedy. Oxford 1968

Montgomery, Robert L. jr. *Symmetry and sense: the poetry of Sir Philip Sidney.* Austin 1961

Myrick, Kenneth. *Sir Philip Sidney as a literary craftsman.* Cambridge, Mass. 1935; Lincoln, Neb. 1965

Nashe, Thomas. *Works,* ed R. B. McKerrow. 1904–10

Osborn, James M. *Young Philip Sidney, 1572–1577.* New Haven 1972

Parker, Robert W. 'Terentian structure and Sidney's Original *Arcadia*', *ELR* 2 (1972) 61–78

Puttenham, George. *The art of English poesy* (1589), ed Gladys Doidge Willcock and Alice Walker. Cambridge 1936

Rees, Joan. 'Fulke Greville and the revisions of *Arcadia*', *RES* 17 (1966) 54–7

Robinson, Forrest G. *The shape of things known: Sidney's 'Apology' in its philosophical tradition.* Cambridge, Mass. 1972

Rose, Mark. *Heroic love: studies in Sidney and Spenser.* Cambridge, Mass. 1968

Rudenstine, Neil L. *Sidney's poetic development*. Cambridge, Mass. 1967
Sannazaro, Jacopo. *Arcadia and Piscatorial eclogues* (1504), tr. Ralph Nash.
    Detroit 1966
Scaliger, Julius Caesar. *Poetices libri septem*. 3rd edn 1586
Smith, G. Gregory. ed *Elizabethan critical essays*. Oxford 1904
Spenser, Edmund. *Minor poems*, ed Ernest de Sélincourt. Oxford 1910
    Poetical works, ed J. C. Smith and E. de Sélincourt. Oxford 1912
Spingarn, J. E. ed. *Critical essays of the seventeenth century*. Oxford 1909
Tillyard, E. M. W. *The English epic and its background*. 1954.
Wallace, Malcolm William. *The life of Sir Philip Sidney*. Cambridge 1915
Whetstone, George. *Sir Philip Sidney: his honourable life, his valiant death
    and true virtues*. 1587
Whitney, Geoffrey. *A choice of emblems*. Leiden 1586. Facs. edn Amster-
    dam 1969
Young, Richard B. *English Petrarke: a study of Sidney's 'Astrophel and
    Stella'*. New Haven 1958
Zandvoort, R. W. *Sidney's 'Arcadia': a comparison between the two
    versions*. Amsterdam 1929
Zouch, Thomas. *Memoirs of the life and writings of Sir Philip Sidney*.
    York 1808–9

Index